SOCIOLOGICAL STUDY OF RELIGION

Edited By
V. G. Nayar
&
M. G. Nayar

AF795790

COSMO PUBLICATIONS
2001 INDIA

All rights reserved. No part of this publication may be reproduced, or stored in retrival system, or transmitted in any form or by any means without the prior permission of Cosmo Publications.

THE SOCIOLOGICAL STUDY OF RELIGION
First COSMO Print 2001

ISBN 81-7755-139-6

Published by
MRS. RANI KAPOOR
for COSMO PUBLICATIONS Div. of
GENESIS PUBLISHING PVT. LTD.
24-B, Ansari Road, Darya Ganj,
New Delhi-110 002, INDIA

Printed at
Mehra Offset Press

CONTENTS

Preface

There are two possible approaches to the sociology of religion. One is to emphasis the *sociology* of religion, to show how sociological thought about religion illumines sociology and how religious behaviour and belief expand and contribute to concepts in general use in sociology. With this emphasis religion becomes an instance to illuminate sociology. The other emphasis is upon the sociology of *religion.* Sociology here becomes one approach to our way of thought about religion. It finds its place alongside other approaches, such as those of history or psychology. It may find itself in a hierarchy, above or below these other approaches, the hierarchy being decided by appropriateness to the subject of religion. With this emphasis religion is partially illuminated by sociology, for sociology is not the only searchlight upon religion.

In what follows our bias will be towards the latter, the sociology of *religion.*

While it is hoped that the book will interest the general reader it is written with two groups of readers in mind - those who at the beginning of their studies in sociology need a guide to that important area of study, religion, and those who need some assessment of the help the sociology of religion can bring to the life and work of the religious institutions.

Chapter-1

INTRODUCTION

Chapter-1

INTRODUCTION

It is widely appreciated that the study of cultural forms and processes has been greatly stimulated in recent years by a more sophisticated and flexible Marxism than that which existed in the decades of Stalinist orthodoxy. Whereas the older, economistic Marxism relegated religion and other cultural phehomena to the category of mere epiphenomena—part of a superstructure determined by the economic base—recent Marxist-inspired debates about ideology and culture have allowed a higher degree of relative autonomy to such phenomena. The socilogy of religion has much to gain from a careful consideration of developments in the analysis of ideology, and in return it has much to offer, particularly by a reappraisal of the light thrown on ideology by the classical sociologists of religon (Durkheim and Weber, featured in Section I(a)) and by some social anthropologists' work on symbolic structures and processes (as exemplified by Evans-Pritchard, Mary Douglas and Clifford Geertz, in Section I (b)).

Classical statements and their development

Durkheim's special contribution to the study of religion as ideology was to show its symbolic representation corresponds to something socially real (leaving aside any supernatural reference, which cannot be studied sociologically) and yet in an imaginary way. As he puts it, 'if in the midst of these mythologies and theologies we see reality clearly appearing, it is none the less true that it is found there only in an enlarged, transformed and idealized form, (Durkheim, 1915, p.468). Like Marx, Durkheim made clear that religion and ideology have a social basis, particularly in patterns of social relations and organization, but they also have a degree of autonomy, following certain rules peculiar to culture. In rejecting the crude Marxist historical materialism of his own day, Durkheim had something in common with those present day Marxist who would agree with his statement of the need to avoid producing a theory of religion that was 'a simple restatement of historical materialism' (ibid., p.471).

It was Max Weber, above all , who produced the most sensitive and complex account of the 'elective affinities' between social groups (classes, status groups, occupations, sexes) and sets of beliefs or ideologies (meaning systems, legitimations, theodicies). The contrasts hedrew between religious messages that contain theodicies of good furtune for the privileged, and those which contain theodicies that offered compensation to the underprivileged, are still instructive for the sociology of religion. Similarly, his perceptive discussions of the different ideological inclinations of various intellectual strata, provide a link with Marxist insights, such as those of Gramsci on 'organic intellectuals' (the leaders of thought in each class.) Like Durkheim, and no doubt Gramsci also, Weber rejected a crudely reductionist explanation of the relation between beliefs/ ideologies and material-base/interests. Beliefs and ideologies could not be reduced to a mere function or reflection of material circumstances and interest:

> It is not our thesis that the specific nature of a religion is simply a 'function' of the social situation of the stratum which appears as its characteristic bearer, or that it represents the stratum's 'ideology' or that it is a 'reflection' of the stratum's material or ideal interest situation.
>
> *(Weber, 1969, p.22, and in this volume.)*

Nevertheless, Weber was far from falling over into the opposite, idealist, extreme, which would have led to the unsociological conclusion that social relations and social circumstances do not affect beliefs and values. He wanted to arrive at a formulation which would do justice to material circumstances and interests and also to the channelling effects of ideas in determining people's actions:

> Not ideas, but material and ideal interests, directly govern men's conduct. Yet very frequently the 'world imges' that have been created by 'ideas' have, like switchmen, determined the tracks along which action has been pushed

> by the dynamic of interest. 'From what' and 'for what' one wished to be redeemed and, let us not forget, 'could be' redeemed, depended upon one's image of the world.
>
> *(Weber, op. cit., pp. 34-4, and in this volume.)*

The Marxist tradition for a long time reflected the rather ambiguous and sometimes contradictory accounts of ideology to be found in the various writings of Marx and Engels. In the early writings of the young Marx, which were of a philosophical nature, he considered religion in the context of alienation, a condition giving rise to false consciousness and a systematised pattern of beliefs that he called ideology. In their later historical and political writings, Marx and Engles (especially the latter), tended to explain religious phenomena as directly motivated by class interests. Thus, English religiosity was contrasted, by Englesh, with working-class radicalism and bourgeois free-thinking on the Continent, and explained in terms of the greater cunning of the English bourgeoisie in safeguarding their class interests by spreading religion among the wokers and pretending to be religious themselves (see the extract from Engles' *Introduction to Socialism: Utopian and Scientific,* on pp. 17-20). This reductionist explanation of ideology as a simple function of class situation and interests is inadequate, as well be made clear in the course of this book, especially in the discussion of 'Religion and social control' in Section II.

Marx's analysis of ideology was potentially much more subtle and suggestive when he avoided the pitfalls of a reductionist class interest theory and focused instead on homologies or parallels between the principles of symbolisation in different ideological spheres (e.g religion and economics) and related these to principles of structuration in the relevant social formation. However, Marx did not pursue the analysis of symbolisation very far and tended to fall back on the notion of ideas simply being a 'reflection' of the 'real' world. As in the statement in *Capital* that:

> The religious world is but the reflex of the real world. And for a society based upon the production of commodities, in which the producers in general enter into social relations with one another by treating their products as commodities

and values, whereby they reduce their individual private labour to the standard of homogeneous human labour - for such a society, Christianity with its *cultus* of abstract man, more especially in its bourgeois developments, Protestantism, Deism, etc., is the most fitting form of religion.

(Capital, Book 1, quoted in Marx and Engels, On Religion, p.135, and in this volume.)

Recent developments in the analysis of ideology have been concerned with improving explanation of how and why ideology takes a particular form and of how it works. Two important developments are discrenible: Firstly, more attention has been given to what Geertz has called 'autonomous process of symbolic formulation', which entails examining ideologies as systems of interacting symbols and the ways in which they provide plausible interpretations of problematic social reality for particular groups (see extracts from Geertz in this book, pp. 76-83). This has led to a greater appreciation of the complexity and variability of symbolic processes, which cannot be differentiated simply in terms of false consciousness versus true consciousness (a subject taken up in this book). Secondly, there is now an awareness of the field of ideology in relation to classes and groups as being one of contestation and 'lived relationship', not a mechanical process. *(This will be evident in Sections II, III and IV.)*

Culture, ideology and rationality

Although this book acknowledges that many of the developments in the analysis of ideology have derived from debates within Marxism, it also recognises that many of the classical works on the sociology of religion were implicity concerned with religion's ideological character and effects. A bridge between these classical studies and recent developments, including the Marxist-inspired debates, is provided by Clifford Geertz's discussions of religion and ideology as cultural systems. Geertz defines culture as 'an historically transmitted pattern of meanings embodied in symbols, a system of inherited conceptions expressed in symbolic forms by means of which men communicate, perpetuate, and develop their knowledge about and attitudes towards life' (C. Geertz, 1966, pp.3-4; this volume p.66).

Geertz defines religion as :

> ... (1) a system of symbols which acts to (2) establish powerful, pervasive, and long-lasting moods and motivations in men by (3) formulating conceptions of a general order of existence and (4) clothing these conceptions with such an aura of factuality that (5) the moods and motivations seem uniquely realistic.
>
> *(op., cit., p.4)*

Ideology, for its part, refers 'to that part of culture which is actively concerned with the establishment and defence of patterns of belief and value' whilst bearing in mind that 'the patterns of belief and value defended may be, of course, those of a socially subordinate group, as well as those of a socially dominant one, and the "apology" therefore for reform or revolution' (Geertz, this volume, p.83.) The differenc between science and ideology as cultural systems is to be sought in the sorts of symbolic strategy for encompassing situations that they respectively represent. 'Where science is the diagnostic, the critical, dimension of culture, ideology is the justificatory, apologetic, one' (Geertz, op. cit.).

Science can itself, however, become part of an ideologial system of beliefs and values, as in Comtean positivism, and Stalinist dialectical materialism. In these kinds of belief system science is seen as an alternative set of beliefs and values which can replace those of traditional religions. The notion of 'Science' comes to form a central component of such ideologies —that is, science is the measure of all things. On the other hand, some belief systems claim to be sciences, such as astrology, scientology and some forms of meditation. These systems of belief, however, do not welcome critical appraisal of their predictions or techniques, and might be better seen as ideologies rather than sciences. Only complete relativists try to maintain that there is no difference between education into some form of critical rational thinking, and indoctrination, or socialiation into an ideology, such that the notion of an educated public, open to reasoned argument, is virtually meaningless. (See P.Feyerabend, 1975.) Relativists, however, cannot use reasoned arguments to support their view that there is no such thing as science, for they do not accept that rational criteria for assessing such arguments exist.

The problem of whether or not these are thought to be any universal standards of rationality arises in acute form whenever people from the modern West try to understand and explain cultures in which modern forms of 'rationality', as found in sciences and technologies, are absent. An earlier generation of anthropologists, working in the first few decades of life, including the beliefs and ritual practices, of people living in preliterate societies. These belief systems, often termed 'primitive religions', 'witchcraft' and 'magic', were explicitly or implicitly compared with literate peoples to cure illnesses using magic, or to explain why someone fell ill as the result of the work of withchraft. A classic of this someone fell ill as the result of the work of withchraft. A classic of this kind of anthropological research, based upon fieldwork, was that of Evans-Pritchard, as in the selection from his study of Azande witchcraft in this volume.

The work of empirical, field research orientated anthropologists led to many social scientists adopting a relativistic position about other cultures; that is to say, some of them adopted and approach which refused to make judgements, on the basis of modern scientific assumption, about other culters' values, beliefs and rituals practices, such as those involved in magic and witchraft. All beliefs, values, rituals and symbols were seen as having some plausibility in their own social settings, and should bot be judged by western standards of rationality. Such relativism seemed to be consistent with a broadly liberal, tolerant approach, which many western social scientists accepted. It was challenged by events in Europe, especially with the rise of fascism and Nazism during the economic crises of the early part of the twentieth century. It was all very well to be tolerant of other cultures which were made known to Europeans and Americans by anthropologists; it was quite another matter to be tolerant of the new ideologies which emerged in Europe. The belief systems of tribal groups could be invested with a degree of plausibility by westerners, but not those of fascists, Naziz and racists, by such groups of liberal-minded social scientists. Relativism was found to have its limitations in this period of European and American history.

The effects of these developments are still operating in recent debates about nationality and cultural relativism. For instance, some writers, such as Steven Lukes (1970, in this volume) argue that there are some universal rational criteria which must be used in understanding what members of any society are trying to assert, criteria which include the concept of negation, the laws of identity and non-contradiction, within logic. Lukes holds a position which is influenced by those who thought that social scientists cannot be complete relativists, and he can be seen as an example of someone inclined towards a non-relativist position, but who avoids the simple error of cultural ethnocentrism. Others have taken a less universalistic position about the existence of some basic logical laws and concepts which operate in all cultures, and are more inclined to raise questions about the supposed rational, scientific, ethical and technological superiority of the west at the end of the tewntieth century compared with some other cultures. In part, this is held on the grounds that western culture is not a unity, and is full of contradictions which can produce a sense of futility and aimlessness among some groups. (Hirst and Wooley are close to a position of this kind).

Religion, conflict and legitimation

Some of these cultural contradictions within western capitalist societies have been the subject matter of debates about the role that religion has played in ideological contestation, particularly with regard to the Industrial Revolution in England. This was a subject that attracted the attentions of Weber, Marx and Engles, and also of some French historians who contrasted the revolutionary enthusiasm of their own country with the religious enthusiasm of the England. It was suggested that the channelling of ideological enthusiam in a religious direction, particularly by Methodism, Evangelicalism and the Sunday school movement, was a crucial distraction in the formation of the English working class. This topic is examined at length in Section II, where we consider some of the various theses that have been put forward on this subject, especially the Halevy thesis (deriving from the French historian of that name) and that of E.P. Thompson in his *The Making of the English Working Class.* The arguments as they relate to the part played by the Sunday schools in this period are considered in the extract from Thomas Walter Laqueur's *Religion and Respectability: Sunday Schools and Working Class Culture 1788-1850.*

Another major area where the contradictins and lack of unity to be found in contemporary western culture appears in sharp focus is in the variations which exist in relationship to religion. Christianity has been the major religion historically in the west, but it is no longer so dominant as perhaps it once was. Sociologists have contributed to the analysis and understanding of the role of religion in modern societies, especially in the emphasis they have given to the social and psychological functins of religion, as distinct from its cognitive beliefs. (Here the work of Durkheim, Marx, Weber and Freud, has been especially significant.) As a cognitive explanatory system, Christianity has appeared weak when compared with the sciences of physics, astronomy, biology and even the social sciences. However, as a symbolic system offering values backed by sacred authoruty, legitimation to a variety of political views and positions and emotional, therapeutic compnesations throughout the lifecycle to those who can find comfort in religious symbolism and rituals, it remains largely unrivalled. Even modern political ideologies such as communism, fascism and national socialism have not achieved the hold over both the collective and the personal lives of people in the ways in which traditional religons, and the more recent froms of religious sectarianism, have achieved in the past and the present. (The ideological potency of such sectarian religious movements is illustrated in the case of Jamaica).

In Britain, there is a particular ideological use of some of the symbols of Christianity which is found in the 'civil religion', as it might be called, of the rituals surrounding the monarch and the other members of the Royal Family. It is here that some sociologists and social theorists perceive an ideiological role for Britain's civil religion in the creation and legitimation of major cultural and political values, especially in the area of gender roles and sexual morality. (See J. Weeks, 1980, in this book.) These cultural values come to appear to be backed up by the sacred authority of the Church, in part because the monarch is Head of the Church of England and of the Chruch of Scotland, as well as being Head of State. (See R. Bocock, 1985) Other sociologists and social theorists do not attach much, if any, weight of the civil religion of Britain in the maintenance of its economics and political structures are seeing the cultus of royalty as not much more than a popular diverson, created and sustained by the mass media, and of no major political or socio-cultural significance. The economic and political structures are seen by these sociologists as being maintained and reproduced by more direct material interests and pressures operating upon different classes. (See B. Turner, 1983, in this book.) It is possible to argue that both of these positions have some plausibility if a distinction is made between the role of civil religion in reproducing patriarchal cultural definitions of gender and sexuality, and the legitimation of capitalism as a mode of production on the one hand, and the actual social and economic processes involved in the reproduction of capitalist social relations in the spheres of production and consumption on the other. If such a distinction is made then there is no necessary contradiction between the two broad types of analysis.

CONCLUSION

We are suggesting that, on the one hand, a purely materialistic social theory, which perceives only material interests lying behind ideologies and religions, cannot do justice to the relative autonomy of religious symbolism and values in many societies both in the past and in the world since the end of the Second World War. On the other hand, social theories, in sociology or elsewhere, which treat religious symbolism in isolation from the social formation in which such symbolism is loated, fail to acknowledgw that religion is part of a wider cultural, economic and political set of relations. In so doing such approaches ignore the 'elective affinity' between a status group or class and a particular road to salvation, and the influence this had on the development or religious symbolism - an influence which whilst it is not fully determining is often important in giving a particular stamp to a religious belief system. In this way, it is possible to see ideological elements in a particular religion, that is, aspects of its belief and value systems which bear the imprint of the classes and status groups which have been its main bearers, or carriers, and in whose interestes it may have been modified. But this is a two-way process - the carriers, themselves, are constituted in part by ideology and bear its imprint.

Chapter-2

A due Sense of Religion: Quiet Lives or Misty Views ?

Chapter-2

Like marriage the study of society is not to be taken in hand unadvisedly, lightly or wantonly. There are many aspects to such study. There is the picture of how things are in society. There is the review of what people do, of human action which maintains or changes society. There is the thinking which is done about society, theory of society or social theory. These aspects linked together make up sociology.

Let us begin with definitions of sociology put forward by some of the masters of sociology. Morris Ginsberg's definition serves well—sociology... as the study of society, that is, of the web or tissue of human interactions and interrelations. It is concerned with all that happens to human begins in virtue of their relations to each other. It follows that the principal headings of society studied by sociology are social structure (groups, associations and institutions), social function and social control (how structures work) and social change (short-and long-term trends). An example of fruitful distinction in social structure was that made by Tonnies between community and association, where community was a social group living and belonging together with several interests and association was a group meeting for a particular interst. Examples of social function would be law, the poli ce, education, while examples of social change would be mobility, evolution, urbanization. Max Weber brings interpretation into his definition: 'sociology is the science which attempts the interpertive understanding of social action. Interpretation introduces philosophy, the outlook and assumptions of the interpreter, the cultural climate in which he studies and interprets. Weber is surely right that sociology does contain interpretation Durkheim did not think so, although his studies did interpret. Durheim held that sociology was a rational inquiry into the facts of human society, that social facts were to be treated as things, that social phenomena were external to individuals so that methods appropriate to psychology did not suit sociology and that social study must not have its conclusions influenced by some previous philosophy. On the other hand Durkehim held the doubtful position that philosophical conclusions could be drawn from sociological studies. He put forward the views that the scientific inquiry of sociology could find a basis for ethics and that sociological inquiry could throw light on the major questions of philosophy such as those about free will and form and matter.

The methods of sociological inquiry are the formulating of an hypothesis, the assembling of facts to test the hypothesis, assessing the impact of the facts upon the hypothesis, the drawing of conclusions and making generalizations. Ginsberg put stress on the comparative method of varying 'the circumstances of a phenomenon with the object of eliminating variable and inessential factors, and so arriving at what is essential and constant. If sociology is a scienvce it is an inductive science, beginning with what is the case and going on to generalizations where it can. It is in the first place descriptive, beginning with what can be counted and measured, better described as sociography. It goes on to structures and movements and only after this, according to Le Bras, does sociology properly begin with analysis, hypothesis and generalization. Sociology then aims to discover types and to seek causes.

Le Bras, the leading exponent of sociological studies of religion in Francein this century, provides a suitable bridge for crossing from the definition of sociology to the definition of religion. In the irst place it is possible to define religion so widely that it covers every human aspiration-as does this definition of religion as 'a system of beliefs and practices by which a group of people struggules with ultimate problems of human life. Every church, religion political party or philosophy with adherents qualifies here. Since no human being or group can escape ultimate questions of why he or they exist, of birth, decay and death, the definition has all the comprehensiveness of a tautology. On such a definition all have prizes, nothing escapes religion. It has the merit of eliminating any problem of sceularization, of which more later, as ruthlessly as any old-style logical positivist eliminated metaphysics. It is unfortunately a merit which turns out like Lord Melbourne's praise of the

Order of the Garter to be no merit at all. 'I like the Garter; there is no damned merit in it' may never have done for an ancient order of chivalry any more than 'I like a broad definition of religion because it eliminates my problems' may do for the sociologist of religion. Besides, common sense holds there are some things, persons, groups, institutions which are religious and others which are not and in offended to be told otherwise, just as an atheist is offended when the liberal missionary suggests he is really a Christian. If the all-inclusive deefinition of religion as the object of ultimate concern in pressed then absurdities arise. What of the man or group whose ultimate concern is the performance of the stock market? Is the daily reading of the *Financial Times* to be held a religious act? On a common sense view ultimate concern may be directed to non-common sense view ultimate concern may be directed to non-religious as well as to religious objects and in itself can be no criterion of religion.

The inclusive definition does, however, have the merit of showing religion as bound up with culture but fails to clarify the relationship of religion and culture. Before returning to culture we must seek an exclusive definition o religion. Le Bras defines it in terms of relations with the sacred, which distinguishes religion from philosophy; he goes on to see the sacred as inspiring respect and fear and distinguishes it from magic. However, the definition of religion in terms of the sacred also will not stand. The sacred is the area towards which ultimate concern is directed. The man whose ultimate concern lies in the stock market sees the stock market and its affairs as sacred. For him other areas are profane, outside the temple. Yet for another man whose ultimate concern lies elsewhere the stock market is profane.

Robertson devotes much attention to the definition o religion. He notes that the category or religion has arisen in cultures dominated by the Judaeo-Christian tradition and argues for a definition in terms of culture and of another world. He thus define religion in terms of religious culture. 'Religious culture is that set of beliefs and symbols (and values deriving directly therefrom) pertaining to a distinction between an empirical and a super-empiririical, transcendent reality; the affairs of the empiririical being subordinated in significance to the non-empirical. This definition has the merit of making a distinction between religious and non-religious culture and of pointing to the beyond. Culture then becomes every set of beliefs and symbols, of which religious culture is one. It is all embracing in the sense used by T.S. Eliot, who writes of culture as including 'all the characteristic activities and interest of a people: Derby Day, Henley Regatta, Cowes, the twelfth of August, a Cup final, the dog races, the pin tables, the dart board, Wensleydale cheese, boiled cabbage cut into sections, beetroot in vinegar, nineteenth century Gothic chruches and the music of Elgar.

The all-embracing nature of culture, implied in Eliot's catalogue, is the sense of culture used in anthropology. It lacks the precision which is to be found in Eliot's distinction between three senses of culture, of which the all-embracing sense is one only. The other two are the culture of the individual and of the group, the third being that of society as a whole. Any definition of religious culture must also follow Eliot's three senses by being the religious culture of the individual, of the group and of the society. The levels of culture reached will be interdependent and the first two particularly dependent upon the third, that o society as a whole. Eliot argues the essential relations of culture to religion. 'No culture has appeared or developed except together with a religion : according to the point of view of the observer, the culture will appear to be the product of the religion, or the religion the product of the culture. Eliot dismisses the view that 'ethical formatioin and some emotional colour to culture which is the ultimate value, and asserts that culture is the incarnation of the religion of the people so that religion and culture are different aspects of the same thing. If we are moving towards an exclusie definition of religion along the lines suggested by Robertson we are not bound to hold that there is a necessary connection between religion and culture. A culture without religion is conceivable and thus the relationship of religion and culture is contingent. It may turn out that we do not know of a culture without religion, but that is a matter for inquiry. It follows that we are not bound to agree a definition of religion which is universal. I remember Professor Le Bras saying that he did not think man was by nature religious but that he was made so. There could therefore be cultures which did not make him religious. What is required of our definition is that it should allow of widespread, cross-cultured comparison and that it should not greatly offend common sense, although there may be an arbitrary element in it.

To build on Robertson's definition we may take this remark from a paper by Melfond E. Spiro, that 'the belief in superhuman beings and in their power to assist or harm man . . . is the core variable which ought to be designated by any definition of religion. Religious belief and behaviour can be to do with this with whom the believer strives to be united, or as means to obtain for the believer spiritual or material goals.

> 'The beliefs in superhuman beings, other-worldliness, and spiritual alues vary independently. Thus ancient Judaism, despite its obsession with God's will, was essentially this wordly in orientation. Catholicism, with all its other-wordly orientation is, with certain kinds of Hinduism, the most "materialistic" of the higher religions. Conucianism, intensely this-wordly, is yet concerned almost exclusively with such values as filial piety.

Accepting the core variable of religion as belief in superhuman beings, we go on to deine religion in terms of a social institution among other social institutions, influencing and being influenced by surrounding culture and having the marks of any social institution—belief systems, action systems and value systems, but all directed towards superhuman beings. Those who are members of such a social institution are required to use their minds in certain ways, to behave in certain ways and to submit to certain standards of judgment.

There are at least two aspects of definition. One is to draw out the logical significance of a concept; the other is to point to cases and instances. In the next chapter we shall turn to these ostensive definitions, but we may pause at this point to consider two literary examples. Both illustrate religious cultures within which there is belief in a superhuman being. Both show an interaction of belief, action and values. One presents an integrated religious culture, the other a split culture. The first portrays the landed gentry of the seventeenth century and the second a character from one of Thomas Hardy's novels.

Lord David Cecil's account of the Osborne family, a cavalier country family, *Two Quiet Lives,* shows how such families accepted the plain facts of existence—love, death, money, poetry. In their religious outlook they were not materialists. Religious belief provided a sublime background. They passed briefly through this world to an eternity of bliss or torment. As immortal souls their destiny hung on their attainments in virtue. They were magnanimous and possionate in moral sensitivity. They were imaginative with a delight in beauty. 'Their religion expressed itself in the jewelled and courtly mode of George Herbert.

A way of life followed to incarnate these values and this artistic sense: ceremonious manner, respect for convention and hierarchy. There was no dissonance between the ideal and the real, the poetic and the prosaic, no distinction between a man's public and private personality. 'Accepting equally the earthly and the spiritual, their version embraced all experience in one harmony.

Thomas Hardy in *Far From the Madding Crowd* portrays a culture which is religious but with degrees of religion and which in the person of Gabriel Oak lacks that integration of religion in culture shown in *Two Quiet Lives.*

> 'His Christian name was Gabriel, and on working days he was a young man of sound judgment, easy motions, proper dresss, and general good character. On Sundays he was a man of misty views, rather given to postponing, and hampered by his best clothes and umbrella: upon the whole, one who felt himself to occupy morally that vast middle space of Loadicean neutrality which lay between the Communion people o the parish and the drunken section, - that is, he went to church but yawned privately by the time the congregation reached the Nicene creed, and thought of what there would be for dinner when he mean to be listening to the sermon.

'Since he lived six times as many working-days as Sundays, Oak's appearance in his old clothes was most peculiarly his own—the mental picture formed by his neighbours in imagining him being always dressed in that way.

Chapter-3

A Strange Compelling Fascination: The Sociological Study of Religion

Chapter-3

In marking out the area studied by the sociology of religion we may begin with religious experience and take as our guide Karl Mannheim. Among his more influential books is *Diagnosis of our Time,* subtitled 'wartime essays of a sociologist'. One of these essays, 'Towards a New Social Philosophy, sets out four essential spheres of religious experience : personal communion with God, personal relationships, the pattern of social life. religious behaviour. Personal communication with God is much valued in all religions. Some persons specialize, in it, the mytics. The general body of believers is encouraged to it by methods of prayer, sacrifice and orders of worship. Forms of social organization are devised to promote it, such as monasteries and retreat houses. Priests and other officers of religious bodies are set aside to encourage and teach it.

It is argued that in a complex society where other spheres of religious experience are weakened this sphere is strengthened by privatization. By privatization in this context is meant the freedom of a person to choose his religion and practice it is his own way. The conditions for privatization are tolerance on the part of society and inability on the part of a church or religion to enforce obedience or conformity. The individual is free to choose his wares in the religious supermarket. Yet how free is he? If there are a no pressures for religious conformity are there none against? The theory of privatization sees a man as an atom in a mass, forgetting his membership of many other groups, family, neighbourhood, work or interest, which may all exercise some influence for or against religious experience. Nor does it follow that the atomized individual, if he existed elsewhere than on desert island and if he sought religious experience, would choose communion with God.

Religious experience in personal relationships has an echo in Christinaity, whose Lord promised to be in the midest where two or three are gathered together. The small group has its place in the majority of religions, the master and disciples, the band of brothers, the family. Cathechizing in many of the Reformation churches was the duty of the head of the househol, continuing until recently in the Chruch of Scotland, where the minister's vists before Communion Sunday were to check how well the head had done his duty. The Church of England required heads of families to send their children and apprentices to church for catechetical instruction. Religions with ancestor worship have household ceremonies. The Christian church's central act of worship, the Eucharist, began in the small group of master and disciples and has continued as, among other things, a reunion of God;'s family, while its administration centred on the bishop God's family of clergy. A newly ordained deacon in the church of England requires a title, which is an appointment with pay, so that he shall not be financial charge on the bishop who by ordination makes him a member of his family.

It is argued that the social conditions which encourage privatization also encourage religious experience in personal reltaionships but in forms outside the chruches and the traditional religions. The same conditions of tolerance and the religious bodies' inability to command apply. There is some evidence to support who claim Christian faith but no loyalty to present forms of the church and in the utopain communes of the American west coast. Such groups pose problems only to those religions which set up an institution requiring membership. There follows the question, in which sociology may take some interest, of why some new movements of personal relationships remain within the existing forms of the churches and why some go outside? The medieval church kept the Franciscans but not the Waldesians. The Church of England kept the Evangelicals but not the Methodists. The models for these problems are historical. Religious bodies face nothing new. Human history is also littered with the wrecks of utopain communes.

Religious experience expressed in the pattern of social life means that the social order reflects and incorporates the values of a given religion. The perfect form of this was but by Hooker in *The Laws of Ecclesiastical Polity*. Church and state were one. The Church of England was society in its religious order under king, convocations of bishops and clergy; the state was society in its political order under kind and parliament. Church and state were two sides of the same coin. Paul Tillich invented three terms to describe possible relationships between religion and patterns of social life. The terms deal with the attempt of religion to apply norms to society. For Tillich if society was autonomous, then religion attempted to apply no norms. If society was heteronomous, then religion imposed norms but was itself a separate institution over against society. If society was theonomous, then religion did not impose but created a situation where its values were spread in society and reflected by society. The theonomous society had its models in Hooker already mentioned and in Israel of the Old Testament. These models were fragile. Religion's tendency to domination and society's tendency to independence threatened to break them. Theonomous society was the most desirable type, rare and fleeting in reality.

These possible relationships of religion and society are to be distinguished from that put forward by the advocates of the social gospel. Hooker and Tillich deal with implications. If the Christian gospedl be such, then certain implications for the ordering of society follow. If Christ has redeemed men from sin and set them free, then a measure of freedom must follow in political life, albeit with safeguards. The social gospel is a matter of identification. A certain ordering of society, such as capitalism, is taken to be sin; to overthrow it is redemption.

When Mannheim wrote his wartime essays the threat of the corporate state mastering the individual seemed strong. The war was fought against the Fascist corporate state with its presecution of minorities in alliance with the Bolshevik corporate state which was and is a secular form of the heteronomous society with the Communisgt party and doctrine playing, the part of religion. The question to him was the balance of freedom and order in postwar planning. Mannheim feared that without a coherent social philosophy the balance would not be struck. More than a generation later is seems that his fears have been to some extent realized. What has happened has been a late but partial triumph of Rousseau. In

Western societies the state has, surprisingly, been over-sensitive to the claims of the individual for self-expression in certain departments of life. If, as Rousseau said, man is naturally good why restrain him? Away, then, with consorship and with restraints on what at other times have been held to be sexual perversions. His private life is his own; what he does in it is his own affair and cannot be bad if he is left to himself. At the same time the state takes to itself certain ends which are judged to be morally desirable - such as racial and financial equality—and sets up legislation to promote them. Western states have abondoned private life to the philosophy of Rousseau but retained and extended in the public sphere policies which deny Rousseau. The social philosophy is not coherent, nor has the contribution of religion to it been coherent. Religion has been restrained by the empiricist emphasis in philosophy, to which we return below, and has concentrated on the fourth sphere of religious experience, the one to which the sociology of religion has given most attention.

The fourth sphere is religious behaviour, which unlike the other three spheres is more open to observation. The practice of religion, the attendance at church or temple, the rites of passage, the expressions of belief, the working of institutions and their officers, all come into an understanding of religion and have been much studied. The types of institutional form which religions take is of some interest.

Much attention has been given within Christianity to institutional types. The basic distinction of types was made by Troeltsch into church and sect.

> 'The Church is that type of organization whch is overwhelmingly conservative, which to a certain extent accepts the secular order, and dominates the masses; in principle, therefore, it is universal, i.e., it desires to cover the whole life of humanity. The sects, on the other hand, are comparatively small groups; they aspire after personal inward perfection, and they aim at a direct personal fellowship between the members of each group. From the very beginning, therefore, they are forced to organize themselves in small groups, and to renounce the idea of

dominating the world.

The sects have in recent years received much sociological attention, partly perhaps because they are easier to handle. The work in this field of Bryan, Wilson, both for his own studies and for those he has inspired, is notable. He refers to four sub-types of sect within Protestant Christianity, classifed according to their policy of mission towards the outside world : conversionist, adventist or revolutionary, introversionist or pietistic, and agnostic or manipulationist. The first seeks to alter men and the world. The second predicts a drastic alteration of the world. The third rejects the world and stands for high inner values. The fourth seeks to attain the world's goals through mysticism. In a later classification he adds thaumaturgical, reformist and utopain sects. A further type between church and sect is the denomination, into which some sects turn. The sociological status of the denomination was brought out by David Martin.

The church-sect distinction has been broadened in another way by Werner Stark, who has divided the church type into established and universal churches. The effect of the distinction is less strong than it might be because the criteria are vague and limited, being mainly to do with a church's relation with the political order rather than with its missionary policy. Troeltsch in the phrase quoted above shows the universal intention of the church, whether it be established or not, 'to cover the whole life of humanity'. Stark's first three volumes range over his threefold classification. His instances of established religion are to be found principally in the Church of England and in the Russian Orthodox Church. In both he underlines the concept of the sacred ruler and of the nation entrusted with a sacred mission. In the case of Russia, when monarchy no longer rules, there are democratic and proletarian reversals (volume one). The second volume is devoted to sects, while the third deals with two instances of the universal church, Roman Catholicism and Calvinism, each treated undeer the heads of conservatism and revolution.

The relationship of church and society, of Christianity and civilization, can take various forms or types. Nowhere have the alternatives been so clearly set out as in H. Richard Niebuhr's *Christ and Culture.* The first type Niebuhr shows is opposition, where Christ is seen to call men to abandon the world and to 'come out from among them and be separate'. The second type is that of agreement between Christ and culture. 'In our time', Niebuhr comments, 'answers of this kind are given by Christians who note the close relation between Christianity and Western civilization, between Jesus' teachings or the teachings about him and democratic institutions; yet there are occasional interpretations that emphasize the agreement between Christ and Eastern culture as well as some that tend to identify him with the spirit of Marxian society.

The first two types are poles apart, but the third type is synthetic. Christ is a Christ of culture but also a Christ above culture. Christ is the fulfilment of culture but is yet apart from it and above it. Niebuhr takes the thought of Thomas Aquinas as representing this type. The fouth type holds Christ and culture apart and in tension. In this type 'life must be lived precariously and sinfully in the hope of a justification which lies beyond history'. Luther represents this type. The fifth and final type is the conversionist. Human nature is fallen and perverted. This perversion is reflected and passed on by culture. The opposition of Christ to culture is therefore recognized, but the solution is not separation from the world or endurance. 'Christ is seen as the converter of man in his culture and society, no apart from these, for there is no nature without culture and no turning of men from self and idols to God save in society. It is in Augustine that the great outline of this answer seems to be offered; John Calvin makes it explicit.' Niebuhr points out that these alternatives present themselves to the churches at different historical times and in different social circumstances.

Lord Melbourne, Queen Victoria's first Prime Minister, has already made his entrance. He appears in the unexpected guise of *homo religiosus* in a paragraph of Lord David Cecil's *Lord M.* Not a regular churchgoer and against too much churchgoing, his reply to the Archbishop of York's invitation to evening service was 'No my Lord, once is orthodox, twice is puritanical'. 'Things are coming to a pretty pass when religion is allowed to invade private life' was his comment on an evangelical sermon. Pious emotionalism horrified him. He recommended the Church of England as being 'least meddlesome', Rome was insufficiently calm. He thought and read much in theology; he took in every new theological work and wrote copious notes in their margins. It was partly hisotical interest, partly ironical amusement, but he was also serious. 'He realized the sadness of human life too well not to long for the comfort of a religious faith.' A mystical element in him reached out after religion. 'The subject of religion exercised over him a strange compelling fascination.'

This strange, attractive man, who could not bear to hear the novels of Dickens read because there was enough misery in the world already and yet as Home Secretary put down the risings of agricultural labourers with vigour, has collected to himself many of the indicators of religion here : belief, the psychology of belief, religious practice in the form of churchgoing; liturgy, the sermon, the religious institution, the church, its officers, the theologians; comparative institutions of religion and comparative religion itself; social influence of religious ideas and institutions; the intellectual mystical and emotional elements in religion; natural and revealed theology; the history and geography of religion, all these appear in him.

Glock's summary of the dimensions of religious belief and practice is as follows: 'the experiential (subjective religious experience or emotion); the ritualidstic (specific practice expected of religious adherents); the ideological (the actual beliefs held by adherents); the intellectual (knowledge of basic tenets of belief); the consequential (the secular effects of religious belief, practice and experience)'. This summary provides categories which embrace the indicators of the religion of Lord Melbourne.

Not a subscribing sort of fellow, Lord M called himself, but how does sociology subscribe to these categories and indicators of religion? It does so by seeing in each one a social dimension and by seeing each one in a social dimension. These are not the same things. For example, the study of the church as a social institution means considering the church over and above its theological formulations and intentions as composed of certain social groups, and also considering the church as one social institution among many.

We can now look more closely at the work of the sociology of religion. Its widest interest is the sociology of religions, which are social institutions or systems of belief and practice and which in theological terms are more than human struggles with ultimate problems. Religions are such systems in response to God or gods, to superhuman beings with dimensions of the sacred, the transcendent or of what men take to be such. Some have argued that religions are illusions, but the point is not that religions are the fulfilment of human needs or the solutions to human problems but that they are responses to divine activity. The divine, the sacred, the transcendent initiate and act in ways that are not necessarily predictable in terms of human need or problems. Such a definition of religion embraces the major religions, Christianity, Islam, Buddhism, Hinduism, but excludes systems of belief an practice which reject the divine along with dimensions of the sacred and the transcendent such as Marxism or certain forms of humanism. There may be secondary features of the latter which have parallels in religions, for example the parallel of the dictatorship of the proletariat in Marxist theory with the reign of the saints in sectarian Christianity, but on this definition there is a basic, primary distinction between religions and systems of belief and practice which are not religions. This definition makes use of the sense of *religio* as binding men to God.

A further narrowing may occur. In certain cultures the sociologist of religion may concentrate upon one religion. The Indian may concentrate upon Hinduism in the same way that the useful introduction to the subject by T.B. Bottomore, *Sociology*, draws upon Indian examples to illustrate sociological themes because the author was lecturing to Indian stuents. The West produced sociology and thus the sociologist of religion has tended to focus his studies upon Christianity, which, although a religion of universal implication and outreach has had and continues to have a powerful influence upon Western culture. Within Christianity sociologies of the Church of England, of Roman Catholicism, of Protestantism, of sects can be developed, or sociologies of the forms of Christianity in one country, region or city and of their relationship with the rest of culture.

The sociologist may approach religion differently. He may take religion *in se, in mundo* and in relation to the divine and the transcendent, *coram deo*. For the sociologist religion *in se* is the observable social grouping created in response to the divine initiative : the church, the sect, the religious community. Religion is subdivided into the elements of the social group, the hierarchy, laity, worshippers, catechumens. It is seen in its various activities, worship, teaching administration. It is seen historically in terms of growth, change, contraction. It is seen geographically in its spread through a country, continent or the world. The sociologist in studying religion *in se* asks what does the church, sect, parish do? What does it think it does? Is it the same? What are the roles of the group, individual officer, actual, manifest, hidden roles? Many of the variables of sex, age, class, level of education are brought into use in these studies. Note that the questions asked are loaded. Later we shall have to consider the mental equipment the sociologist of religion brings to this task.

Religion *in mundo* stands not like Saint Athanasius against the world, necessary though it was for the saint and for the church then and at other times, but in relation to other social groupings - the groupings of government, occupation, leisure and many others in a complex society. The interaction of religion with other social groupings is a matter of great interest to the sociologist. Note that it is interaction; the movement is both ways. Religion works upon other social groupings; indeed is often intertwined with them. Social groupings also work upon religion. There are some who suppose that the traffic is one way, that religion is a product of or at the mercy of current social trends, or that forms of religion create a certain kind of society around them. A simple view will not do. The interaction is subtle and manifold. History, geography, anthropology, political science and economics play their part in the sociological study of religion *in mundo*. From another aspect it is a study of the circumstances in which the gospel of a particular religion is preached and a study of the ideas used in preaching it. The sociology of the Christian religion, with which the West is mainly concerned, follows. It is a study of the circumstances and content of the Christian religion. Circumstances and content are closely related. The preaching of a religion creates a response which is institutionalized. There is something to be seen, a practice, a new social group, an influence upon society as a whole, acceptance is visibly part of the world and can be studied in the same way as any other visible part of the world is open to scientific study.

Circumstances influence the response. They affect what can and what cannot be heard. Industrialization and urbanization are two broad labels for processes of much complexity bearing upon society. Industrial society is perhaps the best name for the kind of society now becoming worlwide, which finds its economic basis in inustrial production and its population in large cities. The study of the influence upon religion of industrialization and urbanization is a major task of the sociology of religion.

Circumstances also influence the preaching. Studies of ideology, the formation of ideas systems, reveal how much the content of preaching is influenced by social circumstances. The debate over the relationship of the Pruitan ethic and the spirit of capitalism, begun by Max Weber and continued by many others, reveals a real question. The conception of religion as social control comes from the fact that religion can be so used. The kings of France before the Revolution were more fierce with heresy than the French bishops. Disaffection in the main agency of social control, the church, was a greater threat to the throne than to the high officers of the church.

Religion *coram deo* is least accessible to the sociologist. The theologian, the biblical scholar, the philosopher of religion, the theological poet may approach. In so far as Dante had these skills he outside the Bible expresses best and deepest of all Christian religion *coram deo*. The *Doivine Comedy* springs out of faith. Perhaps then only the religious sociologist, he who accepts the truth of a given religion and works within its framework, may enter here? No, there is work for the sociologist of religion in studying the relationship of the religious community with the divine, in analysing the concepts of worship and teaching which communicate this relationship and noting the impact of this relationship upon the religious community and society at large. At this point the psychology of religion becomes an ally and perhaps a will of the wisp. Just as the assumptions of the sociologist have to be checked, so do those of the psychologist.

How is the study of the sociology of religion to be tackeld? Using whatever methods are appropriate to the particular type of study in hand, history, geography, the collection of statistics, censuses, surveys, attitude studies, the sociology of religion aims to acquire facts. It begins with whatever is the case. It has to select the right facts for the inquiry. Certain leading ideas or hypotheses help the right facts to emerge. the sociology of religion has to take into account the presuppositions used in forming hypotheses, in selecting areas for study, in judging that certain facts might be worth acquiring and not others. Any fact-collecting starts with a *critique des bases*. We must know where we begin and why we begin there. We must review our assumptions and methods.

Our next step takes us into the realm of explanation. Some distinctions may be helpful at this point. The sociologist of religion has rightly not been content to stop at definition. Indeed, definition of a logical sort has often been his starting-point, while ostensive definition which points to cases and describes has not seemed to him the whole of his work. Rather his task has been to explain religion. The explain religion may seem honourable, presumptuous or threatening according to how explanation is understood. There are various meanings to 'explain'. Which ones are appropriate to the sociology of religion? To explain may be a matter of spelling out the details. Explanation in this sense is harmless an is the process of ostensive definition already mentioned. it makes something plain or intelligible, as far as may be, and removes difficulties.

To explain may then go on to interpret. Interpretation puts something said into other words. Sometimes the transfer is straight. 'What you have said in Russian is as follows in English.' Sometimes the transfer is not. 'Where you say that what you really mean is this', so that a new and different meaning is assigned to the speaker's words. An explanation which begins by stating an implied meaning can go on to assign a different one.

Explanation may take another approach. To explain here may be to account for something by showing the cause of it or revealing its oirigin. 'I can explain this by showing how it all began or I can explain their behaviour by showing that the real cause for it is as follows.' It is not difficult to see from the second and third senses of 'explain' how the phrase 'explain away' arose, which is by explanation to do away with or modify something and so take away its force or significance.

The assumptions of the sociologist of religion as he sets about explanation need careful scrutiny. What is he trying to do? In which sense is he explaining? If he is interpreting are the categories of sociology adequate or apporporiate for the religious phenomenon with which he is dealing? If he is looking for causes or for origins is he lookin in the right direction, or is such a search appropriate? Answers to these questions should also make clear whether he is not after all trying to explain away religion.

The step then which follows the collecting of facts is the sorting of them. How do they group? What are the types of institution, parish, exercise of power, influence in society, moral emphases? The third step is interpretation. What do the facts and the categories mean? What are the causes of these facts and these types? The first two steps are take-off for deeper questions, which need much sensitivity in answering as well as appreciation of theological and philosophical bias. The generalizations which emerge here are few and have to be related to wider sociological generalizations. Perhaps we can only say so far that there is a relationship between religion and society (which the sociology of religion must assume anyway!), and that religious attitudes and practices. Other generalizations such as that a religious institution tends to diversify itself at a time of growth or that adults of the workin classes have never, except in small numbers, been members of the Christian churches, are invitations to further research, particularly of a geographical an cross-cultural kind.

In the sociology of religion the work of interpretation in the search for meaning and causes has often shaded into explaining away. Some of the pioneers' explanations of religion as social function, the cement of society (Durkheim), as universal neurosis, an escape from the problems of personality and society (Freud), or as an escape from the social situation or as imposed social control (Marx and Engels) have taken explanation that far.

What we have described so far is the sociology of religion, which is doing sociology, handling sociological problems, within the context of religion. The sociology of religion should be distinguished from religious sociology. Religious sociology is clinical. Some within the churches have seen sociology and religious sociology as useful tools in the carryingg out of their tasks. In this century the churches, particularly in France, the USA and this country, have nationally or through private initiatives developed sociographical methods for collecting information about themselves and about some features of the society in which they are placed. This is proper and intelligent. It is to use tools of administration which are available to any institution. Yet the tools have a double edge. Sociology has its own questions to ask the churches, springing from the relationships of religion and society or the relationship of preaching of the gospel and its response. These questions set up a healthy process of self-analysing within the churches as to their business. What are they doing and saying ? What should they be doing and saying?

One of the main distinctions between the sociology of religion and religious sociology is over the defining of problems. In religious sociology it is the religious executive who defines the problem. He wishes to use sociological methods to study a management problem, where to build churches or employ clergy. In the sociology of religion it is the sociologist or social philosopher who wishes, for example, to test an hypothesis about the function of an institution in a setting of religion. The sociology of religion attempts to put the study of social problems in religion on a basis of good scientific theory. Sociology in religious sociology is a sort of technology. The sociology of religion looks for a secure theoretical basis from which a better technology may emerge.

Yet King David sinned in conducting a census of the people of Israel (2 Samuel xxiv). The King was offered the choice of three punishments : seven years of famine in the land, three months' flight before his enemies or three days' pestilence. David resolved the matter by falling into God's hands as he should have done in the first place. His offence was to rely on the known armed might of the nation rather than oon the infinite mercy and strength of God. On the other hand students of the Bible will know the canonical book of Numbers, in which God requires Moses to count the people brought out of Egypt (chapter I) with the tribe of Levi reserved for a separate census (chapters 3 and 4).

Those of us in the churches who are interested in the social aspects of religion can never be sure if we follow in the steps of King David or of Moses. Some Roman Catholics argued after Vatican II that the previously undertaken studies in the sociology of religion were now out of court. God had unpredictably raised up Pope John, they said, created a new situation and thus up Pope John, they said, created a new situation and thus delivered a judgment upon those studies similar to that upon King David's census accompanied by the punishment of confusion in the ranks of Rome. Thus *Herder Correspondence:* Vatican II

> seems to have overtaken and to some extent bypassed the believers in sociological study as a primary remedy of the church's pastoral malaise. A living liturgy, a theology and preaching in closer touch with life, a revivification of the Christian language, better religious teaching a keygma drawing heavily on Scripture, are the new solutions offered and most widely believe in by those who wish to renew the Chruch's life. What sociology claimed to offer was a better knowledge of people—of life; but more dynamic and more profound ways of acquiring this knowledge have been made possible by *aggiornamento* theology and by the conciliar decress.

The situation may now appear less new than formerly, and still it requires study. In order to make decisions the officers of the church need some basic information about the situation and the resources they command. In this sense the task of Moses never ends, although no devout son of the Church can be foolish enough to deny the initiative to God or to forget that God's judgment of resources may be different from ours. god chose the weak things of the world, that he might put to shame the things that are strong, St Paul tells the Corinthian Church (I Corinthians i. 27), and when he opens the eyes of the young man can show the mountain full of chariots and horses of fire around Elisha, the man of God (2 Kings vi. 17).

Fortunately, then, the church cannot shape its own destiny. Market research will not reveal the Kingdom of God, which does not come by observation. The ultimate problems are not spoken to by a sociological word but by a theological word. Sociology may help to bring the theological word within speaking istance. It cannot make it heard. There can be no determinism in the sociology of religion, only intelligent guesses among probabilities, which the churches have always had to make. Sociology and the sociology of religion may help to make the probabilities clearer.

There are other benefits to the churches in these studies. One is a theological assumption. Sociology and the sociology of religion start from the goodness of God's world, that it is worth looking at, that human society and history reveal sufficient sense and regularity that orerly information can be drawn from study of them. Another is a stretch of perspective from the year to the generation or century, which may allow a proper confidence in and discrimination about the work to which the churches are called.

As an introduction to matters of philosophy which make up the next chapter neither we nor the churches should forget Karl Mannheim's warning that 'sociology in its historical origins is a secularized, perhaps the most secularized approach to the problems of human life. Mannheim may not be right, for we have already set up definitions of religion referring to super-human beings with the dimensions of the sacred and the transcendent which are agreeable to at least some sociologists, but the approach to religion of some sociologists of religion suggests that they are rivals to the theologian and the evangelist. If, as they think, the claims of religion are false, they have the gospel of enlightenment, which helps men to be truly men throuh self-knowledge. Know yourself by understanding religion for the darkness it really is and free yourself from it. The certainty of the missionary who declares the revelation of the one, true God has its counterpart in the certainty of the apostle of enlightenment. Unless the philosophy behind the sociology of religion is carefully reviewed the church may find it mistook for a helpful ally a dangerous rival.

Chapter-4

The Philosopher's Stone: Philosophy in the Sociology of Religion

Chapter-4

Philosophy was Mannheim's interest. It touches particularly his third sphere of religious expression. It lies behind that unity of natural and supernatural is Dorothy Osborne's quiet life and in the separation of Gabriel Oak's Sunday from his weekdays. It is now time to consider its bearing on the sociology of religion. We start with the fac t that a man's total view of reality affects how he handles any part of reality, even if he rejects a total view of reality or, like Camus, supposes it to be absurd. If there are more things in heaven and earth than are in his philosophy, then his philosophy is not likely to be a good one and what he does and how he handles parts of reality may be in spite of his philosophy and not because of it. A scientist will be influenced by, though rarely conscious of, his views of reality, such as that it is rational, that it makes sense to explore it, that all things work together for good to them that love God, that every scientific advance is a step towards the classless society or that every piece of work he does is a step towards an FRS. Yet these elements, in his view, will have practical consequences in how he handles his material or colleagues, in how he plans his next steps and in when he perseveres or gives up. If this is so with a physical scientist, how much more with the student of religion? Much of his study will consist in what he brings to it of his own outlook, of sympathy or repulsion, respect or contempt.

A paper by Edvard Vogt, 'Objectivity in the Sociology of Religion', makes a list of variables which may contribute to the sociologist's thinking : his personality in temperament, interests, values; his social position in his family, community and nation; his cultural and academic backhground; his religious position. This latter is the most important. A socioloist of religion may not be committed to any religion or ideology. It is unlikely. It is more likely that he is. If so the alternatives are that he is committed to some militantly anti-religious position, to an a-religious humanistic position or to a religious position. It makes some difference whether he is an official or ordinary or marginal member of his religious or ideological organization.

Vogt has led us into the sociology of knowlede, which is the asking of why and from what point of view people say things. Over and above the plain statement there is the question why and under what social conditions the speaker says or believes a certain thing to be the case. A man may believe that 'all Irishman are rogues'; the sociology of knowledge looks at his past experience with Irishmen, at his present job with a construction company employing increasing numbers of Irishmen or his home in an area of Irish immigration. These social factors may move him to see all Irishmen in such a way that they appear to him to be rogues. The sociology of knowledge is to do with the stance of the beholder and with those factors which turn his attention in certain directions. The bearing of the sociology of knowledge in the sociology of religion is first upon the sociologist himself in the discovery of bias and then upon the statements of religion. What is said about the interchanges between God and man may properly be considered by the sociology of knowledge and we return to the subject in the treatment of sociology and theology. It should be added that the sociology of knowledge tells us nothing about the truth or falsity of a statement, only about the orientation of the speaker. Therefore the most biased of speakers may sometimes be right and the most objective wrong. As Lord Melbourne said of the Reform Bill 'what all the wise men said would happen has not happened and what all the damned fools said has come to pass'. It follows therefore that the sociology of knowledge throws no light upon epistemology and should be distinguished from it. Epistemology is that branch of philosophy which deals with the truth or falsity of propositions, with how we know such and such to be the case. Information about social bias takes us no nearer the truth.

Bottomore makes the suggestive remark that 'epistemology is the basis of a sociology of knowledge, not vice versa'. Thus the first step is to establish the truth of a proposition, then to look at the bias of the speaker. The same priority serves in literary criticism: read the work first, then do your source criticism.

A further distinction must be drawn between the sociology of knowledge and ideology. If the sociology of knowledge is to do with the stance of the speaker, ideology is to do with his intentions. Reinhold Niebuhr comments that there is an ideological taint upon all social judgments, including those of the social scientists. Marxism put forward the theory of ideology but restricted the ideological taint to economic interests, when any interest or passion can colour judgment. For Marxism ideology tended to be a defect of the opponent's position, the Marxist position being free from it. Niebuhr goes on to ask why the ideological taint should be so strong in the social sciences and gives two answers. The first is the complexity, contingency and variability of the material handled by the social scientist, about that unlike the physical scientist, the social scientist, about which he cannot avoid making value judgments. The second is that unlike the physical scientist, the social scientist, cannot stand back from his material; he is part of it and is committed to positions and values within it.

The view taken here opposes the view of Barbara Wootton in *Social Science and Social Pathology* that 'the success of scientific investigation always has depended, and always must depend, upon the complete exclusion of elements of value.' Lady Wootton went in to claim that medicine is ousting moral judgments from criminal judgments and from definitions of the good life, quoting with approval a statement by a Luxembourg commission on crime: 'We do not pass moral judgments, but we try to see only the man as he is. If he is incorrigible, no longer rehabitable, or his progress is bad, we still pass no moral judgement'. There are three main rasons why this position is false. The decision to exclude moral judgments can only be taken on moral grounds and the attempt to eliminate value judgments is as successful as King Canute's to stem the tide; they keep coming in. The third reasons lies in the obvious failure in the time since the book was written of medicine to define the good life. The problems raised for the good life by new knowledge in medicine are not to be solved in terms of medicine itself but as always in those of theology, philosophy and ethics.

Ideology, in the sense made popular by Marx and Engels and used in sociology, is a statement which may be true or false but which conceals an intention. For example, it is held that employers intend to keep their workers poor, uncomplaining and hardworking. Therefore they commend in ideal terms obedience, work and poverty. An unfair critic of George Eliot might accuse her of ideology in the opening chapter of *Adam Bede,* when Adam regrets that his workmen stop when the church clock strikes six and do not finish the carpentry they have in hand. ('If only my men went on to the sound of the buzzer', I have heard an employer of today say, but *autre temps, autres moeursm,* which after all is a large part of the sociology of religion.) Ideology is to be looked for both in the writings of the sociologists of religion and in the statements of religion. Ideology is a useful concept, but shares the limitation of the sociology of knowledge in not establishing truth of falsity. Both of them help to solve why this is said rather than that and what the speaker is getting at or wishes to hide. They are part of the philosopher's detective armoury.

Another bias in philosophy to be detected is that of development. Mark Pattison wrote to Newman, 5 April 1878: 'Is it not a remarkable thing that you should have first started the idea - and the word Development, as the key to the history of church doctrine, and since then it has gradually become the dominant idea of all history, biology, physics, and in short has metamorphosed our view of every science, and of all knowledge? Newman's doctrine of development was devised to explain how the Roman Catholic Church had lost an exact likeness of the primitive church but still was the true church. His doctrine of development changed theological thinking from static to dynamic and made its fortune in other spheres of thought. The philosopher's task is to detect where it is rightly or wrongly used.

The two main branches of philosophy most influential in the nineteenth and twentieth centuries, idealism and empiricism, have made their mark upon the sociology of religion. Idealism helped to create the cultural climate of the nineteenth century. In its Hegelian form it integrated, was rational, put a primacy upon spirit, was favourable to religion as an interpretative force in human society as it was to any other dynamic expression of the human spirit such as science and technology and encouraged concepts of evolution and progress. Idealism was a confident philosophy and up to the First World War appeared to have captured the educated mind. William Temple was a skilled interpreter of idealism as congenial to Christian thought. The other nineteenth-century rival was Marxism which, it has been shown, turned Hegelianism on its head in stressing the primacy of matter and relegating spirit to a secondary place. In so doing, Marx and Engels were bound to attack religion. The criticism of idealism for them implied the criticism of religion. For the idealist philosoher, religion held a special place in society as the expression and interpreter of spirit; thus a sociologist who was an idealist would give much attention to religion in his study of society. He would tend to describe religion as having an integrating role and indeed to describe religion in terms of social function. At the same time he would take a comparative approach to religion as partial expression in different cultures of the same ultimate truths. The Hegelian was not a relativist; for him truth was anchored in the absolute, however partial some of its expresssions might be.

Changes in philosophy are changes in fashions rather than victories in war. Empiricism, which itself has an ancient history, rapidly replaced idealism after the First World War. It was less that idealism was out-argued, rather that a new generation of philosophers came on the scene who preferred Hume to Hegel. Empiricism is the philosophy of settling for what your senses give you. There is no grand theory, no unifying principles, no special place for any particular expression of the human spirit. There remains the simple test of putting every concept or statement against human experience. It human experience recognizes it, it passes. Empiricism is interested in what is there and reluctant to generalize. Changes in fashion may be swift and to extremes; skirts to from very short to very long. Thus the 1930s saw the extreme from of empiricism, logical positivism. Positivism itself is an older form of empiricism. Empiricism is agnostic about any reality beyond that delivered by the human senses. Positivism is dogmatic that there is no such reality beyond. The logical positivism of the 1930s was a ruthless attempt to cut out all grand theory or metaphysics, all ancient philosophical problems about the existence of God or the immortality of the soul, by restricting reality to scientifically testable assertions and to statements which were logically true, such as 2 + 2 = 4. The weakness of logical positivism was that its method of restriction, the verification principle, was not open to its own test. Thus the whole campaign against traditional philosophy came to nothing, lost like the battle for want of a nail. The effects upon the doing of philosophy were not entirely harmful. Those who had been through the mill of logical positivism learned to be careful about the proper use and function of language. Yet other effects were harmful; the loss of confidence in the purpose of philosophy; the loss of contact with the great questions which had claimed the atttention of the past, the diversion into minor interests. Logical positivism and its successor, linguistic philosophy, contributed towards a climate of empiricism within which the sociology of religion was undertaken in most of this century.

Mention should be made of a third strand of philosophy in these centuries, but particularly in this century, which had much the same effect upon the sociology of religion as empiricism, namely existentialism. Existentialism, whether religious or atheistic, was the assertion of the unique individual over against the all-embracing system of idealism and over against the tendency of empiricism to reduce reality to something less than personal. Existentialism asserts the deciding I, *'le monde, c'est moi'*, I am the world and I create its values. As a protest it has its values but as a normative account of reality existentialism is less than adequate.

The valuable contribution of empiricism to the sociology of religion was the promotion of fieldwork. It made its professors leave the speculations of the armchair and study and go to look at cases. Indeed there have been a great deal of surveys and inquiries with much collecting of evidence. Empiricism, however, is committed to no theories of integration and therefore does not encourage the inquirer to take some theory of explanation to his material. Yet it does, if not encourage, tempt the inquirer to reductionism and to relativism.

An example of reductionism is the seeing of the function of religion as adjustment to environment. As Mannheim points out, if adjustment to environment is made 'a measuring-rod for human action, a dehumanization of life is bound to ensue'. It is one of the major problems of social work that much of what is done is its name is adjustment to environment by virtue of the terms of reference of its statutory and voluntary agencies. The unwary social worker and administrator find themselves in the ironical situation of professing and seeking to raise human dignity and ending by lowering it. Administrative change such as reorganization of local authority social services is no answer. Something can be hoped for from the development of the counselling ideology, which is an ideology with the desirable intention of raising the profession of social work as much as raising the client. The two boioks of Halmos are an interesting return to idealist philosophy. In *The Faith of the Counsellors,* 1965, Halmos argued that certain professional workers in the social services shared a set of assumptions about man and society. In *The Personal Service Society* he went on to show.

> that all practising counsellors testify that the positive - loving, compassionate, sympathetic, co-operative, creative, or what you will—polarity has an edge over the negative polarity of our strivings . . . In my opinion this belief is not based on a verifiable psychological proposition: it is a doctrine . . . The professional role havin been assumed, the doctrine arises from the role. It is 'situationally determined', and therefore, it is ideological.

Doctrines may change and ideological positions be reversed. Halmos argued that because of the failure of political solution to social problems the ideology, which he outlined, of social work was adopted. Yet there are also those in social work who argue that non-politicial social work fails and therefore its ideology should be political.

Reductionism also empties the power of symbols and thus despirtualizes life. Mannheim names some of the archetypes or primordial images: the Hero, the Sage, the Virgo, the Saint, the Repentant; or dominating the realm of Christian imagination : Baptism, Absolution, Agape, the Eucharist, the Good Shepherd, the Cross, Redemption. Reductionism misses his further point that without experiencing the power of such symbols 'no consistent conduct, no character formation and no real human co-existence and co-operation are possible' The result of emptying symbols is the fragmenting of experience. Idealism is less open to it.

Relativism is an error springing from a harmless fact that one thing may be related to another but going on to deny that things are related to any absolute or that judgements may vbe expressed about the relationship or the things. 'This is one thing, that is another, and that's all there is to it' sums it up. Common sense does add value judgments to its consideration of things and their relationship. Some things are better, nobler, wiser, more useful than others. Common sense applies a hierarchy of values. Relativism in the sociology of religion denies a hierarchy of values. No religion is better than another; all are going the same way perhaps—to secular extinction or to God, who cares? A classic instance of relativism is Ruth Benedict's well known *Patterns of Culture,* nortably in such remarks as

> 'the observer will see the bizarre developments only in alien cultures, not in his own. Nevertheless this is obviously a local and temporary bias. There is no reason to suppose that any one culture has seized upon an eternal sainty and will stand in history as a solitary solution of the human problem. Even the next generation knows better. Out only scientific course is to consider our own culture, so far as we are able, as one example among innumerable others of the variant configurations of human culture.

Our earlier discussion of religious culture shows that such a position is false. If a culture incarnates a religion and that religion has disclosed what Ruth Benedict calls eternal sainty then that culture will stand in history as a solitary solution of the human problem. It is conceivable whatever view may be taken of past cultures; there are many who would hold that the Christian revelation has disclosed eternal sainty. Relativism is not a position given much support by logic or philosophy. It is rather a reaction to the overwhelming impact of complex evidence.

Relativism is subject to the criticism of the sociology of knowledge. The point is taken up in P. Berger's *Rumour of Angels* in the chapter 'Relativizing the Relativizers'. Berger argues that the sociologuy of knowledge relativizes the present. 'While other analytic disciplines free us from the dead weight of the past, sociology frees us from the tyranny of the present. Once we grasp our own situation in sociological terms, it ceases to impress us as an inexorable fate.' The effect is to reverse the position of Feuerbach, who 'regarded religion as a gigantic projection of man's own being . . . instead of a dialogue between man and a superhuman reality, religion became a sort of human monologue.' Berger suggests that since Feuerbach 'the entire historical-psycholoical-sociological analysis of reliious phenomena . . . has been primarily a vast elaboration of the same conception and the same procedure'. But this is a relative position. It has nothing to do with the truth of the matter. Hegel's dialectic, which Feuerbach turned upside-down, could be right. It is logically possible and consistent to hold that religion is a dialoue between man and a superhuman reality.

Mascall devotes a chapter of *The Openness of Being* to Berger's views. He agrees that 'if the secularisers and relativisers claim the right to apply the criterion of the sociology of knowledge to the beliefs of traditional supernaturalist believers, they cannot, if they are consistent, refuse to allow those criteria to be applied to their own desupernaturalized views'. He goes on to ask what happens when the diagnostic method of sociology of knowledge is applied to the sociology of knowledge itself. The consequences need not be destructive, he thinks, 'provided it were firmly kept in mind that the question of origin and the question of truth are distinct; if the question of origin were held to supersede or to invalidate the question of truth it would have the same suicidal and self-destructive character which infects all types of scepticism'.

Empiricism does not accord to religion a central place in its scheme of reality (indeed it is questionable whether empiricism has a scheme of reality in the sense in which idealism has). A consequence has been that under the dominant influence in western culture of empiricism, secularization has been presented as a problem. There is also a problem of secularization for the idealist, but it is less acute. For him secularization is a matter of the rise and fall of religious institutions and observances, but the basic principle of interpretation and integration of the universe is secure. For the empiricist everything is at stake in the decline of religious institutions and observances, because the through them alone religion exerts its influence and not through a sympathetic philosophy as well. If for ideological reasons the sociologist of religion welcomes the decline of religious institutions he is likely to draw attention to secularization. All of this has no bearing on whether secularization is the case or whether other processes working against secularization are to be found.

Our earlier definition of religion with its grasp of the transcendent and the super-empirical leads us to a classical problem of philosophy, namely, the relationship of finite and infinite. How can we, finite human beings, know and speak of the infinite, the transcendent, the super-empirical? Are they not by definition separate from us, with a great gulf fixed which no man can cross? In brief the answer to the first question is that we can, and the answer to the second is no. To take language first, language does much of the job for us as a vehicle of wonder and awe, in poetry, in expressin archetypal symbols, in lifting use out of ourselves. Language is a chief means of communication within a culture; if our culture has incarnated the Christian religion which, whatever else it is, is a transcendent religion, then its language has been adapted to carry some of the significance of transcendence. By transcendence is meant here not the going deep into human experience but that which is other, outside and beyond us and yet taking the initiative in meeting us. If there is a linguistic consequence of the Incarnation it is that human language conveys a sufficient knowledge of God. 'He that hath seen me has seen the Father' (St.John, xiv. 9). Language alsoi approaches the infinite by negation. The very negatives which speak of that which is *not* finite, *above* our world, *beyond* our experience, point in the right direction. Thus positively and negatively language does its work and leaves open the possibility of relationship between finite and infinite.

If we are to explore this relationship there are a number of ways of doing so. First we can consider those human experiences of awe and wonder which lift us up and point beyond our normal experience and towards the transcendent. Secondly, we can consider and refine those traditional arguments from finite to the infinite—the arguments for the existence of God may not take us all the way to the full revelation of religion but they take us some of the way. Thirdly, we can make use of the analogy of being or of faith. Analogy is a helpful concept in relating one thing to another, which allows for similarities and differences between them. The analogy of being provides steps in the relationship of finite and infinite. If we are successful by these means we shall have made possible for the theologian natural theology. Natural theology is the movement from human experience by reason towards what religion gives in revelation. Many theologians deny the possibility of natural theology on the grounds of the utter seperation of finite and infinite and of the corruption of human reason. The former ground is taken by Karl Barth and the latter by Luther, who said that 'reason is the devil's harlot and can do nothing but slander all that God says or does'. Natural theology does not remove from revelation its task of declaring the hidden things of God and is certainly not a superior kind of religious knowledge. Nor does natural theology take anything from faith, for what God chooses to reveal is accepted by some and not by others. 'O righteous Father, the world knew thee not, but I knew thee; and these knew that thou didst send me' (St John, xvii. 25). Both natural and revealed theology present a position or point of view requiring the commitment of faith.

Yet the establishment of natural theology is essential to sound work in the sociology of reliion and in comparative religion to preserve both from reductionism and relativism. Explanation is the filling out of one finite statement with other finite statements, but unless finite statements in religion are open to the infinite there is no escape from reductionism and relativism. In the sociology of reliion Jerusalem has much to do with Athens. Indeed all roads both in the sociology of religion and in comparative religion lead to Jerusalem, in the sense of the heavenly city, which is the mother of us all, or else they are dead ends.

Chapter-5

THE SOCIOLOGIST OF RELIGION AND THE THEOLOGIAN

Chapter-5

As a playwright T.S. Eliot was a theologian writing plays. In *The Cocktail Party,* Helen Gardner says 'the divine broke into the pattern of ordinary relationships in the form of the heroic' In *The Confidential Clerk* 'we are asked', she says, 'to feel its presence in a life of the utmost banality', that of Eggerson the clerk. It is indeed a reversal of wordly values.

Leonard Woolf was a friend of Eliot, printed and published *The Waste Land,* helped him to become a naturalized Englishman but claimed no part in his conversion to the Church of England. He wrote in his autobiography that he could produce a psychological explanation but that he had no 'sympathetic understanding'of it.

We may begin by seeing theology, whatever more it may be, as the understanding and explanation of the religious dimension of life, using 'religious' in the sense already defined with its grasp of the super-empirical and transcendent. Eliot lives in this religious dimension, understands it intellectually and sympathetically and explains it in his plays and poetry, Woolf sees it in Eliot but claims no sympathetic understanding of it. Should the sociologist of religion understand religion and in what sense? Is Eliot or is Woolf the model?

In order to answer the question let us first explore theology and take as our guide T.F. Torrance's *Theological Science.* Torrance first locates 'authority neither in individualism nor in some intuitional seat, but in a reality that is wholly given and transsubjective, and simply and absolutely authoritative through its giveness'; and quoting A.E. Taylor, whose view of authority this is, makes theology 'a genuine, assured yet progressive science of God'. Science is required not because God is a problem but because we are. Because our relations with God have become problematic we must have a scientific theology, Torrance puts it. He goes on :

'Scientific theology is active engagement in that cognitive

relation to God in obedience to the demands of His reality and self-giving. In it we probe into the problematic conditions of the human mind before God and seek to bring knowledge of Him into clear focus, so that the truth of God may shine through to it unhindered by its opacity and the human mind may acquire clear and orderly forms through which to apprehend and concieve His reality.'

Later Torrance says: The theological knowledge pivots upon what is *given*, given from beyond it, and which does not depend on our discovering it.' And 'Theological thinking is theological, not just from our own centres, but from a centre in God, from a divine ground ... It pivots upon the fact that God has made himself known and continues to make himself known, that He objectifies Himself for us, so that our knowledge is a fullfilled meeting with objective reality.' (Eliot then has a fulfilled meeting with objective reality, but Woolf has an unfulfilled one.) Torrance concludes that he has tried to show that

> 'Christian theology has its place of inquiry within the field of rational knowledge, and to claim that in accordance with its attempt to behave in terms of the nature of its own proper object, it must be allowed to adapt and modify language, to shape and form its concepts, and to delimit or expand its use of terms, like any other branch of knowledge or scinece, Because of the unique nature of its own proper object – there is only one Lord God – its use of language and thought forms will not unnaturally often be unique.

There is a further question. How do we recognize the selfgiving of God and the things of God? We must here seek the aid of natural theology outlined at the end of the previous chapter. Our answer lies in the rhetorical question of Austin Farrer: 'Unless I had some mental machinery for thinking the bare notion of God, could I recognize his revelatory action as that of God?

Theology, then, has its place in rational knowledge. We have already seen that sociology has its place. Should the sociologist know theology? It is possible to answer no, on the ground that each has different objects of study. It is more fruitful to take a broader view of rational knowledge which relates studies in one sphere to studies in another. Philosophy is the link, while the method is dialogue. For theology all knowledge relates to the fundamental knwoledge given by its object. If this braoder relationship of theology and sociology applies to the sociologist in general, it applies in particular to the sociologist of religion to theology?

An answer to this question begins with theological views of religion, for religion is not theology. It is also worth remembering, as Torrance points out, that the dialouge above mentined is not between science (and its various forms including sociology) and religion, but between science and theology, There is a series of views held by theologians about religion ranging from severe criticism amounting almost to rejection to acceptance. Let us take an example of each extreme. The most famous attack on religion be theologian in this century is Karl Barth's. In his *Church Dogmatics* he has a section entitled 'The Revelation of God as the Abolition of Religion'. 'The English translation 'abolition of religion' for the German '*die Aufhebung der Religion'* unfortunately fails to bring out the ambiguity of *Aufhebung* which implies less destruction and cancelling out and more lifting up. Barth begins by setting the scene:human religion is 'the realm of man's attempts to justify and to sanctify himself before a capricious and arbitrary picture of God', while the church is 'the locus of true religion, so far as through grace is lives by grace'. First of all religion is unbelief. Revelation is what counts; man can make no move towards revelation, by himself he will go in the wrong direction. 'From the standpoint of revelation religion is clearly seen to be a human attempt to anticipate what God is His revelation will to do and does do. It is the attempted replacement of the divine work by a concept of God arbitrarily and willfully evolved by man.' So it follows that 'religion is the contradiction of revelation, the concentrated expression of human unbelief'. Barth will have not that religion is 'a kind of outstretched hand which is filled by God in His revelation', on the contrry 'in religion man bolts and bars himself against revelation by providing a substitute'. Therefore revelation contradicts and displaces religion, for what is achieved in religion is never the truth, an anti God is worshipped intead of the Lord God. The revelation in Jesus Christ replaces all man's attempts at justification and sanctification, at conversion and salvation. Religion can also be seen as man's attempt to master the world, to make the world serviceable to him, who is only a creature.

For Barth what is true religion? 'Religion is never true in itself and as such.' It can only be true in the way that man is justified, from without; i.e., not of its own nature and being but only in virtue of a reckoning and adopting and separating which are foreign to its own nature and being'. However, Barth goes on to bring out the ambiguity of *Aufhebung:* 'The abolishing of religion by revelation need not mean only its negation: the judgment that religion is unbelief. Religion can just as well be exalted in revelation, even though the judgment still stands.'

What of the Christian religion? The Christian religion is the true one only as we listen to the divine revelation.'[9] It also is justified from without. It is under the same judgment as all other religions, it is not acquitted by any inner worthiness. Indeed, Barth goes on to suggest that church history is a history of unbelief, because the Christian religion is tempted to stand on its own merits and not on the grace it receives.

We may pause before considering the second theological view of religion to ask whether the positon of Barth can allow any talk with the sociologist of religion. Why should the theologian waste time with one who explores the vagaries of human sin and error? After all, the theologian is familiar enough with them and his task is to communicate and expound that word of grace in the Christian revelation which alone can heal. Yet the fact is that those who have held Barth's position have often proved to be the most sympathetic students of other religions. Henrik Kraemer is a notable example. His uncompromising *The Christian Mesage in a Non-Christian World (1938),* prepared for the Madras conference of the World Missionary Council, holds both the distinctiveness of the Christian revelaton in what Kraemer calls biblical realism and a view of other religions, and indeed of religion in general, which is akin to Barth's. The book is also a careful and sympathetic analysis of the religions of the world. Kraemer's own service as a missionary in Java and the Dutch East Indies was marked by the regard in which he was held by those of other faiths and religions. (As a student at the first graduate School of Ecumenical Studies at the Bossey Ecumenical Institute near Geneva, of which Kraemer was director, I remember Kraemer's vivid accounts of the Javanese shadow plays and of the spiritual truths the plays were designed to communicate.)

Two reasons may be put forward in explanation. The first lies in the ambiguity of Barth's *Aufhebung*. It is the same ambiguity as in St John's 'lifting up' of the Son of Man: is it lifting up on the cross or exaltation in glory? The ambiguity leaves upon the possibility of dialogue. It should be said that the view taken in Kraemer is not mainly a 'know your enemy' view, in which study is undertaken in order to defeat him. There is this element, but it is not sufficient to cancel or explain the sympathey. The second reason is that the more a theologian is seized by the majesty and graciousness of God the greater his charity towards human endeavours including religion. This was apparently so of Barth whose distinctive intellectual approach made him more rather than less interested in and sympathetic towards human initiatives in music, politics and world religions. At the same time Barth's position allowed him to stand without compromise at the point where he and other Christians in Germany felt it right to resist the attempt by Hitler and the government of the country to·subvert the Evangelical Churh by introducing doctrines from the Nazi creed of national and racial superiority. The church struggle and the setting up of the Confessing Church drew inspiation from Barth, whose view of religion cannot but be coloured by the preversions which 'the German Christians', the accommodators, were prepared to allow.

The second theological view of religion, that of acceptance, comes from Hans Kung, influential among a new generation of Roma Catholic theologians and an appreciative interpreter of Barth to the Roman communion. Kung begins with the fact that Christians are a minority in the world; of its population of three and a half billion, about 925 million are Christians, less than a third. In this situation it is hard to maintain the old doctrine of outside the church no salvation. Kung goes on to show that the Second Vatican Council has moved away from outside the church no slavation to affirming that men can be saved outside the church. Its *Constitution on the Church* declares :

> 'Those who, while guiltlessly ignorant of Christ and Gospel and of his Church, sincerely seek God and are brought by the influence of grace to perform his will as known by the dictates of conscience, can achieve salvation. Nor does divine Providence deny the assistance necessary to salvation to those who, without having attained, through no fault of their own, to an explicit knowledge of God, are atriving, not without divine grace, to lead a good life.'

King criticises this as too negative; it contradicts the New Testament view of the church and the Christians tradition derived from it, it makes life harder for missionaries who can hardly invite non-Christians to join the community of the church when all men of good will are already in the church and it makes non-christians into members of the church against their will. King's criticism is that Vatican II has used the well-worn liberal trick of fishing without a net.

King thinks that the right way to proceed is to make a positive assessment of the world religions in relation of God's universal plan of salvation which invloves also a reconsideration of the place and task of the church in the world which is not the church. This positive assessment rests on God's free and all-embracing grace, for God is the God of all men; God is known not just through natural theology but as the God of grace. Vatican II also support this view :

> 'One is the community of all peoples, one their origin, for God made the whole human race to live over the face of the earth. One also is their final goal, God. His providence, His manifestations of goodness, His saving design extend to all men, until that time when the elect will be united in the Holy City, the city ablaze with the glory of God, where the nations will walk in His light'.

Kung puts forward a Christian universalism. Basing himself on the scriptures he gives these elements to it: despite whatever truths they have concerning the true God, the world religions are in error, yet the world religions do, though in error, proclaim the truth of the true God. (Though they are far from God, God is not far from them.) As against the 'extraordinary' way of salvation which is the church, the world religions can be called the 'ordinary' way of salvaton for non-Christian humanity. The world religions teach truths about the Gospel of Chirst which, in their error, they do not know as that which it really is: the truth. They recognize man's need of salvation, they recognize God's graciousness, they listen to their prophets. But Kung adds that it is the Gospel of Jesus Christ that is able to liberate the truth of the world religions form their entanglement in error and sin. Thus the world religions are ambiguous: 'on the one hand, embraced, upheld and penetrated by God's grace, and yet on the other hand, in the bonds and oppression of man;s betrayal and wickedness.' King holds that Christian faith stands for radical universalism, but one grounded and made concrete in, and centred upon, Jesus Christ. If so, there is a consequence first for every human being. 'Every human being is under God's grace and can be saved: whatever he be, of this or that nation or race, of this or that caste or class, free or slave, man or woman, or even inside or outside the Church of Christ. Every human being can be saved, and we may hope that everyone is.' And then a consequence for every world religion is under God's grace and can be a way of salvation : whether it is primitive or highly evolved, mythological or enlightened, mystical or rational, theistic or non-theistic, a real or only a quasi-religion. Every religion can be a way of salvation and we may hope that every one is.'

There is a strong ideological element in Kung argument. It comes in the attempt to accommodate the Christian Church's minority position, which may beocme more marked as the population of non-Christian countries grows, to a world mission and to the proclaiming of a distinctive gospel of a unique revelation of God's graciousness in Jesus Christ. The dangers of revelaton of also apparent, as also danger of an end to dialogue, for why bother to talk if we are all going the same way to the same destination? Also the urge to mission may be relaxed through King's view as effectively as through the view which he criticised put forward in Vatican II's *Constitution on the Church.*

We are now in a position to answer the question of te relationship of the sociologist of religion to theology. The views of the theologians about religion to theology. The views of the theologians about religion are of the first importance to the sociology fo religion. What the theologians say about religion has considerable impact on the belief and practice of religious bodies, on how their members see their functions, on how religious bodies relate themselves to the outside world, on their programmes of mission, on their attitudes to other religions. The views given above of Barth and King, of quasi-rejection and acceptance or religion, are widely held and full of practical implications. They happen to be views within Chirstian theology, but Christianity is not the only religion with theologians. The sociologist of religion must know what the theologians. The sociologist of religion must know what the theologians of all religions say, as they assemble a theory within which religion is practised. It is necessary to stress theologians of all religions, since there is a tendency to which we turn later for sociologists to devote attention to what certain theologians, apparently congenial to the sociologists, say. The sociologist, says M.Labbens, needs *'une certaine formation theologgique'*, because to make a sociological study of a religion is not just a matter of observing and describing outward acts but of penetrating a culture.

In additon to knowing what the theologian says in order to see its impact upon religion and socity the sociologist needs to consider the social and cultural climate within which the theologian speaks. Barth in the setting of the German church struggle and Kung in the minority situation of Christians in an increasing world population are illustrations, as is that classic work of Max Weber's, *The Protestant Ethic and the Spirit of Capitalism*, where he considers the ethical teaching of Richard Baxter and other seventeenth-century Puritan divines, first showing what they taught, then its social setting and finally its social and religious impact. One reason for the enduring quality of Weber's main conclusion, 70 years old and going strong, which is a good life span for a sociological conclusion as well as for man, is that it is so well founded on these three stages, beginning with what the theologians said. A further conclusion may be that a careful examinantion of theological statements is the way to pick up enduring hypotheses and conclusions, of which there are not many, in the sociology of religion. Roger Mehl comments that 'a doctrinal symbol or confession of faith has more value for the sociologist than an individual works of theology. The theologians discussed above show what treasures individual works of theology have for the sociologist, especially when they articulate views widely held within churches and religious bodies, but it is possible to agree with Mehl that even more is given in the normative theological statements and symbols of the religious bodies.

Having earlier shown theology to have its place in rational knowledge, having seen the beginning of the sociologist's interest in theology, let us go on to look at the various areas of theological study and at the sociologist's connection with them. Our model once again is Christian theology, but other models can be found for non-Christian theology. An essay by N.P. Williams in *The Study of Theology* entitled 'What is Theology?' sets out this catalogue :

1. The intellectual prolegomena of *Dogmatic Theology* - the *Philosophy and Psychology of Religion,* cinceived as treating, not merely of the bases of religious and theistic conviction, but also of the nature and function of Authority in respect of belief, and the degree (in any) in which this can be ascribed to Scriputer, Traditions or the Church.

2. The study, textual, critical, historical and expository of the Bible, regarded as containing the 'revealed' data for, and the historical prolegomena to, Dogmatic Theology.
3. *Dogmatic Theology* itself, the study of 'revealed truth' concerning the six great Christian ideas of the Trinity, the Incarnaion, the Atonement, the Church, the Sacraments, the Last Things - the crown and summit of sacred learning.
4. *Moral Theology and Casuisty* - the science of Christian conduct. To this may be added as a natural corollary, though its interest is professional rather than general in scope,

5. *Pastoral Theology,* the *ars artium* of guiding and influencing souls.
6. *Ascetical and Mystical Theology.*
7. *Ecclesiastical History* and *Patristics.*
8. *Canon Law*
9. *Liturgiology*

If these are the areas of study in theology, may sociology freely join in? The answer has to be yes, with one qualification, which is that sociology is not Christian religion in particular. Mehl would open the theological range to sociology, as indeed much of it already is. Dogmas and confessions of faith have a date and a certain social context; they answer needs felt by the community. 'It is not true that the great doctrinal formulations of Christianity were undertaken at a time when intellectuals of Greed background had penetrated widely into the church and had brought with them their culture and their concern (which, moreover, was authentically Christian) to make known the Christian message to pagan culturla elites in a language that was accessible to them?' In addition it is hard to seperate form and content in any doctrinal formulation.

> 'When exegetes, who in their way also are sociologists, study the New Testament revelation, they emphasize how much this revelation is couched in categories inherited form Judaism, from prophetism, from late-Judaism, form apocalyptic and Essence sects, etc. At the same time, they underline the dogma of the unity of the Old and New Teataments. The biblical revelation is tied to a certain human group which its own sociology and mentality.'

It is also true that the Word of God comes to men in a given historical and sociological situation.

> 'Jesus' statement that salvation comes from the Jews is both a theological datum and a sociological fact. Christianity declares that God reveals himself not in a non-temporal fashion pur in history, that he makes himself known to a given group of men, to such-and-such a socity. It teaches that this revelation is received (and also partially rejected) through the categories of thought, the ideas, and the schemes which are the particular possession of a given

society. Form that, we are justified in saying that not only does Christianity auhtorize a sociology of Christianity; in certain respects it calls for it.'

Mehl invokes the principle of incarnation to authorize a sociology of Christianity in the same way as Eliot invokes it to speak of culture incarnating religion. At this stage of the sociology of religion the observer is struck not by the boldness but by the timidity of its practitioners. Looking at the list of areas given on pp.48-9 he can see that some have drawn attention, others have drawn very little. Those working within the context of the church have used social studies in certain of these areas, notably in biblical studies (2), in pastoral theology (5), church history (7) and liturgiology (9). In addition the move forward in French religious sociology came from Le Bras adding a social and historical dimension to canon law studies. (8). Sociologists working outside the context of the church have done much as a reflection of a dogmatic truth (3) but rather as a social institution demonstrating certain forms fo human conduct which cuts the church loose from any theological mooring post. Moral theology (4) is the area of some studies and church history (7) of others. We shall later consider examples of these, but at this point can remark that if we want a sociology of Christianity, and the catalogue of areas of theology given above marks out the ground, then we have a long way to go.

In order to achieve a sociology of Christianity or if any other religion, what do we require further of the sociologist apart from competence in his discipline? we have shown that he requires to know theology, its areas, its normative statements and symbols and those individual works of theology which bear upon his interests. More than that we have seen that the areas of theology can give him his own areas of work or dimensions which bear upon his work. Should he also be a believer, an opponent or neutral? The simple answer is that it is desirable that he should be a believer, he can't be neutral; if he is an opponent his work will show it.

The advantage of the believer is that he enters religoin sympathetically to undertake his sociological study; he enters with the spirit of Eliot writing his plays, describing the clerk Eggerson in his garden from which he brings '... marrows, or beetroot, or peas ... for Mrs Eggerson', the ordinary produce of the garden standing for divine graciousness. The believer has the advantage of sympathetic respect for his object of study. Is the believer simply a propagandist making a case for his religion, and blind to the defects obvious to others? The evidence from biblicial studies and from church history, where most of the work has been done by believers, would be that the answer is no. The rules of the discipline, of historical study, literary criticism, scientific study cannot be avoided. The believer's distinctive contribution is his attitude and disposition. Further the believer is declared.

At the beginning of the previous chapter some of the influences which might bear upon the sociologist's thought about religion were set out. The believing sociologist in his studies of religion will not by virtue of his belief escape the climate of the particular community or general culture to which he belongs. He will share with his climate of the day are almost beyond questioning. He will share the same standard of living, read the same papers and watch the same TV programmes, even if he may from different judgments about them. This is to say that the believing sociologist of religion belongs to his day and generation with all its strengths and wearkness.

The strongest argument for the believer undertaking the sociology of religion is that he is the right side of the transcendentimmanent, super-empirical line, or more accurately he is in a position through his commitment to know what is at stake in the distinction made and in the definition of religion used earlier. The case for the Christian believer is well put by Berger:

> 'The Christian faith, when it is true to itself and really is in the world but not of it, provides distance from society and thus creates opportunities for perception ... The Christian sees man as having a destiny over and beyond society ... In thus transcending society, the Christian faith at the same time makes it possible to see society more

clearly.'

While in more general terms Schmidt's refutation of Renan applies :

> 'If religion is essentially of the inner life, it follows that it can be truly grasped only from within. But beyond a doubt, this can be better done by one in whose inward consciousness an experience of religion plays a part. There is but too much danger that the other (the non-believer) will talk of religion as a blind man might of colours, or one totally devoid of ear, of a beautiful musical composition.'

The neutral position is impossible. A man is either for or against religion or a particular form of it. Neutrality can be no more than a disguise, usually for opposition. Opposition may take a number of forms, declared or undeclared, conscious or unconscious. The Marxist form is one. If for the Marxist the purpose of philosophy is not merely to understand the world but to change it, the task of the sociology of religion is also one of liberation. The sociologist has to help in freeing men form the shackles of religion by exposing in his studies the residue of this enslaving ideology of a dying culture so that men may see its true nature. The studies in the sociology of religion in Communist countries are not an objective study of what is there but rather the recording of the remains of a dying superstition so as to hasten its death. There is no further place for religion. In a Communist state it has lost its function of compensating for social enslavement, for in such a state men are by definition liberated. The Western Marxist may be less naive, but for him religious vitality may be some indication of how far wrong the political and economic order is as well as of the effectiveness of the power elite in exercising control through ideology.

A second opponent is the apostle of enlightenment. He also brings a message of liberation. The Marxist delivers from religion by changing the social and economic order and so making it possible for men to be human; the apostle of enlightenment helps men towards their full humanity by bringing them the sociological knowledge of their religious situation. At the best this puts religion 'in its place' among other things, activities and institutions, where it ceases to be the mainspring of culture. The cultured despisers of religion are an old race from Celsus to the opponents of Schleiermacher and it is no surprise that they should be found among sociologists of religion. Barth comments that 'tolerance in the sense of moderation, or superior knowledge, or scepticism is actually the worst form of intolerance', and that in this attitude religion and man are not taken seriously. At worst the apostle of enlightenment is a crusader for another phiolosophy or quasi-religion, perhaps for a sort of sociologism, whereby the facts and observations of sociology make up the whole of reality, all else being fantasy.

The third opponent is not very different from this. He is the apostate, the former member or officer of the church or religious body, who uses the sociology of religion to attack that commitment which he has abandoned, or as a sort of holding device to see what religion is really about, or as s transit-camp where waiting for new orders he looks back to his old station. There is no evidence that those who have turned to the sociology of religion from a religious profession or commitment have through the sociology of religion made their way back to it. It is doubtful if there could be, for the sociology of religion will not solve matters of the truth of religion.

All three opponents have a curious affinity with Barth's position over religious. For them it is a form of human corruption, from which one must escape oneself and free others. Yet like the tentacles which enfolded Laocoon and his sons it is almost impossible to escape it, perhaps the only course is to warn people of the reach of the tentacles. Over it all, as Lord Melbourne felt of religion, there is a strange compelling fascination. The apsotle of enlightment and the apostate have ears eager to hear news of disaster or weakness in the churches or religious bodies, reanging from falling numbers of people attending services or falling ordination figures to cries of decline and fall by the spokesmen of the church. Some sociologists or religion only take note of a certain kind of theologian, who reduces theology to anthropology and the chruch to a social function: Tillich, Bultmann, the American *Death of God* theologians are frequently quoted in their writings. These theologians, in the case of the former two somewhat unfairly, are seen as identifying their work with the sociologist's and sharing a common faith in enlightment by education and in sociology as a provider of answers to the basic human questions.

For these reasons it is advisable to ask after the religious positon and commitment of the sociologist of religion. Bias and ideology can take many forms and may affect his work in many ways. The sociologist of religion may be conscious of it and declare his hand, but whether he does or not his work will declare it.

Chapter-6

ALLIES:
THE BACKGROUND OF HISTORY AND THE SUPPORT OF OTHER DISCIPLINES

Chapter-6

A. HISTORY

We have met perspective already in the sociologist's view of religion. We meet perspective again in the relations of sociology to history, for history brings the dimension of time. Whatever is the case now has a past, which itself has an influence upon and connection with the present. It is therefore helpful to study the historical background and those past links in the chain which have brought us to the present situation. The present may look very different in its connection with the past from what it does when treated alone. This applies greatly to the sociology of religion.

There are many difficulties in the path of the historian. The past has gone but it has left much behind, but what it has left is a small fraction of all that was and happened, of all the words and deeds and events and situations. Even though it is a small fraction, what the past has left is very considerable in memories, in documents, in buildings and places, but among this wealth the historian has to select in terms of a particular area of study, such as the setting of military camps in the Roman Empire, or in terms of a particular interest, such as doctrines of kingship in medieval Europe. The historian adopts the time perspective but he cannot avoid a philosophical perspective. He cannot know what actually happened; too much has gone for that to be possible. He can only select; his selection will be in the light of his philosophy, as will be the interpretation he puts on those events, documents and persons which have claimed his attention. Consequently the past is never fixed but infinitely malleable. The future is unknown, the present is given, but past is free—as far as human knowledge is concerned. 'The judgment of history' can at best be a partial judgment and one which changes. A strong psychological justification for the Christian doctrine of final judgment at the last day is the desire for the past to be fixed somewhere—in the mind of God—and for the past to be under moral control. However, this leads us to philosophies of history, for they provide us with principles for assessing the past by giving pointers to what really counts in the past. What does really count? Wars, economic transactions, the common people, the artists, the philosophers themselves, the religions? What are the events on which history turns? There is no way of telling from within history. The principles of selection which the historian brings from outside will provide his emphases and answers to these questions. Once again the final answer lies in the mind of God.

The sociologist of religion in calling history to his aid will escape none of these problems. His area of study and his interest in it is given, but he must face the limitations imposed by his own philosophical standpoint and by the material he is handling.

Looking at the relationship the other way round we can see that sociology brings benefits to history as the sociology of religion does to the history of religion. The historian G.R. Elton writes of what sociologists have taught historians. The 'asking of new questions is the chief lesson which sociologists have taught to historians, who have learned to consider the "structural" problems of society—the analysis of social hierarchies, relationship of classes, mobility among them, the importance of common assumptions and social myths' He goes on to speak of the contributions of anthropology, economics and social psychology to history in terms which also apply to sociology's contribution:

> 'Anthropology has opened historians' eyes to the significance of social habits, the mixture of the universal and relative which goes to make up the ways in which people accustom themselves to living in groups. The obvious importance of economics and social psychology—the manner in which they enable the historian to construct wholes out of patchy evidence by teaching the general rules governing the behaviour of forces, crowds and individuals—needs no stressing'.

Elton sensibly warns the historian against some of the dangers in learning from non-historians. Points of view change among them and the historians may be backing, if not the wrong horse, one not fancied by the non-historian. For example,

> 'Marxist sociology, long since overtaken by more accurate and more subtle analyses, remains powerful among historians, and its influence is by no means confined to those aware of it; fragments of class struggle theories and economic determinism are found curiously embedded in the work of scholars who at the conscious level do not believe in them but need to satisfy their wish to be thought "deep". "Lonely crowd" and "affluent society" theories are swallowed trustingly by the alert historian who then proves less able to disgorge them again than are his sociological mentors themselves.'

A greater danger than backing an unfancied horse is for the historian to be tied to a horse not out of his own stable. If the historian accepts preconceived notions from other disciplines these notions will falsify his work as a historian. 'Preconceived notions are a much greater danger to historical truth than either deficiency of evidence or error in detail, and nothing entrenches them so deeply as the approval of some other form of study which seems to rest on independent thought.' The danger is of the externally derived scheme becoming doctrine and evidence from history being sought as examples to confirm doctrine. A classic instance in sociology is Comte's *Cours de Philosophie Positive*, in which he aimed to show the laws by which the human mind evolved and then to produce supporting evidence from history: the laws he set forward being the law of the three states, theological, metaphysical and finally positive, and the law of decreasing generality and increasing complexity so that sciences could develop only in a certain order culminating in sociology. Yet, like Comte, the historian knows the importance of multiplicity and the complex texture of history and tries to appreciate interrelations where a simple or rigid framework cannot hold them. This follows from the fact that history is 'ideographic', that is, it particularizes, and not 'nomothetic', that is, designed to establish general laws. History is never likely to have enough cases for the setting up of general laws. Sociology and history are thus different in object and method. Sociology, Elton says, has the object of analysing social relationships and the method of counting heads in categories. History does not go the same way:

> 'History may fairly concern itself with past social relationships, and the historian may often be well advised to count heads; but it should always be recognized that, since history must analyse and relate the story of past change and must concern itself with particular people as well as categories, historical studies derived from sociological influence can never be more than a small part of the whole enterprise.'

An illustration of the historical approach lies in Le Bras' handling of rural French parishes. Each is made up of people, is a 'living world', a collection made up of many categories of inhabitants, who must be looked at separately one after the other. It is only after the careful study of people that the social and judicial system of the parish can be seen.

The contribution of history to the sociology of religion is along three lines. The first is the history of the study itself, the second the history of religion and the third the distinction between historical and non-historical religions. Many of the textbooks give some account of the first—of how the sociology of religion comes through the Enlightenment stream of French thinking from the Encyclopaedists to Comte and the other nineteenth-century European practitioners to the worldwide study of the subject in the twentieth century. The other line of studies in religious sociology is more recent and more modest, beginning in this century formally with Le Bras and then taken up in an increasing number of countries, churches and religions. The history of these studies shows that in the sociology of religion all roads lead to Max Weber, while in religious sociology all roads lead to Gabriel Le Bras.

The second contribution of history to the sociology of religion is the study of the histories of religions in the various way outlined earlier, *in se, in mundo,* and *coram deo.* The change or consistency of belief and practice or organization, the relations of the religious institutions with various societies and cultures, the relations of religions with the transcendent (the concept of secularization is an attempt to explain either a change in or weakening of relations with the transcendent), all come within the range of history. An historical approach is of the greatest help to the sociologist of religion, as it is to those whose interests are directed by pastoral concerns in the promoting of religious belief and practice.

The third contribution of history is to draw the attention of sociologists of religion to the distinction between historical and non-historical religions. Religions are historical or non-historical in two senses. One sense is whether or not they are based upon and treat as of particular importance certain historical facts and events. The other sense is whether or not they treat history itself as of importance; in other words, whether or not they have a philosophy of history. Christianity and Judaism alone stand on particular historical events. Judaism stands on the event of the exodus and its interpretation, as does Christianity, but Christianity treats the exodus as a type for the events of the life, death, resurrection and ascension of Jesus Christ. No other religion is in the same way rooted in historical events, but puts forward rather a teaching, world view and scheme of salvation of a founder. Christianity and Judaism, standing as they do on what has been called 'the scandal of particularity' are open to, though well equipped to withstand, the assaults of historical criticism. Christianity and Judaism certainly have philosophies of history, of God's intentions for the world, for his chosen people and for the destiny of all men. Those religions, which are not historically based in the sense that the teaching and message of Christianity is based on historical events, although they have their origins at a certain point in the past and in certain historical circumstances, may certainly have a philosophy of history. It is a task of the historian and of the philosophy of history to distinguish these philosophies and to sort out how seriously they treat history, what purpose they see in it, in what direction they think it is going, whether it repeats itself in cyclical fashion, or goes forward. It is also a derivative study to consider how these philosophies of history put forward by religions spin off into culture at large; for example, is the concept of progress only possible in a culture influenced by the Christian view of history; can there be such a concept in a Hindu culture?

Mircea Eliade comments that from the point of view of non-Western culture the West and particularly those in it who have lost their Christian faith appear to be obsessed by history. The passion for history, for more and more historical information, dating from the second half of the last century, is comparatively new. He points out that in many religions it is believed that at the moment of death a man remembers all his past life down to the minutest details. 'Considered from this point of view, the passion for historiography in modern culture would be a sign portending his imminent death ... The historiographical consciousness of Europe ... would in fact be the supreme moment which precedes and announces death' From the outside it appears that Western man takes history too seriously because he is imprisoned by it. The view of Eliade has to be set against the view that members of an industrial society have little sense of past and future and live in and for the present. Both may be true: Eliade's view is of a conscious minority and the other of a majority of the population. The place and relative importance given to history and historical studies in any society is a matter of some interest to the sociologist of religion.

B. CHURCH HISTORY AND CANON LAW

Church history and canon law have parts to play in the sociology of religion. Every religion has its institutional history and its code of discipline and the Christian religion is no exception. Church history has a double parentage—in theology and in history. We have already considered the case for the sociologist of religion to have some knowledge and understanding of theology while the philosophical minefields of history have claimed some attention in the paragraphs above. Church history recounts the story of belief and practice in the past, it shows the functioning of the church and elements of it as an institution, both internally and in its external relations with the rest of society. It considers the impact of individuals and of groups within and upon the church. It takes some interest in the development and modification of ideas and symbols. All these studies are of help to the sociologist of religion in his work of describing and explaining the social functioning of the church.

Canon law is worthy of particular notice, not least because an impetus to historical studies in the sociology of religion came from it. The story is well known of how Le Bras, the canonist, went on from the collections of canons to the study of social situations in France implied by the canons and encouraged other to join him in the enterprise. Canon law is then something of a key to social aspects of church history and to the institutional analysis of the church. What is the law contained in canons? 'Canons defined and determine the organization of the church and the conduct and duties of its members. They set forth the norm or standard in these matters accepted and expected by the church.' The purpose of canon law is to promote the eternal welfare of the individual member rather than to serve the good of the church as a society. R.C. Mortimer mentions certain characteristics of canons law, three of which are of particular interest to the sociologist of religion:

> '(I) the sharply-drawn distinction between that part of the law which is invariable and admits of no alteration or exceptions, and that part which is subject to change in accordance with the varying conditions of time and place; (2) arising out of that, the respect accorded in the canon law to local custom and (3) the flexibility shown in applying the law to individuals.'

Changes in canon law are to be studied with care. The history of cannon law from early penitentials through the various collections of the middle ages reveals not only a changing theological scene but also a changing social and political one In England the impact of the Reformation upon canon law was to shift its seat of authority from the Pope, the medieval source of legislative authority from whom the English church broke—'the Bishop of Rome heath no jurisdiction in this Realm of England', Article XXXVII—to the king and people. The effect of this shift was to make the existing canon law binding upon clergy and not upon the laity. A topic to pursure is why by the eighteenth century canon law was conceived as binding only upon the clergy and not upon the laity. Changes have occurred in the area covered by canon law. In most countries areas over which canon law had jurisdiction have come under secular jurisdiction. This has been far from a matter of civil power usurping the functions of the church, but often one of mutual agreement with transfer at the request of the church—and it has been particularly so in England. R.C. Mortimer lists some of these areas of transferred jurisdiction in matters of administration in English law: reduction of competence of ecclesiastical courts by the abolition of the benefit of clergy, abolition of tithes (leaving a situation where, he points out, the Church of England has 'no law about the duty and obligation of the laity to contribute towards the maintenance of the Church and her ministry ... no tithes and no church rates can be levied and collected with the help of the civil power'), the right and duty of ecclesiastical courts to supervise and administer the probate of wills and to decide on questions concerning the validity of marriage contracts, the legitimacy of issue, and the granting of orders of separation. Parliament has also kept under review matters to do with dilapidations, sale and exchange of parsonages, restoration and repair of churches, upkeep of burial grounds, and also the rights of patronage, admissions to benefices, resignations and pensions. Here parliament has acted since 1929 on measures sponsored first by the Church Assembly and since 1970 by the General Synod of the Church of England. There have also been shifts in matters of discipline and penalty. One of the main concerns of the authors of the report *Church and State* 1970, was to establish the proper seat of authority for the Church of England in matters of faith and worship which they recommend to be the General Synod. The revision of the Church of England's canon law, completed in 1969, shows continuity with the past and with civil law. The Archbishops write in the introduction that it is 'a revision of the code of Canons issued in 1603 and covers roughly the same areas of church life, but like that Code it presupposes both the common and statute law of England and the general pre-Reformation Canon Law of the Western Church, except where that Canon Law has been affected by contrary statute or custom in England'.

The enforcement of canon law was and is a problem to Church authorities. Le Bras demonstrated the sociological impact of canon law by examination of inquiries undertaken by bishops and their officers and of attempted methods of enforcement. An example is to be found in his study of the information which such inquiries produced in the diocese of Auxerre in the period 1660-1710. Canon law in the shape of the Fourth Lateran council required of the laity confession and Easter communion. The clergy of the diocese of Auxerre sent returns to the bishop indicating those who failed to meet this requirement. In the country areas of the diocese there were practically no deviants, but a sizeable number in the towns, among them gentry, lawyers, civil functionaries, the professional enemies of the clergy, the *cabaretiers,* the publicans. To them was added those who enjoyed 'common law' marriages, those separated from their partners in marriage, some itinerants, winemakers, but not many labourers. A few whole families were deviant. Le Bras sums up the situation: 'Not much zeal in the towns, an almost total conformity in country areas along with some marks of indifference, an often successful rivalry by the secular world where fairs provide feast-days and "public-houses" a counter-church, an inadequate reaction to this situation by the clergy, of whom the majority conscientiously undertook their duties, while others were negligent or rigorist, leniency on the part of the civil authorities.'

C The geography of religion

'The geography of religion' is a concept put forward by Boulard as a result of his analysis of the maps of religious practice in rural France. 'It is not only individuals that we must classify as practising, indifferent or cut off from the Church, but whole regions as well'. The same point emerges from his analysis of urban surveys of religious practice. It is the cultural region which appears to be the chief factor influencing levels of practice in towns. Levels of practice do not follow the size, social composition, or speed of growth of the town, rather they are linked with those of the surrounding cultural region. The between the two is as marked for those towns which appear to be independent of their immediate neighbour as for small country towns which are most dependent on it.

The distribution of the social institutions of religion in space is, therefore, a comparatively new study, but one as valuable to be sociologist as the study of their distribution in time through history. Some of the distributions of religions on a world scale are mentioned below in the section on population growth, but the initiative of Boulard in relating regional geographical features to religious institutions and practices has proved fruitful. Climate, terrain, geographical boundaries, mountains, rivers, seas, man-made features of town and village and the artifacts of an industrial civilization, density and movement of population are all within the compass of the geographer and all relevant to the inquiries of the sociologist of religion. There is an historical dimension since geographical features change, while historical studies benefit from a geographical approach. for example, analysis of the results of the 1851 census of religion in England will reveal geographical patterns of church attendance. Such historical section trenches provide a point of comparison with the other historical section trenches.

The relationship of geography and religion is not one way. It has long been recognized that man's religious beliefs and practice have helped to shape his environment in such matters as the design of a city or the use of farming land. The factors to which Boulard has drawn attention are those by which geography influences religion.

Boulard has found a worthy disciple in England in J.G. Gay, whose *The Geography of Religion in England* (1971) describes and accounts for distribution of church membership in England, gives its historical background and relates it to geographical factors. His book is of particular value to the student of English religions for the use made of the 1851 census and for the assessment of the present-day strength of the churches and other religions in England, even if his historical assessment is coloured by certain assumptions about secularization. His bibliography, which demonstrates the interrelationship of the sociology and the geography of religion, reveals a number of lines of inquiry to be followed up.

At this stage, where the theoretical connection between the two disciplines is under review, Gay's two theoretical chapters are worth attention. In chapter I, the geography of religion, he places the geography of religion within social geography and distinguishes it from religious geography, the attempt to shape the land or city according to religious doctrine, and from ecclesiastical geography, the administration of the church in geographical terms. He goes on survey studies in the geography of religion beginning with Le Bras and Boulard in France and continuing with studies in Scandinavia and the rest of Europe. A writer on Protestantism in Norway shows that although the population has since the Reformation had the same official religion with the same sort of clergy and religious institutions very great differences in 'religiosity' between the various regions make Norway an interesting test-ground for theories about the importance of geographical factors to religion. The section on the rest of Europe refers to M.P. Fogarty's interesting attempt to map the geographical variations in religious practice over the whole of the continent, which produces a belt of high religious practice, both Catholic and Protestant, running through the centre of Western Europe—the Christian Heartland of Europe. The belt runs from Holland, Belgium, French Flanders and Alsace-Lorraine through the Rhineland into South Germany and Austria, Switzerland and Italy.[6] Fogarty also points to levels of low practice on either side of the belt of high practice.

The section of the chapter devoted to the United States is interesting for its theoretical remarks. Gay quotes a geographer, W.A. Hotchkiss, preparing a master plan for Protestantism in Cincinnati:

> 'The character of the religious institutions of a segment of the earth's surface is an integral part of the chorographic uniqueness of the area. Cincinnati's religion, for example, is as much a part of the uniqueness of the city as its machine tool industry, its Carew tower, or its *Sangerfest.* The functional interrelationship of the religious institutions with all the other patterns, whose total character

differentiates this urban area, is the point of departure from which this study was begun.'

He also showed that religious groups varied over the United States as a whole and within Cincinnati, that organized religion is a visible part of the landscape through its buildings and that organized religion is part of the activity pattern of the whole city or area. Another American writer, W.Zelinsky, reviewing the distribution throughout the country of members of denominations, comments:

'From the scanty evidence available, we have reasonable grounds for proposing the hypothesis that religion is a significant element in the population geography of the US, in the geography of a number of economic, social and cultural phenomena, and in the genesis and persistence of general cultural regions...'

The chapter ends with consideration of the effect of environment. Do certain religions proper in certain climates? The symbols and images of a religion are influenced by its origins. A missionary religion may undergo changes when it spreads outwards from its place of origin. Gay comments that few geographers would now wish to explain. Gay comments that few geographers would now wish to explain religion as a product of environment. The effect of religion upon environment has already been mentioned in the Cincinnati plan, but it is a matter of impact upon people, landscape and countries, through religious buildings, behaviour following religions injunctions and commands, religious practice, such as attendance at ceremonies, and religious activities, such as missions.

The second chapter, the sources, refers mainly to the sources for the geographical study of religion in England but has wider application. The sources listed are denominational statistics, for which the churches and religions have different criteria and which are not therefore easily to be compared, records of the practice of religion, social surveys, marriage statistics, ecclesiastical plant and other distribution patterns and long-term trends such as the impact of penal legislation upon Nonconformists and Roman Catholics. Over and above these sources is the unique Census of Religious Worship in

1851. It can be seen how both the sociology of religion and its geography draw upon the same sources.

D. THE PSYCHOLOGY OF RELIGION

Boundaries between disciplines of thought are arbitrary. To divide sociology from psychology is as arbitrary and as constricting as to divide both from anthropology. Both sociology and psychology undertake to study man. Sociology considers man in his social relationships while psychology considers the mind and emotions of man as directed towards a variety of objects. Religion is to do with man in his social relationships and mind and emotions are all interrelated. Thus the sociology of religion and the psychology of religion must overlap. They have common interests in which they assist each other. They are allies and not rivals. In some inquiries it is hard to say whether they are exercises in the sociology or in the psychology of religion. Their technical language may be used in common: 'suggestion, projection, identification, rationalization'.

Psychology faces the same philosophical problems as those outlined above in the case of sociology. It has the same problems of hidden or sometimes open philosophical assumptions in the explanations it brings to 'explain' the phenomena it assembles, in giving meaning to or finding causes for such phenomena. Like sociology it is a comparatively young discipline but with sufficient growth behind it for schools of thought to have developed with their own policies of explanation, with their theories of reality and of what is permissible as evidence.

The psychology of religion is concerned with belief and action in religion. It first describes and then explains. It asks what beliefs are held, by what processes and with what intensity they are held and expressed and for what reasons they are held. The impact of these beliefs upon the believer and his community is also a matter of study. What do the beliefs do for him and for the community? Are the declared reasons for holding them the real reasons? Every psychologist of religion is a detective seeking to make clues work for him. similar questions can be asked about religious action, worship, prayer, processions, ascesis, systems of government. When the psychologist of religion investigates he brings not only his philosophical assumptions and his emphasis within psychological traditions but also his concepts of normality and abnormality. It is an interesting question to find their derivation. Is it from his philosophy, from current social values, from a religion, from common sense, from some recognized or unrecognized experience of his own? The psychologist of religion like the sociologist of religion categorizes and explains. Categories of personality or of group behaviour are part of his equipment.

An example which combines the use of categories or classification with explanation is to be found in Spiro's account of the basis for religious behaviour. He says that a religious actor 'believes in superhuman beings and performs religious ritual in order that he may satisfy ... substantive desires: desires for rain, nirvana, crops, heaven, victory in war, recovery from illness, and countless others. Everywhere man's mammalian desires (those which can be satisfied by naturalistic goals) must be satisfied, and in the absence of competing technologies which confer reasonable confidence, religious techniques are believed to satisfy those desires.' Spiro adds that these substantive desires can be classified as 'attempts to overcome or transcend suffering'. He brings together both causal and functional explanations in his account of religion. 'Religion persists because it has functions - it does, or is believed to, satisfy desires; but religion persists because it has causes —it is caused by the expectation of satisfying those desire.' He also remarks that 'an adequate explanation for the persistence of religion requires both psychological and sociological variables'.

Much of the discussion of religion is in terms of sociological and psychological explanation. It should not be forgotten that explanation can work the other way. Religion can be a factor in explaining society or psychological behaviour. Some of the classical attempts by pioneers in sociology to explain away religion in sociological terms turn out to be little more than explanations of society in religious terms. They explain society and not religion. This is particularly true of Durkheim's study, *The Elementary Forms of the Religious Life.* For Durkheim society is God: the real purpose of religious rites is that 'they draw clansmen together, and secondly, that the collective enactment of the rites ... renews in them a feeling of solidarity'. In seeking to show religion as a unitive force or symbol of unity in what he took to be the most primitive form of society, that of the Australian Aborigine, and to be no more, he succeeds in showing that the society needed a certain religious support. However, as Spiro again points out, the fact that religion is a sufficient condition for the satisfaction of requirement does not make it a necessary condition. Society is thus explained by religion. Religion may work in society in three ways: by providing social stability, by reducing anxiety and by integrating society. Thus'

> '... religion (a) reduces the probability of psychotic distortion of desires, thereby providing a society with psychologically healthy members, (b) protects society from the socially disruptive consequence of direct gratification of these forbidden desires, (c) promotes social integration by providing a common goal (superhuman beings) and a common means (ritual) by which the desires may be gratified.'

The contribution of the psychology of religion, along with the sociology of religion and its other allies, to religions and the objects of religion, is like that of cooking and digestion to virtue and vice. Sydney Smith may have the last word. In a letter to Arthur Kinglake he worte:

> 'I am convinced digestion is the great secret of life; and that character, talents, virtues, and qualities are powerfully affected by beef, mutton, pie-crust and rich soups. I have often thought I could feed or starve men into many virtues and vices, and affect them more powerfully with my instruments of cookery than Timotheus could formerly do with his lyre'.

Chapter-7

The Spirit of the Age : Some Contributory Factors Bearing upon Religion

Chapter-7

The cultural climate in which we live has no effect upon the truth or falsity of the opinions we hold. It does, however, affect our prejudices, our selection of topics, our bias, our emphases. The cultural climate or spirit of the age is like the air we breathe all around, but with difficulty are we conscious of it. Yet it is possible to analyse the air we breathe, particularly when we fear pollution. Equally it is worthwhile—if in the end vain-to attempt to seize that will-o'-the-wisp, the spirit of the age, particularly as it bears upon those undertaking the sociology of religion. The attempt will serve also to throw some light upon the social conditions within which the religions of the world at present find themselves, whether they have helped to create these conditions or not.

A frequently used starting point for such analysis is change, but this in itself may be no more than the prompting of the spirit of the age, a restless generation seeking some new thing. Richard Hoggart, brought up in a working-class area in Sheffield, was once asked to lecture in that city on change in working class life. He pointed out that he could equally have devoted his lecture to continuity and stability in working-class life. We may therefore begin with continuity and stability. The life cycle continues; we are born, we die, we marry and are given in marriage. It continues from the days of Noah. we have to work, to equip ourselves through learning and training for it. We have to face suffering and tragedy and put together or accept some world view which helps us go give some order to the world confronting us or at least to give us sufficient light for the next step. Whatever culture we find ourselves in we have to do and to face these things. It is these with which religion is mainly concerned. It touches the basic questions of purpose and meaning which we by virtue of our humanity cannot escape. We cease to be human if we escape them. Our maturity lies in the successful facing of them. It appears that the world is so arranged, and this is an argument of natural theology, that the successful facing of them leads to the revelation of a transcendent God.

If this argument is correct religion itself is concerned with the continuities, the constants, the stable things of culture, and thus the sociology of religion is similarly concerned. Yet with this difference, that from the basis of stability and continuity the sociology of religion deals with religion in relation to some of the more changing aspects of culture, which give much of its sting to the spirit of the age, although it is only fair to add that the spirit of the age must owe something to stability and continuity.

In our listing of some of the characteristics of our culture we shall deal with three main topics, people and population growth, cities and the process of urbanization, and industry and industrialization. If as is assumed world population is to grow but at varying speeds in the different continents, the proportions of religious allegiance may alter. In addition the problem of how people live together may become more intense and have implication for religious institutions, belief and behaviour. Cities are places in which an increasing proportion of the world's population live and which impose a certain style of life, while industry and technology provide the means whereby much of the world's work is done. Cities and industry generate values and philosophies which interact with religion and which disseminate the spirit of the age.

A. PEOPLE AND POPULATION

The Washington Population Reference Bureau estimated world population to be 3,443 million on 1 January 1968 and that it would reach 4,500 million by 1983 and almost 7,000 million by 2000. The bureau calculated the rate of increase to be approximately 200,000 a day. The most rapid growth up to that time was in North and Central America. One third of the world's population was under 15 years old, while 58% of it lived in India, the Soviet Union, the United States, Indonesia, Japan and China.

A United Nations report of 1958, *The Future Growth of World population,* provided the following estimates of world population in 1975 and 2000 by continent:

	1975		2000	
Continent m.	Estimated population m.	Percentage	Estimated population	Percentage
Europe (incl. USSR)	751	19.6	947	15.1
Asia	2,210	57.7	3,870	61.8
Africa	303	7.9	517	8.2
N. America	240	6.3	312	5.0
Latin America	303	7.9	592	9.4
Oceania	21	0.5	29	0.5
World	3,828		6,267	

In England and Wales population increased in the nineteenth century by an average of 14% every ten years, although the increase between the censuses of 1951 and 1961 was 5.3%. The Government Actuary made estimates in 1967 of population in the United Kingdom. By 1975 the country's population would be 57.6 million, by 1990 64.2 million, and by 2000 70.3 million. However, forward estimates based on mid-1971 population figures gave a lower rate of increase in England and Wales: 1981, 50.8 million; 1991, 53 million; 2001, 55.5 million and 2011, 58.3 million. As with all estimates certain assumptions were made. In the population estimates the assumptions were a continuing decline in death rates, a certain rate of male to female births and a certain net outward migration.

There are many causes of population growth and not all of them are known. Improved medicine prolongs life span and reduces infant mortality but higher birth rates are not a major factor. In some countries there are more marriages among marriageable women and younger marriages which narrow the generation gap. The effect of population growth is different from country to country. In some with an increased birthrate the population is young, other countries find the prolonging of life span increases the number of the elderly.

Rapid population growth has given rise to anxieties. The basic anxiety is that created by too many people. Does the population of a country reach a point where social discord is inevitable? Experiments with rats in a confined space have shown that above a certain number rats fight and harmony is destroyed. The basic anxiety is of a cosmic Black Hole of Calcutta. There are other fears related to that of social breakdown. It is feared that there will not be enough food to feed a rapidly growing population, when already a sizeable proportion of the world's population is undernourished. At the same time it is feared that since the world's resources of raw materials are limited the rate at which they are now being used will lead in the not too distant future to their exhaustion, while it is douted whether human ingenuity can discover synthetic replacements. It is also feared that an increasing population will so abuse the world as to corrupt its basic elements of land, water and air by pollution and thus to destroy the balance of life, in the first place the ecological balance of natural life and eventually human life itself. The fears, then, are of social conflict, starvation and the extinction of life on a cosmic rubbish heap.

There are confident voices to assure that these fears are unfounded, that human beings can cope with the problems of increased population and that human beings are the basic resource of the world. The practical policies which follow from these fears are mainly those of suspicion and restriction : more social restraints on industry, schemes of planned parenthood and birth control, legalized abortion, the setting up of public institutions to control the private whims of individuals. More positively there are steps to increase the supply of food for a growing population. The trend is towards more overt social control by governments and public authorities in legislation and regulation, which themselves engender frustrations, anxieties and rebellions in the population. Public control goes with population increase.

There are many hazards in calculating population figures; there are even more in estimating religious adherence, when criteria of adherence vary. However, approximations can help. The following table give some indication of the religious population of the world in 1968 against an estimated total population of 3,443 million. The analysis by continent and major religion is instructive and gives a total context for the social story of religion. If this table is taken along with estimates of continental population it can be seen which religions are the more likely to grow in numbers, if other factors do not intervene.

B. CITIES AND URBANIZATION

Towns and cities have grown with increased population and much of the increase of population is in the towns. Before the industrial revolution the bulk of the world's population was rural while the population living in cities small. 'With the exception of Rome at the beginning of the Christian era and of Paris at the end of the Renaissance, the cities of the western world rarely had more than 50,000 inhabitants, before the nineteenth century. From the beginning of the nineteenth century the balance changed. By 1851 England, the leader in this process, was half urban. In the century since then urbanization has spread throughout the world. Recent returns in the more advanced countries like the USA and Great Britain show that some of the largest cities have reached a peak of size and show signs of either dropping in population numbers or of having reached a constant figure.

The rapid urbanization of the world since 1800 may be seen in the following table, which compares the world's urban population with the world's total population 1800-1950 (in millions).

I Year	World Pop.	Towns of 5,000 & over	% World pop.	Towns of 20,000 & over	% World pop.	Towns of 100,000 & over	% World pop.
1800	906	27.2	3.0	21.7	2.4	15.6	1.7
1850	1,171	74.9	6.4	50.4	4.3	27.5	2.3
1900	1,608	218.7	13.6	147.9	9.2	88.6	5.5
1950	2,400	716.7	29.8	502.2	20.9	313.7	13.1

The world's population has increased considerably in this period, but the proportion of population in cities has increased at a far greater rate. The following table gives a comparison of rates of growth in the world's urban population and total population.

Estimated Religious Population of the World in 1968[1] (in thousands)

Religion	N.America	S. America	Europe	Asia	Africa	Oceania	Total
Total Christian	214,258	150,426	442,006	61,473	42,056	14,055	924,274
Roman Catholic	126,468	147,219	226,303	47,622	28,751	4,107	580,470
Eastern Orthodox	3,675	47	114,103	2,819	4,95684	125,684	
Protestant	84,115	3,160	101,600	11,032	8,349	9,864	218,120
Jewish	6,035	705	4,025	2,460	238	74	13,537
Moslem	166	416	13,848	374,167	104,297	118	493,012
Zoroastrian			12	126			138
Shinto	31	116	2	69,513			69,662
Taoist	16	19	12	54,277			54,324
Confucian	96	109	55	371,261	9	57	371,587
Buddhist	187	157	8	176,568			176,920
Hindu	55	660	160	434,447	1,205	218	436,745
Grand total	220,844	152,608	460,128	1,544,292	147,805	14,522	2,540,199

Percentage Increase

2 Period	Total World pop.	World population in cities 5,000 & over	20,000 & over	100,000 & over
1800-1850	29.2	175.4	132.3	76.3
1850-1900	37.3	192.0	193.5	222.2
1900-1950	49.3	227.7	239.6	254.1

In 1800 it is calculated that there were 750 cities of 5,000 or more, 200 of 20,000 and 45 of 100,000.

In 1950 the picture is given in the following Table :

Cities in 1950

Size	Number	Pop. (m.)	% Total world pop.
5,000 & more	27,600	717	30
20,000 & more	5,550	502	21
100,000 & more	875	314	13
500,000 & more	133	158	7
1,000,000 & more	49	101	4

The 1961 census of England and Wales revealed 184 towns with a population of 50,000 or more compared with 157 in 1951. Six areas designated as conurbations contained 16.8 million inhabitants, more than a third of the total; (they were Tyneside, West Yorkshire, south-east Lancashire, Merseyside, west Midlands and Greater London) while urban areas with population over 100,000 had 6.2 million inhabitants, those of 50-100,000 had 4.4 million, and those of under 50,000 had 9.4 million.

Table I shows that the population of large cities with over 100,000 inhabitants increased more than 20 times and Table 2 shows that the growth of large cities was accelerating in the period 1800-1950. Within this growth there are different patterns to be discussed in the different continents. The growth began in Europe, with industrialization, after 1800 and in the nineteenth century was above world average; after 1900 the rate of growth of European cities dropped below world average.

Some examples of growth are the following (in thousands):

Growth of Cities

Tokyo and Yokohama	2,700 (1920)	8,500(1955)	14,770(1965)
Sao Paulo	580(1920)	2,200(1960)	5,383(1966)
Calcutta	1,600 (1921)		4,703(1966)
Johannesburg	280 (1921)		1,000(1955)

The following table shows the share of the world's large cities of over 100,000 among the major continental regions in the period 1800-1950 :

	1800		1850		1900		1950	
Region	Pop. m.	%	Pop. m.	%	Pop. m.	%	Pop. m.	%
World	15.6	100	27.5	100	88.6	100	313.7	100
Asia	9.8	62.8	12.1	44.4	19.4	21.9	105.6	33.7
Europe*	4.8	30.8	12.1	40.0	42.0	47.5	83.1	26.5
USSR	0.57	3.7	1.1	4.1	5.9	6.7	35.1	11.2
Africa	0.30	1.9	0.25	0.9	1.4	1.5	10.2	3.2
America	0.13	0.8	1.8	6.6	18.6	21.0	74.6	23.8
Oceania	—	—	—	—	1.3	1.4	5.1	1.6

* *USSR exculded*

Before 1900 the population growth of the large cities in Asia was below world average and below European and American growth; in the period 1900-1950 it was considerably above.

A comparison of rates of growth of Asian and European and American large cities can be seen in the following table. It is reasonable to take European and American cities together, since American cities recruited a population of immigrants mainly from Europe.

Percentage increase in Population of Large Cities, (100,000 and over)

Period	Asia	Europe and America
1800-1850	25	184
1850-1900	60	220
1900-1950	450	160

This represents a slowing up of population increase in the most industrial parts of the world—and perhaps ultimately a levelling out of the urbanization process throughout the world. Industrialization is taking place in Asia and in parts of Africa, while population growths in industrial cities in South America have been spectacular in recent years.

It is still true that in Asia and Africa the urban population is a smaller proportion of the total population than in the other more industrialized continents & and that their cities are in agricultural countries. The figures for the percentage of population living in cities of 20,000 and more and as follows:

World	21%
Asia	13%
Africa	9%
Central America and Caribbean	21%
South America	26%
USSR	31%
Rest of Europe	35%
North America (Canada and USSR)	42%
Oceania	47%

Since there is a positive relationship between industrialization and urbanization, and most of the world is rapidly becoming industrialized, it is likely that the world will even out at a high level of urbanization. In 1800 before the Industrial Revolution in Europe the population in large cities was distributed over the earth in much the same fashion as the general population; after a period of world industrialization a similar position could be reached on a higher level of urbanization; than in 1800. The European and American pattern of urbanization, and proportion of urban population in total population, might therefore set the pattern for the rest of the world. Thus their present higher level of urbanization is a temporary and passing situation. A high level of urbanization and the prospect of greatly increasing urbanization in these continents outside Europe and America would be for the religions of the world of some significance.

A condition of such a change would be an agricultural revolution in the countries with low urbanization so as to draw men away from the land and to improve farming so that it can support a larger urban population. The following table relates the degree of urbanization to the density of agricultural workers on the land.

% Population in cities of 100,000 & over	Agricultural males per square mile of agricultural land
0-99	136
10-19.9	72
20-29.9	67

In addition to a revolution in agriculture a revolution in industry is a condition of urban growth. It is possible to have large cities in a pre-industrial country—and this is still the situation in parts of Asia and Africa—but the spectacular urban growth of the nineteenth century in Europe and America had an industrial basis, while the attempts of the previously backward countries of Asia and Africa to build an industrial economy are hastening urbanization.

The pre-industrial cities of Europe were court cities, cathedral cities, university towns, fortress towns, markets, ports and country towns. 'Inhabitants of town and country alike were imprisoned within their physical and mental horizons. To escape meant to transcend rather than transform the environment and, as a consequence, men lacked much practical mastery over nature. Manufactures were largely handicraft, as much rural as urban, carried on in close relation to husbandry.' This description would still be true of cities in many countries today.

The industrial revolution produced a new kind of city. The steam engine and the factory system—concentration of capital and labour upon the resources of power—development of regional specialization and therefore of specialized labour forces —were all factors in producing the Birminghams and Manchesters of the nineteenth century. 'The major ingredients of the rapid developments of industrial urban centres in Europe and the United States included the emergence of new fuels, materials and mechanical aids, a closer integration of productive and managerial processes, and improvements in transport and communication.'

The twentieth-century urban developments the metropolitan city, the great city with satellites, 'a gigantic population agglomeration which combines centralization with decentralization, and specialization and differentiation of function with integration and interdependence relationship., although Thomas Miles, Customer for Sandwich, said in 1604 : 'All our creeks seek to one river, all our Rivers run to one Port, all our Ports join to one Town, all our towns make but one City, and all our Cities and Suburbs to one vast unwieldy and disorderly Babel of buildings, which the world calls London!' The city is in constant evolution. War, natural disaster, economic and industrial changes, political changes, improved city government and planning, new architectural ideas and techniques, all contribute to the twentieth century city to distinguish if from its nineteenth-century predecessor, although the one is built often on the other and both are intermingled. The typical industrial city is no longer Dickens' Coketown or like the gloomy portraits of Manchester painted first by Engels and later by Taine, who wrote in 1859 of Manchester:

> '. . . a sky turned coppery red by the setting sun; a cloud, strangely shaped, resting upon the plain; and under this motionless cover a bustling of chimneys by hundreds, all tall as obelisks. Then a mass, a heap, blackish, enormous rows of buildings; and there you are at the heart of a Babel built of brick. A walk in the town; seen close-to it is even more lugurbrious. Earth and air seem impregnated by fog and soot. The factories behind their flanks of fouled brick one after another, bare, with shutterless windows,

like economical and colossal prisons. The place is a great jerry-built barracks, a "work-house" for four hundred thousand people, a hard-labour penal establishment.'

Where the nineteenth-century city survives the task taken on by the planners is to change it, for which 'urban renewal' is the technical phrase. Urban renewal has to adapt the old and often historical central areas to modern conditions and for population much larger than they were originally planned for. It has to prevent the vast 'twilight' areas from further decay, by a combined operation of conservation, rehabilitation and development, as well as meeting modern traffic requirements in the built-up areas, and particularly in the centres of our cities, well documented for the United Kingdom in the Buchanan Report, *Traffic in Towns* (1963). Those who reflect on the function of the city in the twentieth century see possibilities in city life, which were denied either in the cities of the nineteenth century or in rural life still : 'Urbanization can be made a source of pleasure and of dignity.'

The evolving cities of our time show both uniformity and diversity. The diversity among cities appears to be rather that of function than of history, climate or geography.'In no civilization is city life evolved independently of commerce and industry', but the balance may be varied from a largely productive city to a largely commercial city, such as a great port. In addition a city, usually a metropolitan city, may be a political and administrative centre or a university or ecclesiastical centre. Function also changes with size. An analysis of the functions of French cities has been made by J. Coppolani in *le Reseau Urbain de la France* (1959), in which he traces urban function through various small towns to the medium size town of 30-50,000, *la ville maitresse,* usually the administrative enter of a French department, and then the regional capital and the national capital. In a country like France the regional capitals stand upon a great tradition of history and are able to counterbalance the centralizing pressures of the capital city by maintaining a healthy number of administrative, political, educational and other professional institutions which are not entirely dependent upon Paris.

For the city dwellers there is functional diversity. It is often pointed out that before the Industrial Revolution a man's whole life was based on one particular place. It was in the village or in some part of a small town that he had his home and his family, and he also worked, took his leisure and carried out his religious observances. The great mass of the population never stepped outside this *geographical dimension*. After the Industrial Revolution this dimension is broken up. In modern cities the places of residence, work, leisure, instruction and religious practice are now separate and specialized. A new dimension is being drawn, no longer based on the geographical place but on function, the *functional dimension* of human life.

The uniformity of the city is in structure, touched upon already, which means that with minor variations cities have similar structures. Following the classification of Burgess of the famous Chicago school which developed urban studies with such insight and application there is first the business centre based on the original city with a variety of institutions, administrative, financial, political, commercial and cultural, upon which transport converges, active in the daytime, dead at night and with a very small resident population. In Chicago, for example, only 5,000 people live in the 'Loop', but 900,000 go there every day.

Then comes the transitional zone between the business centre and the residential districts. It has often slum, decayed housing which has come down in the world. It is the 'twilight' area into which immigrants first settle. While much of the population may be mobile there is also a stable working-class population which does not want to move. Next come the more prosperous working-and middle-class districts, housing estates of private or municipal construction, and then on their edge the rich residential districts, falling off into the ex-urbanite areas of senior corporation executives whose urban style of life has a more rural setting. The heavy industrial zones are separate from the other areas though sometimes near the transitional zones or working class districts.

In this classification there is a certain uniformity of structure to be found in every city, varied by history of growth, type of predominant industry, geographical layout. Where the variables are taken into account the basic structure provides a useful means of breaking down what otherwise seems a vast amorphous mass beyond human comprehension. This is to say that a city has a certain predictable physical structure and this structure imposes patterns of living and thinking upon those who live in particular areas.

Uniformity also lies in the problems common to the cities of the world. In addition to the problems of structure in the 'twilight' areas or with traffic, there are the social problems of overcrowding, slums, bank robberies, neurosis, loneliness, delinquent youth, theft, violence, prostitution, immigration and racial conflict. A common urban pathology unites the world's cities and often marks them off from the countryside.

Urban pathology leads on to the whole climate of opinion of city life, of the ways of thinking induced by the city, or urban culture. The problem of defining the city has been a puzzle to sociologists, whether to do it in commercial terms for example, or in terms of population size or density, but the most fruitful solution has been along the lines of 'Urbanism as a Way of Life', the title of an influential article by Louis Wirth, a founder of the Chicago school of urban sociology. Wirth put it that 'urbanism as a characteristic mode of life may be approached empirically from three interrelated perspectives: (1) as a physical structure comprising a population base, a technology, and an ecological order; (2) as a system of social organization involving a characteristic social structure, a series of social institutions, and a typical pattern of social relationships; and (3) as a set of attitudes and ideas, and a constellation of personalities engaging in typical forms of collective behaviour and subject to characteristics mechanisms of social control'. Urbanism is indeed more than a concentration of population within a certain areas; it is a complex of human relationship in various conditions. The life of the city dweller is more socialized in the sense that he is more dependent on society. He has many superficial relationships, few deep personal ones. His rhythm of life may be upset by the demands of large-scale industry. He lives in a form of society which is dynamic and changing. Many of his expectations are this-worldly. He is a rationalist with his life depending more on his own choices than on traditional structure. The 'city mentality' described by Park, characterized by its sophistication, objectivity, utilitarianism and rationalism is, on the one hand, a product of the urban environment, and, on the other hand a major force producing and influencing changes in our social heritage, in our economic and political institutions, and in the urban environment itself. As the German proverb puts it, *die Stadtluft macht frei.* 'It is not merely a coincidence that the great centres of learning, invention, innovation, art and culture have historically been in urban areas.' David Riesman's other-directed type, the man who takes his values and standards by built-in mental radar from his group, is a concept derived from urbanization. 'The conditions I believe to be responsible for other-direction the affecting increasing numbers of people in the metropolitan centres of the advanced industrial countries.'

The theme of urbanism as a way of life is usefully developed by another author, N. Anderson, for whom it is necessary to distinguish 'those characteristics of urbanism which concern living in cities and those which relate to urbanism as an outward extending change-stimulating influence emanating from urban centres.' In the city, urbanism has been described as superficial, anonymous, and transient. But this way of life as it extends onward may not be anonymous, although it tends to be contractual and secondary. The superficially, so much a part of urbanism in the city and outside, is not always superficial, for urbanism is also profoundly creative. Transiency is a mark of urbanism where its influence extends, and transiency tends to increase with nearness to urban centres. In contrast to the uniformities of urban life it can be shown that 'urbanism tends to "individual" people, liberating them, putting them in a position favourable to making choices and being creative according to their ability. The individual and not the family is the unit in the labour market and before the law.'

Mobility is a feature of city life, which is more than the movement of people from one to place to another. It is movement from one kind of work to another and from one social class to another. The fact of social mobility in industrialized, urban society is confirmed in the exhaustive study of S.M. Lipset and

R. Bendix, who conclude that "the overall pattern of social mobility appears to be much the same in the industrial societies of various western countries.'

It could be wise, however, to note the following reservation:

> 'Many phenomena are said to be characteristic solely of urban communities. But the evidence indicates that the same traits may generally occur in other community systems as well. Further research is needed to discover whether urban communities can be distinguished from other type of communities in terms of anything more than a certain frequency of interaction paterns.'

We may now turn to the symbol of the city, a powerful symbol for good and ill in religion and literature. Classics of Christian literature are St Augustine's *City of God* and John Bunyan's account of the journey of Christian and Faithful in *Pilgrim's Progress* from the City of Destruction to the Celestial City. The medieval poets and hymn-writers with their strong sense of the corporate nature of Christian living frequently use the image of the heavenly city. Some of the best English hymns are translations, many of them by J.M. Neale, of these medieval Latin hymns and poems, such as 'Jerusalem the golden' from Bernard of Cluny's *Hora Novissima* of about 1130. It speaks of '*socially gaudia*', social joys, as does the almost contemporary upon the Peter Abelard:

'O quanta qualia sunt illa sabbata
quae simper celebrate superna curia.'

while the anonymous hymn for the dedication of a church (from about the sixth century) starts from the image of the new Jerusalem, '*Urbs beata Jerusalem dicts pacis vision*':

'Blessed city, heavenly Salem,
Vision dear of peace and love.'

Later writers of hymns, in spite of a certain individualism in hymnody after the Reformation, have continued this tradition. The opening lines of one of Samuel Crossman's hymns in the seventeenth century are:

'Jerusalem on high
My song and city is.'

God himself is a city of refuge and strength to Christians struggling with evil in this world, as Luther's great Reformation hymn, '*Ein' feste Burg its unser Gott*', so powerfully demonstrates, ending with the line 'The City of God remaineth'. There is also Matthew Arnold's 'On, on to the city of God'.

Elsewhere in literature the city has known varying fortunes. To the late medieval, and men of the Renaissance, who saw a considerable growth of towns, the city represented the best of human civilization, a concentration of wealth and power in which the civilized man took pleasure. William Dunbar's poem 'In Honour of the City of London' takes this attitude:

> *'London, thou art of towns a per se*
> *Sovereign of cities. . .*
> *Manly Power, with craftis naturall,*
> *Fourmeth none farier sith the flode of Noy :*
> *London, thou art the flow of Cities all.'*

Johnson wrote : 'I think the full tide of human existence is at Charing Cross.'

To the eighteenth century the city was a place of ordered civilized life. To the Romantics, in reaction to the Industrial Revolution, and to the new industrial towns, the city was a denial of human life. "The concept of ideal order in human society, the world of man, which had provided Shakespeare and Pope with a frame of reference, had collapsed and could no longer supply images of harmony for the Romantic poets. . . so in Romantic and Victorian poetry the city becomes an image of spiritual exhaustion, or even an image of hell.'[15] It was Shalley who wrote :

> *'Hell is a city much like London,*
> *A populous and smoky city.'*

Blake in dissent from eighteenth-century opinion had foreshadowed this change in writing :

> *'I wander thro' each charter's street,*
> *Near where the chartered Thames both flow,*
> *And mark in every face I meet*
> *Marks of weakness, marks of woe.'*

The Romantic poets make the city a symbol of darkness, chaos and barrenness.'The city dweller became a type of the man isolated not only from his fellows, but from those forms of nature which might lead him to a transcendental sense of unity with the universe:

> *"A sordid solitary thing,*
> *Mid countless brethren with a lonely heart*
> *Through courts and cities the smooth savage*
> *Feeling himself, his own low self the whole."*

The city is peopled by savages, and the noble shepherds of Wordsworth's poetry are corrupted by contact with societies of men and cities. The poet called London a 'wide waste' in *The Prelude*—his famous sonnet on Westminster Bridge runs counter to the rest of Romantic thought on the city—and the term 'waste', linking the city with the desert and the sea, has lone poetic currency through the nineteenth century to Eliot's seminal poem *The Waste Land,* which brings in focus many aspects of the corrupting, depersonalizing, atomizing life of a great metropolitan city.

James Thomson's short poem on William Blake is typical of this attitude to the city :

> *'He came to the desert of London town*
> *Grey miles long;*
> *He wandered up and he wondered down,*
> *Singing a quiet song.*
> *He came to the desert of London town,*
> *Murk miles broad,*
> *He wander'd up and he wander'd down,*
> *Ever alone with God.*
> *There were thousands and thousands of human kind*
> *In this desert of brick and stone :*
> *But some were deaf and some were blind,*
> *And he was alone.*
> *At length the good hour came; he died*
> *As he had lived alone :*
> *He was not missed from the desert wide -*
> *Perhaps he was found at the Throne.'*

The Romantic looked upon the city as a spiritual desert, but saw the possibility of escape to and restoration in nature. A poet like Thomson sees no escape but death : the submen of the city–isolated individuals in the lonely crowd–must endure this 'strange disease of modern life', as Matthew Arnold puts it, until the good hour comes and death releases them. The spiritual desolation and horror of the life of the great city are vividly portrayed in Thomson's long poem *The City of Dreadful Night:* the frustration, rootlessness and insecurity are the reality from which the city-dweller, in Thomson's rejection of Christianity, can never in this life escape.

C. INDUSTRY AND INDUSTRIALIZATION

The part played by industry and commerce in urbanization has been mentioned more than once. It is now time to consider industrialization. We shall find a similar set of terms to city, urbanization and urbanism in industry, industrialization and industrialism; where industry is the institution, industrialization the process and industrialism the set of values. Industry need not detain us long. It is 'the characteristic institution of modern advanced societies' says an enthusiast, Tom Burns, in *Industrial Man,* Perhaps exaggerating the importance of what is a key institution. It would be hard to resist some other claims for the school, the home, the TV network, but it can be conceded that 'Industrial society' The place of industry in the world of work is recognized. We have already noted the shift from agriculture to industry while the following figures give some idea of the distribution of employment in Great Britain as it was in June 1969.

	thousands
TOTAL WORKING POPULATION	25,207
HM Forces and women's services	380
Registered wholly unemployed	483
TOTAL IN CIVIL EMPLOYMENT	24,344
Employers and self employed	1,744
EMPLOYERS IN EMPLOYMENT	
Males	
Females	14,027

Agriculture, forestry, fishing	
Mining and quarrying	833
Manufacturing–total	8,729
Food, drink and tobacco	818
Chemicals and allied industries	516
Metal manufacture and metal goods not elsewhere specified	1,155
Engineering and electrical goods	2,319
Vehicles	822
Textiles, leather, clothing and footwear	1,256
All other manufacturing industries	1,843
Construction	1,443
Gas, electricity and water	397
Transport and communication	1,546
Distributive trades	2,714
Financial, professional and scientific Services–total	3,453
Insurance, banking and finance	691
Educational services	1,355
Medical and dental services	993
Catering, hotels etc	596
Miscellaneous services (excluding catering, hotels, etc)	1,506
Public administration	1,383

Let us consider a single manufacturing unit. We can see it as a community with a network or relationship between managers and men. The management structure has a chain of command, linking line with specialist managers, production with research, education, industrial relations, buying, selling and financial staff. Amongst the employees of the firm there is a variety of trade unions for office workers, skilled, semi- and unskilled men and women. There are clear lines between management and man, defined by company policy, agreement between the employers and trade unions, by legal and government decisions. Alongside this formal pattern there is a network of personal and group relationships of an informal kind made up of friends who live in the same street, belong to the same clubs, have the same interests. These formal and informal patterns make up a situation of work which has been typical for large numbers of people for generations, and, in spite of technical change, is likely to be with us for several more.

Industry influences the society we have. Internationally the balance of trade, exports, imports, the interlinking of industrial firms and government are based on a world-wide industrial network and have created a world-wide industrial society. Many of the wishes and expectations of people are built on increased production. Industry is a source of wealth, not only for its products but through its profitability. Taxes raised from industry help to finance many aspects of local and national government, education, transport, the arts. Locally, industry gives shapes to the community. The prosperity of local industry, the availability of work, the level of earnings, the type of work, the hours and conditions of work all mark any community. Some industries, such as mining or steel, create distinctive communities around them.

Industry in the local community can then be seen as interwoven with it. Seen from the home, industry is the place where the husband, and sometimes the wife, spend the best hours of the day and the best years of their lives. It is a place where the children on leaving school hope for work. From the point of view of local government industry is a source of rates and subject to control in matters such as smoke abatement. Schools see industry as the place where a large number of their pupils go, where further education of different kinds is increasingly encouraged, particularly since the Industrial Training Act of 1964. Industry can be seen from many other points of view: law enforcement, for example, or government departments such as the Department of Trade and Industry. Department of Employment and Department of Health and Social Security. While we may start by seeing industry as a separate institution with a defined purpose we go on to see it in its ramifications with the rest of society. It is perhaps more important to see it in this way than in separation.

Is industry simply a fact of life, like the weather? To some extent it is. It has a limited aim in the production of goods or provision of services. For the majority of industrial managers and workers their roles are laid down and defined by others. Their discretion is limited by what other people expect. Industry is not the only institution in society and who is to say against the institutions of government, education, the church or the home that it is the most important? Work in industry may claim large numbers of the population. Yet industrial work is hardly the highest point in their lives. For many life begins outside the factory gate.

It is an interesting question whether industry in the last 150 years has more shaped English culture than English culture has shaped industry. The habits, values, outlook of those who manage and work in British industry has strong continuity with the pre-industrial organization of work in rural England. The resistance to change in industrial practice or in society around industry is as striking as technological achievement. *The new Society* was the title of a book describing the plant community in American industry. Anyone taking a look beneath some of the more obvious physical changes of England in its buildings or means of communication, as examples, would hesitate to speak of a new society in the attitudes and outlook of the population. Our society is a strange mixture of conservatism and innovation and the population delights to have it so. The impact of changes in organization of work can easily be exaggerated.

The industrial organization of work is becoming worldwide; the interplay of industry and culture is more obvious in a country such as India where industry is new. In such countries it is assumed that industry is more manageable than the weather. It is there as the result of human decisions. The kind, size and growth of industry are so decided. Many factors go into these decisions the aims and policies of government,. local communities and industrial firms in the country and overseas, as well as the policies of international agencies. Values and social philosophy enter the decisions, which reflect the hopes, fears and expectations of a nation. Here more obviously these decisions affect the lives of people and the shape of a society. Whatever affects the lives of people is within the range of the agencies of social control, law, morality and religion.

Industrialization is the process whereby industry is set up. What sets it in motion? There are basically two answers to the question. One stresses the economic factor, the other stresses a wider set of factors in human culture. It is important to note that the economic factor is a matter of stress, for it need not exclude other factors. Karl Marx puts forward the economic factor. In the preface to *A Contribution to the Critique of Political Economy* he speaks of the relations which men enter into for the purposes of production and of how these relations of production in their sum total constitute the economic structure of society—the foundation on which rise legal and political superstructures and to which correspond definite forms of social consciousness.' He goes on: 'The mode of production in material life determines the general character of the social, political and spiritual processes of life. It is not the consciousness of men that determines their existence, but, on the contrary, their social existence determines their consiouness.' Thus a change in the relations of production brought about by new technology is sufficient to account for industrialization. Technological change the economic order and produces industrial society. There is, of course, no need to be Marxist in philosophy to hold the importance of the technological factor. The contributors to *The Cambridge Economic History of Europe* stress it without being committed to the philoslophy.

The other answer to the question covers a wider set of factors. The best known theory is that of Max Weber, who argued that 'the spirit of modern capitalism was born. . . from the spirit of Christian asceticism.' It was an inner-worldly asceticism. The devout man fulfilled his duty to God in hard work. 'Industry', hard work, became 'industry', the industrial process and plant. Weber's theory can also be seen as an explanation of semantic change. Others have qualified his views. R.H. Tawney in *Religion and the Rise of Capitalism*. Accounted for the rise of capitalism in England by the withdrawal of the church's sanctions from public and social life, while K. Samuelson in *Religion and Economic Action* argues that the conditions for the growth of capitalism were to be found in Roman Catholic as well as Protestant countries, while countries under the influence of secular enlightenment also produced capitalism.

W. Arthur Lewis in his study of economic growth writes : 'if a religion lays stress upon material values, upon things and productive investment, upon honesty in commercial relations, upon experimentation and risk bearing, and upon equality of opportunity, it will be helpful to growth.' Weber's theory reverses Marx's theory. Marx had said that economic change had changed religion, while Weber argued that religion had changed economics. While Marx may not be right about the part played by religion in industrialization upon religion, of ways in which religious institutions have accepted the values of industrialism such as rationality, efficiency, standardization and centralization.

Religion, in its ascetic dimension, if Weber is right, was one of a range of factors causing industrialization. Asceticism concentrates a man's energies, while inventiveness can spring from an appreciation of God's creation. If God has made a good world and put man in it to enjoy it and make it prosper, here too is an invitation to explore, change and construct. The industrialist pioneers also had this spirit in them. Nef, who holds that"the origin of the unique industrial civilization which involves us all cannot properly be made the special preserve of economic historians', puts forward in addition to the spiritual and moral factors certain others. The Limitation on violence based on concepts of universal humanity and of the worth of individuals, the aesthetic dimension of life, art in everyday life, a new economy of delight all led at the time of the Renaissance to a new civilization which itself encouraged scientific discovery and technological advance and so prepared the way for industrialization. Another aspect of cultural change is that of institutional change. Changes in political order, discussed in the case in England in Tawney's *Religion and the Rise of Capitalism,* changes in the organization of work, in banking, in property ownership, in the development of wage-labour can themselves be seen as stimulating industrialization.

Much cultural diversity is built into industrial society; its values are therefore many and take different shape in different societies.[11] Some have already been mentioned in the factors causing industrialization. Some may decline once industrial society is established. Others may be generated within industrial society. The values of inventiveness often sharpened to a mania for innovation, of application and discipline, of respect for the given nature and content of the world, once more acute through anxieties about pollution and cosmic destruction, seem to be constant. It might be added that industrial society requiring certain standards of literacy and numeracy of its members is committed to placing value on the individual, however often he may be abused. Improvement in the position of women has come with industrial society. An industrial society based on mass communications tends to live in the present with little sense of history or of thought for the future and to expect instantaneous gratification of desires. Its philosophy is a moderate utilitarianism for most of the time punctuated by violence and cut off from nature. An industrial society tends to be associations rather than a community, with more isolated individuals and groups than in a pre-industrial one. The elements of conflict and protest in industrial society are themselves matters of dispute. The Marxist view is that the relations of production build conflict into industrial society until it is resolved by the proletarian revolution. Another view is that conflict and protest are not a necessary feature of industrial society. An American study which began with the assumption that conflict and protest were essential features of industrialism had to abandon the assumption. 'Labor protest, on a closer look, is on the decline as industrialization around the world proceeds at an ever faster pace. In the mid-twentieth century, workers do not destroy machines. The protest of today is more in favor of industrialization than against it.' This study, which examined industrialization in various parts of the world, came to see 'the inevitable structuring of managers and managed in the course of industrialization' as the most universal phenomenon. There may indeed be protest about such structuring but the protest is within the terms of industrial society.

How does religion fare in industrial society? There are four major positions held as to the impact of industrial society upon religion. The first is that industrial society will destroy religion, the second that it will weaken and relatives it, the third that it will strengthen and absolutize it and the fourth that religion will certainly survive industrial society and in its essentials not be touched by it. The first position is that of Marx. We may begin by considering his concept of alienation, which is profanation in the strict sense of St Paul's doctrine of sin. Sin for St Paul describes the estrangement of every man from God, for 'all have sinned and come short of the glory of God.' Marx removes this concept from the temple, from the divine order, to that of the economic relations of men : the working class is alienated in capitalist society from the just rewards of its labour, each man is alienated from his neighbour and is alienated in his different capacities as worker, citizen, father. Thus alienated man makes religion.

> 'Man makes religion, does not make man. Religion is indeed man's self-consciousness and self-awareness as long as he has not found his feet in the universe. . . Religion is the sigh of the oppressed creature, the sentiment of a heartless world, and the soul of soulless conditions. It is the opium of the people . . .The abolition of religion, as the illusory happiness of men, is a demand for their real happiness. . . The immediate task is to unmask human alienation in its secular form, now that it has been unmasked in its sacred form. Thus the criticism of heaven transforms itself into the criticism of earth, the criticism of religion into the criticism of law, and the criticism of theology into the criticism of politics.'

These well-known worlds state the first position clearly. What can be said against it is that the course of history since the Russian revolution has not brought about the abolition of religion and the Marx has not yet been proved right.

The second position is one favoured by many sociologists of religion and by some western spokesman for the Christian church. An example of the former is Bryan Wilson who, in *Religion in Secular Society,* writes of the loss of influence of religion in western societies, of 'the epiphenomenal character of religious institutions and religious thinking in contemporary society and of 'the process whereby religious thinking, practice and institutions lose social significance.' an example of the latter is to be found in David Edward's *Religion and Change,* a most able but which sees a contracted although continuing work for the Christian religion against the competition of other religions and ideologies. The position is well expressed by the historian. E.J. Hobsbawm in writing of the impact of the industrial revolution: 'Religion, from being something like the sky, from which no man can escape and which contains all that is above the earth, became something like a bank of clouds, a large but limited and changing feature of the human firmament.'

The sense of weakness and relativity among western Christians has led to two courses of action. In relation to other religions the churches have tended to adopt a policy of dialogue rather than crusade. If all religions contain some truth then each may learn from all. Other religions, unlike the abominations of the Amalekites or of Moab, are to be cultivated and learned from rather than cut down. In relation to the citizens of western industrial countries the churches have undertaken adaptation and mission. The adaptation has been of thought forms in worship and in doctrine, of structure of parish and chaplaincy, while mission has been towards those judged furthest from the institutional life of the church. A bold example of such mission with a sad but not unexpected ending was the priestworker movement in France. The priestworkers, accepting much of the Marxist analysis of industrial society, became industrial workers in order to identify themselves with the working class and so to allow Christian faith and life to grow within that class. They have attracted a large literature, much of it incorporated in the footnotes of Gregor Siefer's *The Church and Industrial Society*. The French bishops had to end the experiment in 1954 because the priestworker movement was dividing the church. It would be wrong to suggest that all forms of mission spring from a sense of weakness in the church, but many of those do which make use of sociologist and historical analyses and are directed towards certain social groups.

The third position, that industrial, society strengthens and absolutizes religion, has fewere spokesman. They are to be found for the non-Christian religions which have shown powers of revival in post-colonial days and under western interest.

Also within the Christian religion there are churches, notably the Pentecostal, and groups within and without churches which at the present time are running strongly, while in the past industrial countries have shown fertility in producing new expressions of the Christian church from the days of the English independents and Methodists onwards. At the same time industrial societies have the power to produce anti-religions with 'religious' features like Communism and Nazism, as well as all manner of popular superstitions. The absolutizing force of industrial society is certainly to be seen in the anit-religions while those religions which antedate industrial society have shown the ability to maintain absoluteness. It was only one hundred years ago in industrial Europe that infallibility was decreed of the Pope.

The fourth position is the one upon which common sense is most likely to stake its money. Social forms and societies change. There is nothing absolute about industrial society. Religion is about man's relation with the eternal, with the transcendent, with that which or him who is above the passing social order. Whatever the difficulties or opportunities presented by industrial society, the evidence of history favours this position, for it shas not yet been proved wrong.

This position has been well argued by an American author, Andrew M. Greeley, the title of whose book shows its theme, *The Persistence of Religion* (Eng. ed. 1973). Industrial society has brought changes. Religion has no direct influence over the large corporate structures which have emerged in the last four hundred years. Big Government, Big Business, Big Labor, Big Military and Big Education are not directly influenced either by religion or by church.' Some phenomena previously interpreted by religion are now explained by rational science. 'Man's development of his capacities for abstract thought and expression means that myths are no longer self-sufficient and must be interpreted.' Religion is now a more explicit and individual matter than it was in the past. It is more a matter of free choice. These changes may be large ones, but they do not take away the work of religion in providing a faith which helps men to cope with ultimate questions or in providing a feeling of belonging to a group whose members support each other. In addition religion has other work: integrating the disturbing forces of sexuality with the rest of life, offering a means of knowing superhuman beings and providing leaders to help and strengthen men in their wrestling with the Ultimate.

This section on industrialization should end with some reference to secularization. The concept is implied in the second of the four positions mentioned above. The quotations from Bryan Wilson's *Religion in Secular Society* were his deceptions of the process of secularization. Definition is the first and major problem of secularization for the term is used ambiguously. David Martin considered that it is used by many sociologists in the interests of anti-religious ideology : 'Secularization is less a scientific concept than a tool of counter-religious ideologies.' His book, *The Religious and the Secular,* demolishes that approach and puts forward a critique of other attempts in politics, the arts and history at giving meaning to secularization. These attempts rely on a selective view of history and on assuming certain normative relations of church and society which, if varied, count as satirization. Other approaches to secularization rely on figures of religious practice or on estimates of the influence of religious institutions. None contributes to clarify of thought. The problem of definition is well illustrated by a page of contrasting terms which on a superficial level might appear respectively secular and not-secular but the majority of which on a considered judgment can be either:

Secular and Non-Secular Terms in the Sociology of Religion

1. Transcendental	Not	Secular	Immanental	Either
2. Other-worldly (Monastic)	"	"	This-worldly	
3. Next-worldly	"	"	This worldly	"
4. Supernaturalistic	"	"	Naturalistic	"
5. Non-empirical	Either		Empirical	"
6. Self-denying or self-controlling	"		Hedonistic	"
7. Reverential	"		Irreverent, Indifferent	"

8. Sacralizing	"	Desacralizing	"
9. Depersonalized	"	Personalized	"
10. Archetypal	"	Particularized, Individualized	"
11. Interested in the permanent	"	Interests in the transient	"
12. Traditional	"	Innovatory	"
13. Conventional, automatic	"	Experimental, sincere	"
14. Global, total, closed"		Partial, limited, open	"
15. Dogmatic	"	Flexible	"
16. Authoritarian	"	Autonomous	"
17. Fanatical	"	Tolerant	"
18. Concerned, committee		Apathetic	"
19. Concerned with the intrinsic	"	Manipulative	"
20. Concerned with the arbitrary	"	Concerned with the lawful	"

Robertson has a table to illustrate tendencies towards secularization at the cultural level :

Religious Beliefs, values and Symbols

	Retention of framework	Neutralization of framework	Abandonment of framework
Intellectual emphasis	(a) Rational religion	(c) Immanentism	(c) Positive atheism
Practical emphasis	(b) Instrumental religion	(d) Supernaturalism	(f) Areligiosity

It is necessary to balance this table with a conversion table towards religion :

Secular Beliefs, Values and Symbols

	Retention of framework	Neutralization of framework	Abandonment of framework
Intellectual emphasis	(a) rational secularism	(c) Immanentism	(c) Positive theism
Practical emphasis	(b)Instrumental secularism	(d)Supernaturalism	(f) religious practice religiosity

The framework in both tables is that of religion or secularism. The intellectual and practical emphases are belief and practice within both framework. (a) and (b) show the first loosening of the framework by secularization or conversion; (e) and (f) show arrival within the new framework of belief and practice; (c) and (d) are transitional stages. Immanentism on the intellectual line stands for an 'explicit' transference of commitment from a spiritual conception within a religious tradition to a non-spiritual commitment within the historical framework of that tradition.' in the case of secularization and a movement the other way in the case of conversion. Supernaturalism is the movement from practice to superstition or vice versa.

Secularization, if there is suchs a thing or prcoess, is not irreversible; its countrary in desecularization or conversion may and does occur. Belief and practice are communicable. Religous institutions are missionary bodies. There is no reason from our previous discussions of industrial society to make us hold that it poses insuperable difficulties for religion. Difficulties there are, yet they lie as much in the nature of man himself as in any particular social order he may devise. Furthermore the action of religion is slow and long-term, to be measured in centuries rather than in that short term which the history of industrial society can supply.

> 'The history of European Christianity teaches us that even religion and faith, the strongest forces of change in the world, need many centuries to achieve a superficial conversion and thousands of years if they are to enter into the very heart of the structure of society and reshape it.'[27]

D. Martin's recommendation that '*secularization*' should be erased from the sociological disctionary' is wise.

Chapter-8

THE ELEMENTARY FORMS OF THE RELIGOUS LIFE

E. DURKHEIM

Chapter-8

. . . The study which we are undertaking is therefore a way of taking up again, *but under new conditions,* the old problem of the origin of religion. To be sure, if by origin we are to understand the very first beginning, the question has nothing scientific about it, and should be resolutely discarded [. . .]

What we want to do is to find a means of discerning the ever-present causes upon which the most essential forms of religious thought and practice depend [. . .]

For a long time it has been known that the first systems of representations with which men have pictured to themselves the world and themselves were of religious origin. There is no religion that is not a cosmology at the same time that it is a speculation upon divine things. If philosophy and the sciences were born of religion, it is because religion, began by taking the place of the sciences and philosophy. But it has been less frequently noticed that religion has not confined itself to enriching the human intellect, formed beforehand, with a certain number of ideas; it has contributed to forming the intellect itself. Men owe to it not only a good part of the substance of their knowledge, but also the form in which this knowledge has been elaborated.

At the roots of all our judgements there are a certain number of essential ideas which dominate all our intellecual life; they are what philosophers since Aristotle have called the categories of the understanding : ideas of time, space, class, number, cause, substance, personality, etc. They correspond tothe most universal properties of things. They are like the solid frame which encloses all thought; this does not seem to be able to liberate itself from them without destroying itself,

---

From the *The Elementary Forms of the Religious Life* By E. Durkheim, 1915. Translated by J.W. Swain.

for it seems that we cannot think of objects that are not in time and space, which have no number, etc. Other ideas are contingent and unsteady; we can conceive of their being unknown to a man, a society or an epoch; but these others appear to be nearly inseparable from the normal working of the intellect. They are like the framework of the intelligence. Now when primitive religious beliefs are systematically analysed, the principal categories are naturally found. They are born in religion and of religion; they are a produce of religous thought. This is a statement that we are going to have occassion to make many time in the course of this week.

This remark has some interest of itself already; but here is what gives it its real importace.

The general conclusion of the book which the reader has before him is that religion is something eminently social. Religious representations are collective representations which express collective realities; the rites are a manner of acting which take rise in the midst of the assembled groups, and which are destined to excite, maintain or recreate certain mental states in these groups. So if the categories are of religous origin, they ought to participate in this nature common to all religious facts; they too should be social affairs and the product of collective thought. At least—for in the actual condition of our knowledge of these matters, one should be careful to avoid all radical and exclusive statemnets—it is allowable to suppose that they are rich in social elements.

Even at present, these can be imperfectly seen in some of them. For example, try to represent what the nation of time would be without the processes by which we divide it, measure it or express it with objective signs, a time which is not a succession of years, months, weeks, days and hours!. This is something nearly unthinkable. We cannot conceive of time, excpet on condition of distinguishing its different moments. Now what is the origin of this differentiation? Undoubtedly, the states of consciousness which we have alrady experienced can be reproduced in us in the same order in which they passed in the first place; thus portions of our past become present again, though being clearly distinguished from the present. But howsoever important this distinction may be for our private experience, it is far from being enough to constitute the notion or category of time. This does not consist merely in a commemoration, either partial or integral, of our past life. It is an abstract and impersonal frame which surrounds, not only our individual existence, but that of all humanity. It is like an endless chart, where all duration is spread our humanity. It is like an endless chatt, where all duration is spr-ead out before the mind, and upon which all possible events can be located in relation to fixed and determined guide lines. It is not *my time* that is thus arranged; it is time in general, such as it is objectively thought of be everybody in a single civilization. That alone is enough to give us a hint that such an arrangement ought to be collective. And in reality, observation proves that these indispensable guide lines, in relation to which all things are temporally located, are taken from social life. The divisions into days, weeks, months, years, etc. correspond to the periodical recurrence of rites, feasts, and public ceremonies. A calendar expresses the rhythm of the collective activities, while at the the same time its function is to assure their regularity.

It is the same thing with space [. . .]

All known religious beliefs, whether simple of complex, present one common characteristic : they presuppose a classification of all the things, real and ideal, of which men think, into two classes or opposed groups, generally designated by two distinct terms whcih are translated well enought by the words *profane and sacred [profane, sacre]*. This division of the world into two domains, the one containing all that is sacred, the other all that is profane, is the distinctive trait of religious thought; the beliefs, myths, dogmas and legends are either representations or systems or representations which express the nature of sacred things, the virtues and powers which are attributed to them, or thier relations with each other and with profane things. [. . .]

But if a purely hierarchic distinction is a criterium at once too general and too imprecise, there is nothing left with which to characterize the sacred in its relation to the profane except their heterogeneity. However, this heterogeneity is sufficient to characterize this classification of things and to distinguish it from all others, because it is very particular: *it is absolute.* In all the history of human thought there exists no other example of two categories of things so profoundly differentiated or so radically opposed to one another. The traditional opposition of good and bad is nothing beside this; for the good and the bad are only two opposed species of the same class, namely morals, just as sickness and health are two different aspects of the same order of facts, life, while the sacred and the profane have always and everywhere been conceived by the human mind, as two distinct classes, as two worlds between which there is nothing in common. The forces which play in one are not simply those which are met with in the other, but a little stronger; they are of a different sort [. ..]

Thus we arrive at the first criterium of religious beliefs. Undoubtedly there are secondary species within these two fundamental classes which, in their turn, are more or less incompatible with each other. But the real characteristic of religious phenomena is that they always suppose a bipartite division of the whole universe, known and knowable, into two classes which embrace all that exists, but which radically exclude each other. Sacred things are those which the interdictions protect and isolate; profane things, those to which these interdictions are applied and which must remain at a distance from the first. Religious beliefs are the representations which express the nature of sacred things and the relations which they sustain, either with each other or with profane things. Finally, rites are the rules of conduct which prescribe how a man should comport himself in the presence of these sacred objects [. . .]

However, this defintion is not yet complete, for it is equally applicable to two sorts of facts which, while being related to each other, must be distinguished nevertheless: these are magic and religion.

Magic, too, is made up of beliefs and rites. Like religion, it has its myths and its dogmas; only they are more elementary, undoubtedly because, seeking technical and utilitarian ends, it does not waste its time in pure speculation [. . .]

Here is how a line of demarcation can be traced between these two domains.

The really religious beliefs are always common to a determined group, which makes profession of adhering to them and of practising the rites connected of this group, they are something belonging to the group, and they make its unity. The individuals which compose it feel themselves united to each other by the simple fact that they have a common faith. A society whose members are united by the fact that they think in the same way in regard to the sacred world and its relations with the profane world, and by the fact that they translate these common ideas into common practices, is what is called a Church [. . .]

It is quite another matter with magic. To be sure, the belief in magic is always more or less general, it is very freq-uently diffused in large masses of the population, and there are even people where it has as many adherents as the real religion. But it does not result in binding together thosewho adhere to it, nor in uniting them into a group leading a common life. *There is no Church of Magic.* Between the magician and the individuals who consult him, as between these individuals themsevles, there are no lasting bonds which make them members of the same moral community, comparable to that formed by the belivers in the same god or the observers of the same cult. The magician has a clientele and not a Church, and it is very possible that his clients have no other relations between each other, or even do not know each other; even the relations which they have with him are generally accidential and transietn; they are just like those of a sick man with his physician [. . .]

Thus we arrive at the following definition: *A religion is a unified system of beliefs and practices relative to sacred things, that is to say, things set apart and forbidden—beliefs and practices which unite into one single moral community called a Church, all those who adhere to them.* The second element which thus finds a place on our definition is no less essential than the first; for by showing that the dea of religion is inseparable from that of the Church, it makes it clear that religion should be an eminently collective thing.

Origin of the idea of the totemic principle or mana

The proposition established in the preceding chapter determines the terms in which the problem of the origins of totemism should be posed. Since totemism is everywhere dominated by the idea of quasi-divine principle, imminent in certain categories of men and things and thought of under the form of an animal or vegetable, the explanation of this religion is essentially the explanation of this belief; to arrive at this, we must seek to learn how men have been led to construct this idea and out of what materials they have constructed it.

It is obviously not out of the sensations which the things serving as totems are able to arouse in the mind, we have shown that these things are frequently insignificant [. . .]

Thus the totem is before all a symbol, a material expression of something else. But of what?

From the analysis to which we have been giving our attention, it is evident that it expresses and symbolizes two different sorts of things. In the first place, it is the outward and visible form of what we have called the totenic principle or god. But it is also the symbol of the determined society called the clan. It is its flag; it is the sign by which each clan distinguishes itself from the others, the visible mark of its personality, a mark borne by everything which is part of the clan under any title whatsoever, men, beasts or things. So if it is at once the symbol of the god and of the society, is that not because the god and the society are only one? How could the emblem ofthe group have been able to become the figure of this quasi-divinity, if the group and the divinity were two distinct realities? The god of the clan, the totemic principle, can therefore be nothing else than the caln itself, personified and represented to the imagination under the visible form of the animal of vegetable which serves as totem.

But how has this apotheosis been possible, and how did it happen to take place in this fashion?

In a general way, it is unquestionable that a society has all that is necessary to arouse the sensation of the divine in minds, merely by the power that it has over them, for to its members it is what a god is to his worhshippers. In fact, a god is, first of all, a being whom men think of as superior to themselves, and upon whom they feel that they depend. Whether it be a conscious personality, such as Zeus or Jahveh, or merely abstract forces such as those in play in totemism, the worshipper, in the one case as in the other, believes himself held to certain manners of acting which are imposed upon him by the nature of the sacred principle with which he feels that he is in communion. Now society also gives us the sensation of a prepetual dependence. Since it has nature which is peculiar to itself and different from our individual nature, it pursues ends which are likewise special to it; but, as it cannot attain them except through our intermediacy, it imperiously demands our aid. It requires that, forgetful ofour own interest, we make ourselves its servitors, and it submits us to every sort of inconvenience, privation and sacrifice, without which social life woudl be impossible. It is because of this that at every instant we are obliged to submit ourselves to rules of conduct and of thought which we have neither made nor desired, and which are sometimes even contrary to our fundamental inclinations and instincts.

Even if society were unable to obtain these concessions and sacrifices from us except by a material constraint, it might awaken in us only the idea of a physical force to which we must give way of necessity, instead of that of a moral power such as religious adore. But as a matter of fact, the empire which it holds over consciences is due much less to the physical supremacy of which it has the privilege than to the moral authority with which it is invested. If we yield it is orders, to its not merely because it is strong enough to triumph over our resistance; it is primarily because it is the object of a venerable respect.

We say that an object, whether individual or collective, inspires respect when the representation expressing it in the mind is gifted with such a force that it automatically causes or inhibts actions, *without regard for any consideration relative to their useful or injurious effects.* When we obey somebody because of the moral authority which we recognize in him,, we follow out his opinions, not because they seem wise, but because a certain sort of physical energy is imminent in the idea that we form of this person, which conquers our will and inclines it in the indicated direction. Respect is the emotion which we experience when we feel this interior and wholly spiritual pressure operating upon us [. . .]

Since it is in spiritual ways that social pressure exercises itself, it could not fail to give men the idea that outside themselves there exist one or several powers, both moral and, at the same time, efficacious, upon which they depend. They must think of these powers, at least in part, as outside themselves, for these address them in a tone of command and sometimes even order them to do violence to their most natural inclinations. It is undoubtedly true that if they were able to see that these influences which they feel emanate from society, then the mythological system of interpretations would never be born. But social action follows ways that are too circuitous and obscure, and employee psychical mechanisms that are too complex to allow the ordinary observer to see when it comes. As long as scientific analysis does not come to teach it to them, men know well that they are acted upon, but they do not know by whom. So they must invent by themselves the idea of these powers with which they feel themselves in connection, and from that, we are able to catch a glimpse of the way by which they were led to represent them under forms that are really foreign to their nature and to transfigure them by thought.

But a god is not merely an authority upon whom we depend; it is a force upon which our strength relies. The man who has obeyed his god and who for this reason, believes the god is with him, approaches the world with confidence and with the feeling of an increased energy. Likewise, social action does not confine itself to demanding sacrifices, privations and efforts form us. For the collective force is not entirely outside of us; it does not act upon us wholly from without; but rather, since society cannot exist except in and through individual consciousness, this force must also penetrate us and organize itself within us; it thus becomes an integral part of our being and by that very fact this is elevated and magnified.

There are occasions when this strengthening and vivifying action of society is especially apparent. In the midst of an assembly animated by a common passion, we become susceptible of acts and sentiments of which we are incapable when reduced to our own forces; and when the assembly is dissolved and when, finding ourselves alone again, we fall back to our ordinary level, we are then able to measure the height to which we have been raised above ourselves. History abounds in examples of this sort [. . .]

Besides these passing and intermittent states, there are other more durable ones, where this strengthening influence of society makes itself felt with greater consequences and frequently even with greater brilliancy. There are periods in history when, under the influence of some great collective shokc, social itneractins have become much more frequent and active. Men look for each other and assemble together more than ever. That general effervescence results which is characteristic of revolutionary or creative epochs [. . .]

Also, in the present day just as much as in the past, we see society constantly creating sacred things out of ordinary ones. If it happens to fall in love with a man and if it thinks it has found in him the principal aspirations that move it, as well as the means of satisfying them, this man will be raised above the others and, as it were, deified. Opinion will invest him with a majasty exactly analogous to that protecting the gods. this is what has happened to so many sovereigns in whom their age had faith: if they were not made gods, they were at least regarded as direct representatives of the deity. And the fact that it is society alone which is the author of these varieties of apotheosis, is evident since it frequently chances to consecrate men thus who have no right to it from their own merit. The simple deference inspired by men invested with high social functions is not different in nature from religious respect. It is expressed by the same movements: a man keeps at a distance from a high personage; he aproaches him only with precaustions; in conversing with him, he uses other gestures and language than those used with ordinary mortals. The sentiment felt on these occasions is so closely related to the religious sentiment that many peoples have confounded the two.

In addition to men, society also consecrates things, especially ideas. If a belief is unanimously shared by a people, then, for the reason which we pointed out above, it is forbidden to touch it, that is to say, to deny it or to contest it. Now the prohibition of criticism is an interdiction like the others and proves the presence of something sacred. Even to-day, howsoever great may be the liberty which we accord to others, a man who should totally deny progress or ridicule the human ideal to which modern societies are attached, would produce the effect of a sacrilege. There is at least one principle which those the most devoted to the free examination of everything tend to place above discussion and to regard as untouchable, that is to say, as sacred: this is the very principle of free examination.

All these facts allow us to catch glimpses of how the clan was able to awaken within its members the ida that outside of them there exist forces which dominate them and at the same time sustain them, that is to say in fine, religious forces: it is because there is no society with which the primitive is more directly and closely connected. The bonds uniting him to the tribe are much more lax and more feebly felt. Although this is not at all strange or foreign to him, it is with the people of his own clan that he has the greatest number of things in common, it is the action of this group that he feels that most directly; so it is this also which, in preference to all others, should express itself in religious symbols.

The life of the Australian [Aboriginal] societies passes alternately through two distinct phases. Sometimes the population is broken up into little groups who wantder about independently of one another, in their various occupations; each family lives by itself, hunting and fishing, and in a word, trying to procure its indispensable food by all the means in its power. Sometimes, on the contrary ,the population concentrates and gathers at determined points for a length of time varying from several days to several months. This concentration takes place when a clan or a part of the tribe is summoned to the gathering, and on this occasion they celebrate a religious ceremony, or else hold what is called a corrobbori in th usual ethnological language.

These two phases are contrasted with each other in the sharpest way. In the first, economic activity is the preponderating one, and it is generally of a very mediocre intensity. Gathering the grains or herbs that are necessary for food, or hunting and fishing are not occupations to awaken very lively passions. The dispersed condition in which the society finds itself results in making its life uniform, languishing and dull. But when a corrobbori takes place, everything changes. Since the emotional and passional faculties of the primitive are only imperfectly placed under the control of hsi reason and will, he easily loses control of himself. Any event of some importance puts him quite outside himelf [. . .]

We are now able to understand how the totemic principle, and in general, every religious force, comes to be outside of the object in which it resides. It is because the idea of itis in no way made up of the impressions directly produced by this thing upon our senses or minds. Religious force is only the sentiment inspired by the group in its members, but projected outside of the consciousnesses that experience them, and objectified. To be objectified, they are fixed upon some object which thus becomes sacred; but any object might fulfil this function. In principal, there are none whose nature predestines them to it to the exclusion of all others.; but also there are none that are necessarily impossible. Everything depends upon the circumstances which lead the sentiment creating religious ideas to establish itself here or there, upon this point or upon that one. Therefore, the sacred character assumed by an object is not implied in the intrinsic properties of this latter : *itis added to them.* The world of religious things is not one particular aspect of empirical nature, *it is superimposed upon it* [. . .]

Thus social life, in all its aspects and in every period of its history, is made possible only by a vast symboilsm. The material emblems and figurative representations with which we are more especially concerned in our present study, are one form of this; but there are many others. Collective sentiments can just as well become incarnate in persons or formula : some formula are flags, while there are persons, either real or mythical, who are symbols [. . .]

Our entire study rests upon this postulate that the unanimous sentiment of the believers of all times cannot be purely illusory. Together with a recent apologist of the faith we admit that these religious beliefs rest upon a specific experience whose demonstrative value is, in one sense, not one bit inferior to that of scientific experiments, though different from them. We, too, think that 'a tree is known by its fruits' and that fertility is the best proof of what the roots are worth. But from the fact that a 'religious experience' if we choose to call it this, does exist and that it has a certain foundations—and, by the way, is there any experience which has none?—it does not follow that the reality which is its foundation conforms objectively to the idea which believers have of it. The very fact that the fashion in which it has been conceived has varied infinitely in different times is enough to prove that none of these conceptions expressit adequately. if a scientist states it as an axiom that the sensations of heat and light which we feel correspond to some objective cause, he does not conclude that this is what it appears to the senses to be. Likewise, even if the impressions which the faithful feel are not imaginary, still they are in no way privileged instutions; there is no reason for believing that they inform us better upon the nature of their properties. In order to discover what this object consists of, we must submit them to an exminations and elaboration analogues to that which has substituted for the sensuous idea of the world another which is scientific and conceptual.

This is precisely what we have tried to do, and we have seen that this reality, which mythologies have repreented under so many different forms, but which is the universal and eternal objective cause of these sensations *sui generis* out of which religious experience is made, is society. We have shown what moral forces it develops and how it awakens this sentiment of a refuge, of a shielf and of a gaurdian support which attaches the believer to his cult. It is that which raises him outside himself, it is even that which made him. for that which makes a man is the totality of the intellectual property which constitutes civilization, and civilization is the work of society. Thisis explained [by] the preponderating role of the cult in all religious, whichever they may be. This is because society cannot make its influence felt unless it is in action, and it is not in action cannot make its influence flet unless it is in action, and it is not in action unless the individuals who compose it are assembled together and act in common. Itis by common action that it takes consciousness of itself and realizes its position; it is before all else an active co-operation. The realizes its position; it is before all else an active co-operation. The collective ideas and sentiments are even possible only owing to these exterior movements which symbolize them, as we have established. Then it is action which dominates the religious life, because of the mere fact that it is society which is its source.

In addition to all the reasons which have been given to justify this conception, a final one may be added here, which is the result of our whole work. As we have progressed, we have established the fact that the fundamental categories of thought, and consequently of science, are of religious origin. We have seen that the same is true for magic and consequently for the different processes which have issued from it. On the other hand, it has long been known that up until a relatively advanced movement of evolution, moral and legal rules have been indistinguishable from ritual prescriptions. In summing up, then, it may be said that nearly all the great social institutions have been born in religion. Now in order that these principal aspects of the collective life may have commenced by being only varied aspects ofthe religious life, it is obviously necessary that the religious life be the eminent from and, as it were, the concentrated expression of the whole collective life. If religion has given birth to all that is essential in society, it is becaue the idea of society is the soul of religion.

But, it is said, what society is it that has thus made the basis of religion? Is it the real society, such as it is and acts before our very eyes, with the legal and moral organization which it has labouriously fashioned during the course of history? This is full of defects and imperfections. In it, evil goes beside the good, injustice often reigns supreme, and the truth is often obscured by error. How could anything so crudely organized inspire the sentiments of love, the ardent enthusiasm and the spirit of abnegation which all reglions claim of their followers? These perfect beings which are gods could not have taken their traits from so mediocre, and sometimes even so base a reality.

But, on the other hand, does someone think of a perfect society, where justice and truth would be sovereign, and from which evil in all its forms would be banished for ever? No one would deny that this is in close relations with the religions sentiment; for, they wold say, it is towards the realization of this that all religions strive. But that society is not an empirical fact, definite and observable, it is a fancy, a dream with which men have lightened their sufferings, but in which they have never really lived. It is merely an idea which comes to express our more or less obscure aspirations towards the good, the beautiful and the ideal. Now these aspirations towards the good, the beautiful and the idea. Now these aspirations have their roots in us; they come from the very depths of our being; then there is nothing outside of us which can account for them. Moreover, they are already religous in themselves, thus it would seem that the ideal society presupposes religion, far from being able to explain it.

But, in the first place, things are arbitraily simplified when religion is seen only on its idealistic side : in its way, it is realistic. There is no physical or moral ugliness, there are no vices or evils which do not have a special divinity. There are gods of theft and trickery, of lust and war, of sickness and of death. Christianity itself, howsoever high the idea which it has made of the divinity may be, has been obliged to give the spirit of evil place in its mythology. Satan is an essential piece of the Christian system; even if he is an impure being, he is not a profane one. The anit-god is a god, inferior and subordinated, it is true, but nevertheless endowed with extended powers; he is even the object of rites, at least of negative ones. Thus religion, far from ignoring the real society and making abstraction of it, is in its image; it reflects all its aspects, even the most vulgar and the most repulsive. All is to be found there, and if in the majority of cases we see the good victorious over evil, life over death, the powers of light over the powers of darkness, it is because reality is not otherwise. If the relation between these two contrary forces were reversed, life would be impossible, but, as a matter of fact, it maintains itself and even tends to develop.

But if, in the midst of these mythologies and theologies we see reality clearly appearing, it is none of less true that it is found there only in an enlarged, transformed and idealized form. In this respect, the most primitive religions do not differ from the most recent and the most refined. For example, we have seen how the Arunta place at the beginning of time a mythical society whose organization exactly reproduces that which still exists to-day; it includes the same clans and phratries. It is under the same matrimonial rules and it practises the same rites. But rhe personages who compose it are ideal beings, gifted with powers and virtues to which common mortals cannot pretend. Their nature is not only higher, but it is different, since it is at once animal and human. The evil powers there undergo a similar metamorphosis : evil itself is, as it were, made sublime and idealized. The question now raises itself of whence this idealization comes.

Some reply that men have a natural faculty for idealizing, that is to say, of substituting for the real world another different one, to which they transport themselves by thought. But that is merely changing the terms of the problem; it is not resolving it or even advancing it. This systematic idealization is an essential characteristic of religions. Explaining them by an innate power of idealization is simply replacing one word by another which is the equivalent of the first; it is as if they said that men have made religions because they have a religions nature. Animals know only one world, the one which they perceive by experience, internal as well as external. Men alone have the faculty of conceiving the ideal, of adding something to the real. Now where does this singular privilege come from? Before making it an intial fact or a mysterious virtue which escapes science, we must be sure that it does not depend upon empirically determinable conditions.

The explanation of religion which we have proposed has precisely this advantage, that it gives an answer to this question. For our definition of the sacred is that it is something added to and above the real: now the ideal answers to this same definition; we cannot explain one without explaining the other. In fact, we have seen that if collective life awakens religious thought on reaching a certain degree of intensity, itis because it brings about a state of effecrvescence which changes the conditions of psychic activity. Vital energies are over-excited, passions more active, sensations stronger; there are even some which are produced only at this moment. A man does not recognize himself; he feels himself transformed and consequently he transforms the environment which surrounds him. In order to account for the very particular impressions which he receives, he attributes to the things with which he is in most direct contact properties which they have not, exc-eptional powers and virtues which the objects of every-day experience do not possess. In a word, above the real world where his profane life passes he has placed another which, in one sense, does not exist excpet in thought, but to which he attributes a higher sort of dignity than to the first. Thus, from a double point of view it is an ideal world.

The formation of the ideal world is therefore not an irreducible fact which escapes science; it depends upon conditions which observation can touch; it is a natural product of social life. For a society to become conscious of itself and maintain at the necessary degree of intensity the sentiments which it thus attains, it must assemble and concentrate itself. Now this concentration brings about an exaltation of the mental life which takes form in a group of ideal conceptions where is portrayed the new life thus awakened, they correspond to this new set of psychical forces which is added to those which we have at our disposition for the daily task of existence. A society can neither create itself nor recreate itself without at the same time creating an ideal. This creation is not a sort of work of supererogation for it, by which it would complete its-elf, being already formed; it is the act by which it is periodically made and remade. Therefore when some oppose the idel society, like two antagonists which woudl lead us in opposite directions, they materialize and oppose abstractions. The ideal society is not outside of the real society; it is a part fo it. Far from being divided between them as between two poles which mutually repel eachother, we cannot hold to one wihout holding to the other. For a society is not a made up merely of the mass of individuals who compose it, the ground which they occupy, the things which they use and the movements which they perform, but above all is the idea which it forms of itself. it is undoubtedly true that it hesitates over the manner in which it ought to conceive itself, it feels itself drawn in divergent directions. But these conflicts which break forth are not between the ideal and reality, but between two different ideals, that of yesterday and that of to-day, that which has the authority of tradition and that which has the hope of the future. There is surely a place for investigating when theese ideals evolve; but wheatever solution may be given to this problem, it still remains that all passes in the world of the ideal.

Thus the collective ideal which religion expresses is far from being due to a vague innate power of the individual, but it is rather at the school of collective life that the individual has learned to idealize. It is in assimilating the ideals elaborated by society that he has become capable of conceiving the ideal. It is society which, by leading him within its sphere of action, has made him acquire the need of raising himself above the world of experience and has at the same time furnished him with the means of conceiving another. For society has constructed this new world in constructing itself, since it is society which this expresses. Thus both with the individual and in the group, the faculty of idealizing has nothing mysterious about it. It is not a sort of luxury which a man could get along without, but a condition of his very existence. He could not be a social being, that is to say, he could not be a man, if he had not acquired it. It is true that in incarnating themselves in individuals, collective ideals tend to individualize themselves. Eah understands them after his own fashion and marks them with his own stamp; he suppresses certain elements and adds others. Thus the personal ideal disengages itself from the social ideal in proportion as the individual personality develops itself and becomes an autonomous source of action. But if we wish to understand this aptitude, so singular in appearance, of living outside of reality, it is enough to connect it with the social conditions upon which iit depends.

Therefore it is necessary to avoid seeing in this theory of religion a simple restatement of historical materialism : that would be misunderstanding essentially social, we do not mean to say that it confines itself to translating into another language the material forms of society and its immediate vital necessities. It is true that we take it as evidnet that social life depends upon its mateiral foundation and bears its mark, just as the mental life of an individual depends upon his nervous system and in fact his whole orgnism. But collective consciousness is something more than a mere epiphenomenon of its morphological basis, just as individual consciousness is something morethan a simple efflorescence of the nervous system. In order that the former may appear, a synthesis *sui generis* of particular consciousness is required. Now this synthesis has the effect of disengaging a whole world of sentiments, ideas and images which, once born, obey laws all their own. They attract each other, repel each other, unite, divide themselves, and multiply, though these combinations are not commanded and necessitated by the condition of the underlying reality. The life thus brought into being even enjoys so great an independence that is sometimes indulges in manifestations with no purpose or utility of any sort, for the mere pleasure of affirming itself. We have shown that this is often precisely the case with ritual activity and mythological thought [. . .]

Thus there is something eternal in religion which is destined to survive all the particular symbols in which religous thought has successively enveloped itself. There can be no society which does not feel the need of upholding and reaffirming at regular intervals the collective sentiments and the collective ideas which make its unity and its personality. Now this moral remaking cannot be achieved except by the means of reunions, assemblies and meetings where the individuals, being closely united to one another, reaffirm in common their common sentiments; hence come ceremoneis which do not differ from regular religious ceremonies, either in their object, the result which they produce, or the processes employed to attain these results. What essential difference is there between an assembly of Christians celebrating the principal dates of the life of Christ, or of Jews remembering the exodus from Egypt or the promulgation of the decalogue, and a reunion of citizens commemorating the promulgation of a new moral or legal system or some great event in the national life?

If we find a little difficulty to-day in imagining what these feasts and ceremonies of the future could consist in, it is because we are going through a stage of transition and moral mediocrity [. . .]

But feasts and rites, in a word, the cult, are not the whole religion. This is not merely a system of practices, but also a system of ideas whose object is to explain the world, we have seen that even the humblest have their cosomlogy. Whatever connection there may be between these two elements of the religious life, they are still quite different. The one is turned towards action, which is demands and regulates, the other is turned towards thought, which is enriches and organizes. Then they do not depend upon the same conditions, and consequently it may be asked if the second answers to necessities as universal and as permanent as the first.

When speicific characteristics are attributed to religious thought, and when it is believed that its function is to express, by means peculiar to itself, an aspect of reality which evades ordinary knowledge as well as science, one naturally refuses to admit that religion can ever abandon its speculative role. But our anlaysis of the facts does not seem to have shown this specific quality of religion. The religion which we have just studied is one of those whose symbols are the most disconcerting for the reason. There all apears mysterious. These beings which belong to the most heterogenous groups at the same time, who multiply without ceasing to be one, who divide without diminishing, all seem, at first view, to belong to an entirely different world from the one where we live; some have even gone so far as to say that the mind which constructed them ignored the laws of logic completely. Perhaps the contrast between reason and faith has never been more thorough. Then if there has ever been a moment in history when their heterogeneousness should have stood out clearly, it is here. But contrary to all appearances, as we have pointed out, the realities to which religious speculation is then applied are the same as those which later serve as the subject of reflection for philosophers : they are nature, man, society. The mystery which appears to surround them is wholly superficial and disappears before a more painstaking observation : it is enough merely to set aside the veil with which mythological imagination has covered them for them to appear such as they really are. Religion sets itself to translate these realities into an intelligible language which does not differ in nature from that employed by science; the attempt is made by both to connect things with each other, to establish itnernal relations between them, to classify them and to systematize them. We have even seen that the essential ideas of scientific logic are of religious origin. It is true that in order to utilize them, science gives them a new elaboration; it purges them of all accidental elements; in a general way, it brings a spirit of criticism into all its doings, which religion ignores; it surrounds itself with precautions to 'escape precipitation and bias,' and to hold aside the passions, prejudices and all subjective influences. But these perfectionings of method are not enough to differntiate it from religion. In this regard, both pursue the same end, scientific thought is only a more perfect form of religious thought. Thus it seems natural that the second should progressively retire before the first, as this becomes better fitted to perform the task.

And there is no doubt that this regression has taken place in the course of history. Having left religion, science tends to substitute itself for this latter in all that which concerns the cognitive and intellectual functions. Christianity has already definitely consecrated this substitution in the order of material things. Seeing in matter that which is profane before all else, it reaily left the knowledge of this to another disipline, *tradidit mundum hominum disputationi,* 'He gave the world over to the disputes of men', it is thus that the natural sciences have been able to establish themselves and make their authority recognized without very great difficulty. But it could not give up the world of souls so easily; for it is before all over souls that the god of the Christians aspires to reign. That is why the idea of submitting the psychic life to science produced the effect of a sort of profanation for a long time; even to-day it is repugnant to many minds. However, experimental and comparative psychology is founded and to-day we must reckon with it. But the world of the religious and moral life is still forbidden. The great majority of men continue to believe that here there is an order of things which the mind cannot penetrate except by very special ways. Hence comes the active resistance which is met with every time that someone tries to treat religious and moral phenomena scientifically. But in spite of these oppositions, these attempts are constantly repeated and this persistance even allows us to foresee that this final barrier will finally give way and that science will establish herself as mistress even in this reserved region.

That is what the conflict between science and religion really amounts to. It is said that science denies religion in principle. But religion exists; it is a system of given facts; in a word, it is a reality. How could science deny this reality? Also, in so far as religion is action, and in so far as it is a means of making men live, science could not take its place, for even if this expresses life, it does not create it; it may well seek to explain the faith, but by that very act it presupposes it. Thus there is no conflict except upon one limited point. Of the two functions which religion originally fulfilled, there is one, and only one, which tends to escape it more and more: that is speculative function. That which science refuses to grant to religion is not its right to exist, but its right to dogmatize upon the nature of things and the special competence which it claims for itself for knowing man and the world. As a matter of fact, it does not know itself. It does not even know what it is made of, nor to what need it answers. It is itself a subject for science, so far is it from being able to make the law for science! And from another point of view, since there is no proper subject for religious speculation outside that reality to which scientific reflection is applied, it is evident that this former cannot play the same role in the future that it has played in the past.

However, it seems destined to transform itself rather than to disappear.

We have said that there is something eternal in religion: it is the cult and the faith. Men cannot celebrate ceremonies for which they see no reason, nor can they accept a faith which they in no way understand. To spread itself or merely to maintain itself, it must be justified, that is to say, a theory must be made of it. A theory of this sort must undoubtedly be founded upon the different sciences, from the moment when these exist; first of all, upon the social sciences, for religious faith has its origin in society; then upon psychology, for society is a synthesis of human consciousness, and finally upon the sciences of nature, for man and society are a part of the universe and can be abstracted from it only artificially. But howsoever important these facts taken from the constituted sciences may be, they are not enough, for faith is before all else an impetus to action, while science, no matter how far it may be pushed, always remains at a distance from this. Science is fragmentary and incomplete; it advances but slowly and is never finished, but life cannot wait. The theories which are destined to make men live and act are therefore obliged to pass science and complete it prematurely. They are possible only when the practical exigencies and the vital necessities which we feel without distinctly conceiving them push thought in advance, beyond that which science and complete it prematurely. They are which we feel without distinctly conceiving them push thought in advance, beyond that which science permits us to affirm. Thus religions, even the most rational and laicized, cannot and never will be able to dispense with a particular form of speculation which, though having the same subjects as science itself, cannot be really scientific : the obscure institutions of sensation and sentiment too often take the place of logical reasons. On one side, this speculation resembles that which we meet with in the religions of the past; but on another, it is different. While claiming and exercising the right of going beyond science, it must commence by knowing this and by inspiring itself with it. Ever since the authority of science was established, it must be reckoned with; one can go farther than it under the pressure of necessity but the must take his direction from it. He can affirm nothing that it denies, deny nothing that it affirms, and establish nothing that is not directly or indirectly founded upon principles taken from it. From now on, the faith no longer exercises the same hegemony as formerly over the system of ideas that we may continue to call religion. A rival power rises up before it which, being born of it, ever after submits it to its criticism and control. And everything makes us foresee that this control will constantly become more extended and efficient, while no limit can be assigned to its future influence.

Chapter-9
On Religion

K. MARX and F. ENGELS

Chapter-9

1.1. **Contribtion to the critique of Hegel's philosophy of right**

(first published in 1844)—Marx

For Germany the *criticism of religion* is in the main complete, and criticism of religion is the premise of all criticism.

The *profane* exercise of error is discredited after its *heavenly oratio pro aris et focis* [speech for the altars and hearths] has been rejected. Man, who looked for a superman in the fantastic reality of heaven and found nothing there but the *reflexion* of himself, will no longer be disposed to find but the *semblance* of himself, the non-human [*unmensch*] where he seeks and must seek his true reality.

The basis of irrligious criticism is : *Man makes religion,* religion does not make man. In other words, religion is the self-consciouness and self-feeling of man who has either not yet found himself or has already lost himself again. But *man* is no abstract being squatting outside the world. Man is the *world of man*, the state, society. This state, this society, produce religion, a *reversed world-consciousness,* becaue they are *a reversed world.* Religion is the general theory of that world, its encyclopaedic compendium, its logic in a popular form, its spiritualistic *point d'honneur,* its enthusiams, its moral sanction,its solemn completion, its universal ground for consolation and justification. It is the *fantastic realization* of the human essence because the *human essence* has no ture reality. The struggle against religion is therefore mediately the fight against *the other world,* of which religion is the spiritual *aroma.*

Religous distress is at the same time the *expression* of real distress and the *protest* against real distress. Religion is the sigh of the oppressed creature, the heart of a heartless world, just as it is the spirit of a spiritless situation. It is the *opium* of the people.

The aboltion of religion as the *illusory* happiness of the people is required for their *real* happiness. The demand to give up the illusions about its condition is the *demand to give up a condition which needs illusions.* The criticism of religion is therefore in *embryo the criticism ofthe vale of woe,* the *halo* of which is religion.

Criticism has plucked the imaginary flowers from the chain not so that man will wear the chain without any fantasy or consolation but so that he will shake off the chain and cull the living flower. The criticism of religion disillusions man to make him think and act and shape his reality like a man who has been disillusioned and has come to reason, so that he will revolve round himself and therefore round his true sun. Religion is only the illusory sun which revolves round man as long as he does not revolve round himself.

The taks of history, therefore, once the *world beyond the truth* has disappeared, is to establish the *truth of this world.* The immediate *task of philosophy,* which is at the service of history, once the *saintly fomr* of human self-alientation has been unmasekd, is to unmask self-alienation in its *unholy forms.* Thus the criticism of heaven turns into the criticism of the earth, the *criticism of religion* into the *criticism of right* and the *criticism of theology* into the *criticism of politics* [. ..]

The philosophers have only *interpreted* the world, in various ways; the point, however, is to *change* it.

1.2 **German ideology** (from Chapter 1, written in 1845-6- Marx and Engels)

. . . The fact is, therefore : definite persons who are productively active in definite ways enter into definite social and political relations. Empiric observation must in every single case riveal the connection of the social and poltical organization with production, empirically and wihout any mysticification or speculation. The social organization and the state constantely arise from the life-process of definite individuals, of those individuals not as they or other people imagine them to be, but as they are *really*, i.e. a they act, as they materially produce, consequently as they are active under definite material limitations, provisions and conditions which do not depend on their free will.

The production of notions, ideas and consciousness is from the beginning directly interwoven with the material activity and the material intercourse of human beings, the languages of real life. The production of men's ideas, thinking, their spiritual intercourse, here appear as the direct efflux of their material condition. The same applies to spiritual production as represented in the language of politics, laws, morals, religion, metaphysics, etc. of a people. The producers of men's ideas, notions, etc., are men, but real active men as determined by a definite development of their productive forces and the intercourse corresponding to those productive forces up to its remotest form. Consciousness [*das Bewubtsein*] and the being of men is their real life-process. If in the whole of ideology men and their relations appear upside down as in a *camera obscura* this is due as much to their historical life-process as the inversion of objects on the retina is due to their immediate physical life-process.

In direct opposition to German philosophy, which comes down from heaven to earth, here there is ascension from earth to heaven. That means that we proceed not from what men say, fancy or imagine, nor from men as they are spoken of, thought, fancied, imagined in order to arrive from them at men of flash and blood; we proceed from the really active men and see the development of the ideological reflexes and echoes of their real life-process as proceeding from that life-process. Even the nebulous images in the brain of men are necessary sublimates of their material, empirically observable, materially preconditioned, life-process. Thus, morals, religion, metaphysics and other forms of ideology and the forms of consciousness corresponding to them no longer retain their apparent independence. They have no history, they have no development, but men, developing their material production and their material intercourse, with this, their reality, their thinking and the products of their thinking also change. It is not consciousness that determiens life, but life that determines consciousness. In the first view one proceeds from consciousness as from the living individuals; in the second, in conformity with real life, from the real living individuals themselves, considering consciousness only as *their* consciousness.

Consciousness is therefore from the start a product of society, and it remains such as long as men exist at all. At the beginning consciousness is of course only consciousness of the limited connection with other persons and things outside the individual becoming conscious of itself, at the same time it is consciousness of nature, which at the beginning confronts man as a completely alien, almighty and unassailable power to which man's attitude is a purely animal one and to which he submits like a beast; it is therefore a purely animal consciousness of nature (nature worship).

It is immediately obvious that this nature worship or this definite attitude to nature is determined by the form of society and conversely. Here as everywhere the identity of man and nature is so apparent that the limited attitude of man towards nature conditions their limited attitude to one another and their limited attitude to one another determines their limited attitude towards nature for the very reason that nature has yet hardly been modified by history; on the other hand, consciousness of the necessity of intercourse with surrounding individuals isthe begining of consciousness with surrounding individuals is the beginning of consciousness of living in soiety at all. This beginning is as animal-like as social life itself at this stage, it is mere herd consciousness, and man is distinguished from the sheep only by his consciousness taking the place of instinct or by his instinct being a conscious one.

1. In the manuscript the following is crossed out : 'The ideas that these individuals have are ideas either of their relation to nature or of their relation to one another or of their own constitution. It is clear that in all these cases these ideas are the conscious expression—true or illusionary—of their real relations and activity, of their production, their intercourse, their social and political organization. The opposite assumption is possible only when besides the spirit of the real materially determined individuals another spirit apart is presupposed. If the concious expression of the real relations of these individuals is illusory, if in their ideas they turn reality

upside down, this again is a result of their limited material activity and their consequent limited social relations.'

1.3 Manifesto of the Communist Party

(Extracts from Chapter II and III, written in 1847-8)—
Marx and Engels

. . . The charges against communisim madefrom a religious, a philosophical, and, generally, from an ideological standpoint, are not deserving of serious examination.

Does it require deep intuition to comprehend that man's ideas, views and conceptions, in one word, man's consciousness, changes with every change in the conditions of his material existence, in his social relations and in his social life?

What else does the history of ideas prove, than that intellectual production changes its character in proportion as material production is changed? The ruling ideas of each age have ever been the ideas of its ruling class.

When people speak of ideas that revolutionize society, they do but express the fact that within the old society the elements of a new one have been created, and that the dissolution of the old ideas keeps even pace with the dissolution of the old conditions of existence.

When the ancient world was in its last throes, the ancient religions were overcome by Christianity. When Christian ideas succumbed in the eighteenth century to rationalist ideas, feudal society fought its death battle with the then revolutionary bourgeoisie. The ideas of religious liberty and freedom of consience merely gave expression to the sway of free competition within the domain of knowledge.

'Undoubtedly', it will be said, 'religious, moral, philosophical and juridical ideas have been modified in the course of historical developmen. But religion, morality, philosophy, political science,and law, constantly survived this change.'

'There are, besides, eternal truths, such as Freedom, Justice, etc. that are common to all states of society. But communism abolishes eternal turths, it abolishes all religion, and all morality, instead of consituting them on a new basis, it therefore acts in contradiction to all past historical experience.'

What does this accusation reduce itself to? The history of all past society has consisted in the development of class antagonisms, antagonisms that assumed different forms at different epochs.

But whatever from they may have taken, one fact is common to all past ages, viz., the exploitation of one part of society by the other. No wonder, then, that the social consciousness of past ages, despite all the multiplicity and variety it displays, moves within certain common forms, or general ideas,, which cannot completely vanish except with the total disappearance of class antagonisms.

The communist revolution is the most radical rupture with traditional property relations, no wonder that its development involves the most radical rupture with tradittional ideas.

. . .As the parson has ever gone hand in hand with the landlord, so has Clerical Socialism with Feudal Socialism.

Nothing is easier than to give Christian asceticism a Socialist tinge Has not Christianity declaimed against private property, against marriage, against the State? Has it not preached in the place of these, charity and poverty, celibacy and mortification of the flesh, monastic life and Mother Church? Christian Socialism is but the holy water with which the priest consecrates the heart-burnings of the aristocrat....

1.4 Capital, Book I

[Extracts, first published in 1867] - Marx

...The religous world is but the reflex of the real world. And for a society based upon the prouction of commodities,in which the producers in general enter into social relations with one another by treating their products as commodities and values, whereby they reduce their individual labour to the standard of homogeneous human labour—for such a society. Christianity with its *cultus* of abstract man, more especially in its bourgeois developments, Protestantism, Deism, & c., is the most fitting form of religion. In the ancient Asiatic and other ancient modes of production, we find that the conversion of products into commodities and therefore the conversion of men into producers of commodities holds a subordinate place, which, however, increases in importance as the primitive communities approach and nearer to their dissolution. Trading nations, properly so called, exist in te ancient world only in its interstices, like the gods of Epicurus in the Intermundia, or like Jews in the pores of Polish society. Those anicent social organisms of production are, as compared with bourgeois society, extremely simple and transparent. But they are founded either on the imature development of man individually, who has not yet severed the umbilical cord that unites him with his fellowmen in a primitive tirbal community,or upon direct relatins of subjection. They can arise and exist only when the development of the productive power of labour has not risen beyond a low stage, and when, therefore, the social relations within the sphere of material life, between man and man, and between man and nature, are corresondingly narrow. This narrowsness is reflected in the ancient worship of nature, and in the other elements of the popular religons. The religous reflex of the real world can, in any case, only then finally vanish, when the practical relations of every-day life offer to man none but perfectly intelligible and reasonable relations with regard to his fellowmen and to nature...

1.5 **Anti-Dühring** [written in 1878]—Engels

....All religion... is nothing but the fantastic reflection in men's minds of those external forces which control their daily life, a reflection in which the terrestrial forces assume the form of supernatural forces. In the begining of history it was the forces of nature which were first so reflected and which in the course of further evolution underwent the most manifold and varied personifications among the various people. This early process has been traced back by comparative mythology, at least in the case of the Indo-European peoples, to its origin in the Indian Vedas, and its further evolution it has been demonstrated in detail among the Indians, Perisans, Greeks, Romans, Germans and, so far as material is available, also among the Celt, Lithuanians and Slave. But it is not long before, side by side with the forces of nature, social forces begin to be active–forces which confront man as equally alien and at first equally inexplicable, dominating him with the same apparent natural necessity as the forces of nature themselves. The fantastic figures, which at first only reflected the mysterious forces of nature, at this point acquire social attributes, become representatives of the forces of history. At a still further stage of evolution, all the natural and social attributes of the numerous gods are transferred to *one* aimighty god, who is but a reflection of the abstract man. Such was the origin of monotheism, which was historically the last product of the vulgarized philosophy of the later Greeks and found its incarnation in the exclusively national god of the Jews, Jehovah. In this convenient, handy and universally adaptable form, religion can continue to exist as the immediate, that is, the sentimental form of men's relation to the alien natural and social forces which dominate them, so long as men remain under the control of these forces. However, we have seen repeatedly that in existing bourgeois society men are dominated by the economic conditions created by themselves, by the menas of production which they themselves have produced, as if by an alien force. The actual basis of the reflective activity that gives rise to religion therefore continues to exist, and with it the religious reflection itself. And although bourgeois political economy has given a certain insight into the causal connection of this alien domination, this makes no essential difference. Bourgeois economics can neither prevent crises in general, nor protect the individual capitalists from losses, bad debts and bankruptcy, nor secure the individual workers against unemployment and destination. It is still true that man proposes and God (that is, the alien domination of the capitalist mode of production disposes. Mere knowledge, even it it went much further and deeper than that of bourgeois economic science, is not enough to bring social forces under the domination of society. What is aboe all necessary for this, is a social *act.* And when this act has been accomplished, when society, by taking possession of all means of production and using them on a planned basis, has freed itself and all its members from the bondage in which they are now held by these means of production which they themselves have produced but which confront them as an irresistible alien force, when therefore man no longer merely proposes, but also disposes—only then will the last alien force which is still reflected in religion vanish, and with it will also vanish the religious reflection itself, for the simple reason that there will be nothing left to reflect.

1.6 **Introduction to the English edition of 'Socialism : Utopian and Scientific'** (written in 1892)—Engels

... I have mentioned the fact that, about forty or fifty years ago, any cultivated foreigner settling in England was struck by what he has then bound to consider the religious bigotry and stupidity of the English respectable middle class. I am now going to prove that the respectable English middle class of that time was not quite as stupid as it looked to the intelligent foreigner. Its religous leanings can be explained [...]

Thus, if materialism because the creed of the French Revolution, the God-fearing English bourgenis held all the faster to his religion. Had not the reign of terror in Paris proved what was the upshot, if the religious instincts of the masses were lost? The more materialism spread from France to neighbouring countries, and was reinforced by similar doctrinal currents, notably by German philosophy, the more, in fact, materialism and free thought generally became on the Continent, the necessary qualifications of a cultivated man, the more stubbornly the English middle class stuck to its manifold religious creeds. These creeds might differ from one another, but they were, all of them, distinctly religious Christian creeds.

While the Revolution ensured the political triumph of the bourgeoisie in France. In England Watt, Arkwright, Cartwright, and others initiated an industrial revolution, which completely shifted the centre of gravity of economic power. The wealth of the bourgeoisie increased considerably faster than that of the landed aristocracy. Within the bourgeoisie itself, the financial aristocracy, the bankers etc., were more and more pushed into the background by the manufacturers. The compromise of 1689, even after the gradual changes it had undergone in favour of the bourgeoisie, no longer correspond to the relative position of the parties to it. The character of these parties, too, had changed, the bourgeoisie of 1830 was very different from that of the preceding century. The political power still left to the aristocracy, and used by them to resist the pretensions of the new industrial bourgeoisie, became incompatible with the new economic interests. A fresh struggle with the aristocracy was necessary, it could end only in a victory of the new economic power. First, the Reform Act was pushed through, in spite of all resistance, under the impulse of the French Revolution of 1830. It gave to the bourgeoisie a recognized and powerful place in Parliament. Then the Repeal of the Corn Laws, which settled, once for all, the supremacy of the bourgeoisie, and especially of its most active portion, the manufacturers, over the landed aristocracy. This was the greatest victory of the bourgeoisie, it was, however, also the last it gained in its own exclusive interest. Whatever triumphs it obtained later on, it had to share with a new social power, first its ally, but soon its rival.

The industrial revolution had created a class of large manufacturing capitalists, but also a class—and a far more numerous one—of manufacturing work people. This class gradually increased in numbers, in proportion as the industrial revolution seized upon the branch of manufacture after another, and in the same proportion in increased in power. This power it proved as early as 1824, by forcing a reluctant Parliament to repeal the acts forbidding combinations of workman. During the Reform agitation, , the working men constituted the Radical wing of the Reform party, the Act of 1832 having excluded them from the suffrage, they formulated their demands in the People' s Charter, and constituted themselves, in opposition to the great bourgeois Anti-Corn Law party, into an independent party, the Chartists, the first working men's party of modern times.

Then came the Continental revolution of February and March 1848, in which the working people played such a prominent part, and, at least in Paris, put forward demands which were certainly inadmissible from the point of view of capitalist society. And then came the general reaction. First the defeat of the Chartists on the 10th April, 1848, then the crushing of the Paris working men's insurrection in June of the same year, then the disasters of 1849 in Italy, Hungary, South Germany, and at last the victory of Louis Bonaparte over Paris, 2nd December, 1851. For a time, at least, the bugbear of working class pretensions was put down, but at what cost! If the British bourgeois had been convinced before of the necessity of maintaining the common people in a religious mood, how much more must be feel that necessity after all these experiences? Regardless of the sneers of his Continental compeers, he continued to spend thousands and tens of thousands, year after year, upon the evangelization of the lower orders, not content with his own native religious machinery, he appealed to Brother lonathan, the greatest organizer in existence of religion as a trade, and imported from America revivalism. Moody and Sankey, and the like, and, finally, he accepted the dangerous aid of the Salvation Army, which revives the propaganda of early Christianity, appeals to the poor as the elect, fights capitalism in a religious way, and thus fosters an element of early Christian class antagonism, which one day may become troublesome to the well-to-do people who now fine the ready money for it [...]

And now came the triumph of British respectability over the free thought and religious laxity of the Continental bourgeois. The workmen of France and Germany had become rebellious. They were thorouogly infected with socialism, and, for very good reasons, were not at all particular as to the legality of the means by which to secure their own ascendency. The *pure robustus,* here, turned from day to day more *malitiosus.* Nothing remained to the French and German bourgeoisie as a last resource but to silently drop their free thought, as a youngster, when seasickness creeps upon him, quietly drops the burning cigar he brought swaggeringly on board, one by one, the scoffers turned pious on outward behaviour, spoke with respect of the Church, its dogmas and rites, and even conformed with the latter as far as could not be helped. French bourgeois dined *maigre* on Fridays, and German ones sat out long Protestantsermons in their pews on Sundays. They had come to grief with materialism. '*Die Religion muss dem Volk erhalten werden.*' —religion must be kept alive for the people —that was the only and the last means to save society from utter ruin. Unfortunately for themselves, they did not find this out until they done their level best to break up religion for ever. And now it was the turn of the British bourgeois to sneer and to say 'Why, you fools, I could have told you that two hundred years ago!'

However, I am afraid neither the religious stolidity of the British, nor the *post festum* conversion of the Continental bourgeoise will stem the rising Proletarian tide. Tradition is a great retarding force, is the *vis inertiae* of history, but, being merely passive, is sure to be broken down, and thus religion will be no lasting safeguard to capitalist society. If our juridical, philosophical, and religious ideas are the more or less remote offshoots of the economical relations prevailing in a given society, such ideas cannot, in the long run, withstand the effects of a complete change in these relations. And, unless we believe in supernatural revelation, we must admit that on religious will ever suffice to prop up a tottering society.

Chapter-10

The Sociology of Religion

M. WEBER

Chapter-10

The rise of religion

To define 'relgion', to say what it *is,* is not possible at the start of a presentation such as this. Definition can be attempted, if at all, only at the conclusion of the study. The essence of religion is not even our concern, as we make it our task to study the conditions and effects of a particular type of social behaviour.

The external courses of religious behaviour are so diverse that an understanding of this behaviour can only be achieved from the viewpoint of the subjective experiences, ideas, and purpose of individuals concerned —in short, from the viewpoint of the religious behaviour's 'meaning' (*Sinn*).

The most elementary forms of behaviour motivated by religious or magical factors are oriented to *this* world. 'That it may go well with thee ... and that thou mayest prolong the days upon the earth' (Deut. 4:40) expresses the reason for the performance of actions enjoined by religion or magic [...] Furthermore, religiously or magically motivated behaviour is relatively rational behaviour, especially in its earliest manifestations. It follows rules of experience, though it is not necessarily action in accordance with a means-end schema. Rubbing will elicit sparks from pieces of wood, and in like fashion the simulative actions of a magician will evoke rain from the heavens. The sparks resulting from twirling the wooden sticks are as much a 'magical' effect as the rain evoked by the manipulations of the rainmaker. Thus, religious or magical behaviour or thinking must not be set apart from the range of everyday purposive conduct, particularly since even the ends of the religious and magical actions are predominantly economic....

Religion of non-privileged classes

...From the time of its inception, ancient Christianity was characteristically a religion of artisans. Its saviour was a semi-rural artisan, and his missionaries were wandering apprentices, the greatest of them a wandering tent maker, so alien to the land that in his epistles he actually empoloys in a reverse sense a metaphor relating to the process of grafting. The earliest communities of original Christianity were, as we have already seen, strongly urban throughout ancient times, and their adherents were recruited primarily from artisans, both slave and free. Moreover, in the Middle Ages the lower middle class remained the most pious, if not always the most orthodox stratum of society. But in Christianity as in other religious, widely different currents found a warm reception simultaneously within the lower middle class. Thus, there were the ancient pneumatic prophecies which cast out demons, the unconditionally orthodox (institutionally ecclesiastical) religiosity of the Middle Ages, and the monasticism of the mendicant type. In addition, there were certain types of medieval sectarian religiousity such as that of the *Humiliati,* who were long suspected of heterodoxy, there were Baptist movements of all kinds, and there was the piety of the various Reformed churches, including the Lutheran.

This is indeed a highly checkered diversification, which at least proves that a uniform determination of religion by economic forces never existed among the artisan class. Yet there is apparent in these lower middle classes, in contrast to the peasantry, a definite tendency towards congregational religion, towards religion of salvation, and finally towards rational ethical religion. But this contrast between the middle class and the peasantry is far from implying any uniform determinism [...]

Yet it is still true in theory that the middle class, by virtue of its distinctive pattern of economic life, inclines in the direction of a rational ethical religion, wherever conditions are present for the emergence of a rational ethical religion. When one compares the life of a lower-middle-class person, particularly the urban artisan or the small trader, with the life of the peasant, it is calear that middle-class life has far less connection with nature. Consequently, dependence on magic for influencing the irrational forces of nature cannot play the same role for the urban dweller as for the farmer. At the same time, it is clear that the economic foundation of the urban man's life has a far more rational essential character, viz., calculability and capacity for purposive manipulation. Furthermore, the artisan wand in certain circumstances even the merchant lead economic existences which influence them to entertain the view that honesty is the best policy, that faithful work and the performacne of obligations will find their reward and are 'deserving' of their just compensation. For these reasons, small traders and artisans are disposed to accept a rational world view incorporating an ethic of compensation. We shall see presently that this is the normal trend of thinking among of non-privileged classes. The peasants, on the other hand, are much more remote from this notion of compensation and do not acquire it unitl the magic in which they are immersed has been eliminated by other force. By contrast, the artisan is very frequently active in effecting the elimination of this very process of magic. It follows that the belief in ethical compensation is even more alien to warriors and to financial magnates who have economic interests in war and in the political manifestations of power. These groups are the least accessible to the ethical and rational elements in any religion.

The artisan is deeply immersed in magical encumbrances in the early stages of occupational differntiation. Every specialized art that is uncommon and not widely disseminated is regarded as a magical charisma, either personal or, more generally, hereditary, the acquisition and maintenance ofwhich is guaranted by magical means. Other elements of this early belief are that the bearers of this charisma are set off by taboos, occasionally of a totemic nature, from the community of ordinary people [peasants], and frequently that they are to be excluded from the owernship of land. One final element of this early belief in the magical charisma of every specialized art must be mentioned here. Wherever crafts had remained in the hadns of ancient groups possessing raw materials, who had first offered their arts as intruders in the community and later offered their craftsmanship as individual strangers settled within the community, the belief in the magical nature of special arts condemned such groups to pariah status and stereotyped with magic their manipulations and their technology. But wherever this magical frame of reference has once been broken through (this happens most readily in newsly settled cities], the effect of the transformation may be that the artisan wil learn to think about his labour and the small trader will learn to think about his enterprise much more rationally than any peasant thinks. The craftsman in particular will have time and opportunity for reflection during his work, in many instances. Consequently, the workers in occupations which are primarily of the indoor variety, e.g., in textile mills in our climate, are strongly infused with sectarian or religious trends. This is true to some extent even for the workers in modern factories with mechanized weaving, but very much more true for the workers at the looms in the textile mills of the past.

Wherever the attachment to purely magical or ritualistic views has been broken by prophets or reformers, there has frequently been a tendency for artisans, craftsman arnd middle-class people to incline toward a rather primitively rationalistic ethical and religious view of life. Furthermore, their very occupational specilization makes them the bearers of an integrated pattern of life of a distinctive kind. Yet there is cerainly no uniform determination of religion by these general conditions in thelife of artisans and middle-class groups [...]

Only a congregational religion, especially one of the rational and ethical type, could conceivably win followers easily, particularly among the urban lower middle classes, and then, given certain circumstances, exert a lasting influence on the pattern of life of these classes. This is what actually happened.

Finally, the classes of the greatest economic disability, such as slaves and free day laborers, have hitherto never been the bearers of a distinctive type of religion. In the ancient Christian comunities the slaves belongs to the lower middle classes in the cities [...]

Handicraft apprentices have at all times tended to share the characteristic religion of the lower middle classes, since they are normally distinguished from the independent lower middle classes only by the factor of *Karenzzeit* [the time during which a person employed at some manufactory is pledged to refrain from entering any rival establishment in that locality]. The apprentice group also tended to evince a conspicuous inclination toward various forms of unoffficial religion of the sect type, which found particularly fertile soil among the lower occupational strata of the city, in view of their work a day struggles with everyday needs, the fluctuations in the price of their daily bread, their quest for jobs, and their dependence on fraternal asistance. Furthermore, the class of small artisans and craft apprentices was generally represented in the numerous secret or half-tolerated communities of 'poor folk' that espoused congregational religions which were by turn revolutionary, pacifistic-communistic and ethical-rational, chiefly for the technical reason that wandering handicraft apprentices are the available missionaries of every mass congregational religion. This process is illustrated in the extra-ordinarly rapid expansion of Christianity across the tremendous area from the Orient to Rome in just a few decades.

Insofar as the modern proletariat has a distinctive religious position, it is characterized by indifference to or rejection of religions common to large groups of the modern bourgeoisie. For the modern proletariat, the sense of dependence on one's own achievements is supplanted by a consciousness of dependence on purely societal factors, economic conjunctures, and power relationship guaranteed by law. Any thought of dependence upon the course of natural or meterological processes, or upon anything that might be regarded as subject to the influence of magic or providence, has been completely eliminated, as Sombart has already demonstrated in fine fashion. Therefore, the rationalism of the proletariat, like that of the bourgeoisie of developed capitalism when it has come into the full possession of economic power, of which indeed the proletariat's rationalism is a complementary phenomenon, cannot in the nature of the case easily possess a religious character and certainly cannot easily generate a religion. Hence, in the sphere of proletarian rationalism, religion is generally supplanted by other ideological surrogates.

The lowest and the most economically unstable strata of the proletariat, for whom rational conceptions are the least congenial, and also the proletaroid or permanently impoverished lower middle-class groups who are in constant danger of sinking into the proletarian class, are nevertheless readily susceptible to being influenced by religious missionary enterprise. But this religious propaganda has in such cases a distinctively magical from or, where real magic has been eliminated, it has certain characteristics which are substitutes for the magical-orgiastic supervention of grace. Examples of these are the soteriological orgies of the Methodist type, such as are engaged in by the Salvation Army. Undoubtedly, it is far easier for emotional rather than rational elements of a religious ethic to flourish in such circumstances. In any case, ethical religion scarcely ever arises primarily in this group.

Only in a limited sense is there a distinctive class religion of disprivileged social groups. Inasmuch as the *substantive* demands for social and political reform in any religion are based on god's will, we shall have to devote a brief discussion to this problem when we discuss ehtics and natureal law. But insofar as our concern is with the character of the religion as such, it is immediately evident that a need for salvation in the widest sense of the term has as one of its foci, but not the exclusive or primary one, as we shall see later, disprivileged classes. Turning to the 'sated' and priviledged strata, the need for salvation is remote and alien to warriors, bureaucrats, and the plutocracy.

A religion of salvation may very well have its origin within socially priviledged groups. For the charisma of the prophet is not confined to membership in any particular class, and furthermore, it is normally associated with a certain minimum of intellectual cultivation. Proof for both of these assertions is readily available in the various characteristic prophecies of intellectuals. But as a rule, the aforementioned relationship between salvation religion and privileged classes changes its character as soon as the religion has reached lay groups who are not particularly or professionally concerned with the cultivation of intellectualism, and certainly changes its character after it has reached into the disprivileged social strata to whom intellectulism is both economically and socially inaccessible. One characterisitc element of this transformation, a product of the inevitable accomodation to the needs of the masses, may be formulated generally as the emergence of a personal, divine or human-divine saviour as the bearer of salvation with the additional consequence that the religious relationship to this personage becomes the precondition of salvation.

We have aleady sene that one form of the adaptation of religion to the needs of the masses is the transformation of cultic religion into mere wizardry, A second typical form of adaptation is the shift into savior religion, which is naturally related to the aforementioned change into magic by the most numerous transitional stages. The lower the social class, the more radical are the forms assumed by the need for a savior, once this need has emerged [...]

The religious need of the middle and lower bourgeosie expresses itself less in the form of heroie myths than in rather more sentimental legend, which has a tendency toward inwardness and edification. This corresponds to the peace-bleness and the greater emphasis upon domestic and family life of the middle classes, in contrast to the ruling strata. This middle-class transformation of religion in the direction of domesticity is illustrated by the emergence of the god-shifted *bhakti* piety in all Hindu cults, both in the creation of the Bodhisattva figure as well as in the cults of Krishna, and by the popularity of the edifying myths of the child Dionysos, Osiris, the Christ child, and their numerous parallels [...]

The soteriological myth with its god who has assumed human form of its savior who has been deified is, like magic, a characteristic concept of popular religion, and hence one that has arisen quite spontaneously in very different places. On the other hand, the notion of an impersonal and ethical cosmic order that transcends the deity and the ideal of an exemplary type of salvation are intellectualistic conceptions which are definitely alien to the masses and possible only for a laity that has been educated along rational and ethical lines. The same holds ture for the development of a concept of an absolutely transcendent god. With the exception of Judaism and Protestantism, all religions and religious ethics have had to reintroduce cults of saints, hereoes or functional gods in order to accommodate themselves to the needs of the masses. Thus, Confucianism permitted such cults, in the form of the Taoist pantheon, to continue their existence by its side. Simlilarly, as popularized Buddhism spread to many lands, it allowed the various gods of these land to live on as recipients of the Buddhist cult subordinated to the Budha. Finally, Islam and Catholicism were compelled to accept local, functional, and occupational gods as saints, the veneration of which constituted the real religion of the masses in everyday life.

The religion of the disprivileged classes, in contrast to the aristocratic cults of the martial nobles, is characterized by a tendency to allot equally to women. There is great diversity in the scope of the religious participation permitted to women, but the greater or lesser, active or passive participation (or exclusion) of women from the religious cults is everywhere a function of the degree of the group's relative pacification or militarization (present or past) [...]

What gave Christianity its extraordinary superiority, as it conducted its missionary enterprises among the lower middle classes, over its most important competitor, the religion of Mithra, was that this extremely masculine cult excluded women [...]

The specific importance of salvation religion for politically and economically disprivileged social groups, in contrast to privileged groups, may be viewed from an even more comprehensive perspective. In our subsequent discussion of castes and classes we shall have a good deal to say about the sense of honor or superiority characteristic of the non-priestly classes the claimed the highest social privileges, particularly the nobility. Their sense of self-esteem rests on their awareness that the perfection of their life pattern is an expression of their underived, ultimate, and qualitatively distinctive *being*. indeed, it is in the very nature of the case that this should be the basis of the elite's feeling of worth. On the other hand, the sense of honor of disprivileged classes rests on some concealed promise for the future which implies the assignment of some function, mission, or vocation to them. What they cannot claim to *be,* they replace by the worth of that which they will one day *become,* to which they will be called in some future life here or hereafter; or replace, very often concomitantly with the motivation just discussed, by their sense of what they signify and achieve in the world as seen from the point of view of providence. Their hunger for a worthiness that has not fallen to their lot, they and the world being what it is, produces this conception from which is derived the rationalistic idea of a providence, a significance in the eyes of some divine authority possessing a scale of values different from the one operating in the world of man.

This psychological condition, when turned outward toward the other social classes, produces certain characteristics contrasts in what religion must provide for the various social strate. Since every need for salvation is an expression of some distress, social or economic oppression is an effective source of savation beliefs, though by no means the exclusive source. Other things being equal, classes with high social and economic privilege will scarcely be prone to evolve the idea of salvation. Rather, they assign to religion the primary function of legitimizing their own life pattern and situation in the world. This universal phenomenon is rooted in certain basic psychological patterns. When a man who is happy compares his position with that of one who is unhappy, he is not content with the fact of his happiness, but desires something more, namely the right to this happiness, the consciouness that he has earned his good fortune, in contrast to the unfortunate one who must equally have earned his misfortune. Our everyday experience proves that there exists just such a psycholgoical need for reassurance as to the legitimacy or deservedness of one's happiness, whether this involves political success, superior economic status, bodily health, success in the game of love, or anything else. What the privileged classes require of religion, if anything at all, is this psychological reassurance of legitimacy. [...]

In practically every ethical religion found among privileged classes and the priests who serve them, the privileged or disprivileged social position of the individual is regarded as somehow merited from the religious point of view. What varies is only the form by which good fortune is legitimized.

Correspondigly different is the situation of the disprivileged. Their particular need is for release from suffering. They do not always experience this need for salvation in a religious form, as shown by the example of the modern proletariat. Furthermore, their need for religious salvation, where it exists, may assume diverse forms. More important, it may be conjoined with a need for just compensation, envisaged in various ways but always involving reward for one's own good deeds and punishment for the unrighteousness of others. This hope for and expectation of just compensation, a fairly calculating attitude, is, next to magic (indeed, not unconnected with it), the most widely diffused form of mass religion all over the world. Even religious prophecies, which rejected the more mechanical forms of this belief, tended as they underwent popularization and routinization to slip back into these expectations of compensation. The type and scope of these hopes for compensation and salvation varied greatly depending on the expectations aroused by the religious promises, especially when these hopes were projected from the earthly existence of the individual into a future life [...]

A theodicy of disprivilege, in some form, is a component of every salvation religion which draws its adherents primarily from the disprivileged classes. Whenever a developing priestly ethic met a theodicy of disprivilege halfway, the theodicy became a component of congregational religion, as happened with the pious Hindu and with the Asiatic Buddhist. That these religious lack virtually any kind of social-revolutionary ethics can be explained by reference to their theodicy of rebirth, according to which the caste system itself is eternal and absolutely just. The virtues or sins a former life determine birth into a particluar caste, and one's behavior in the present life determine one's chances of improvement in the next rebirth. Those living under this theodicy experienced no trace of the conflict experienced by the Jews between the social claims based on God's promises and the actual conditions of dishonor under which they lived. This conflict precluded any possibility of finding ease in this life for the jews, who lived in continuous tension with their actual social position and in perpetually fruitless expectation and hope. The Jews' theodicy of disprivilege was greeted by the pitiless mockery of the godless heathen, but for the Jews the theodicy had the consequence of transforming religious criticism of the godless heathen into ever-watchful concern over their own fidelity to the law. This preoccupation was frequently tinged with bitterness and threatened by secret self-criticism [...]

It would be erroneuos to portray the need for salvation, theodicy, or congregational religion as something that developed only among disprivileged social classes or as a product of resentment, and hence merely as the outcome of a 'slave or as a product in morality'. This would not even be true of ancient Christianity, although it directed its promises most emphtically to the poor in spirit and in worldly goods [...]

Not even Jesus' own warnings, according to the tradition, of the dangers presented by wealth to the attainment of salvation were motivated by asceticism. Certainly the motivation of his preaching against wealth was not resentment, for the tradition his preserved many evidences of Jesus' intercourse, not only with publicans (who in the Palestine of that period were mostly small moneylenders), but also with many wealthy people of the upper class. Furthermore, resentment cannot be regarded as the primary motivation of Jesus' doctrines regarding wealth, in view of the Gospels' impressive indifference to mundane affairs, an indifference based upon the importance attributed to eschatological expectations. To be sure, the rich young man was bidden to unconditionally take his leave of the wolrd if he desired to be a perfect disciple. But itis stated that for God all things are possible, even the salvation of the wealthy. The rich man who is unable to decide to part with his wealth may nonetheless achieve salvation, despite the difficulties in the way. There were no `proletatian instincts' in the doctrine and teaching of Jesus, the prophet of acosmistic love. He brought to the poor in spirit and to the good people of this world the happy tidings of the immediate coming of the Kingdom of God and of freedom from the domination of evil spirits. Similarly, any proletarian denunciation of wealth would have been equally alien to the Buddha, for whom the absolute precondition of salvation was unconditional withdrawal from the world.

The limited occurrence of the factor of *ressentiment* and the dubiousness of applying teh conceptual schema of `repression' almost universally appear most clearly when the Nietzschean scheme is applied erroneously to the altogether inappropriate example of Buddhism. constitutes the most radical anti-thesis to every type of *ressentiment* morality. Buddhism clearly arose as the salvation doctrine of an intellectural class, originally recruited almost entirely from the privileged castes, especially the warrior caste, which proudly and aristocratically rejected the illusions of life, both here and hereafter. Buddhism may be compared in social provenience to the salvation doctrines of the Greeks, particularly the Neo-Platonic, Manichean, and Gnostic manifestations, even though they are radically different in content. The Buddhist *bhikshu* does not begrudge the entire world, even a rebirth into paradise, to the person who does not desire *Nirvana.*

Precisely this example of Buddhism demonstrates that the need for salvation and ethical religion has yet another source besides the social condition of the disprivileged and the rationalism of the middle classes, which are poducts of their practical way of life. This additional factor is intellectualism as such, more particularly the metaphysical needs of the human mind as it is driven to reflect on ethical and religious questions, driven not by material need by by an inner compulsion to understand the world as meaningful cosmos and to take up a position toward it.

Chapter-11

Civilization and its Discontents

S. FREUD

Chapter-11

...The two process, that of the cultural development of the group and that of the cultural development of the individual, are, as it were, always interlocked. For that reason some of the manifestations and properties of the super-ego can be more easily detected in its behaviour in the cultural community than in the separate individual.

The cultural super-ego has developed its ideals and set up its demands. Among the latter, those which deal with the relations of human beings to one another are comprised under the heading of ethics. People have at all time set the gratest value on ethics, as though they expected that it in particular would produce especially important results. And it does in fact deal with a subject which can easily by recognised as the sorest sport in every civilization. Ethics is thus to be regarded as a therapeutic attempt–as an endeavour to achieve, by means of a command of the super-ego, something which has so far not been achieved by means of any other cultural activities. As we already know, the problem before us is how to get rid of the greatest hindrance oto civilization–namely, the constitutional inclination of human beings to be aggressive towards one another; and for that very reason we are especially interested in what is probably the most recent of the cultural commands of the super-ego, the commandment to love one's neighbour as oneself. In our research into, and therapy of, a neurosis, we are led to make two reproaches against the super-ego of the individual. In the severity of its comands and prohibitions it troubles itself too little about the happiness of the ego, in that it takes insufficient account of the resistances against obeying them–of the instinctual strength of the id [in the first place], and of the difficulties presented by the real external environment [in the second]. Consequently we are very often obliged, for thereapeutic purposes, to oppose the super-ego, and we endeavour to lower its demands. Exactly the same objections can be made against the ethical demands of the cultural super-ego. It, too, does not trouble itself enough about the facts of the mental constitution of human beings. It issues a command and does not ask whether it is possible for people to obey it. On the contrary, it assumes that a man's ego is psycholgoically capable of anything that is required of it, that his ego has unlimited mastery over his id. This is a mistake; and even in what are known as normal people the id cannot be controlled beyond certain limits. If more is demanded of a man, a revolt will be produced in him or a neurosis, or he will be made unhappy. The commandment, `Love thy neighbour as thyself', is the strongest defence against human aggressiveness and an excellent example of the unpsychological proceedings of the cultural super-ego. The commandment is impossible to fulfil; such an enormous inflation of love can only lower its value, not get rid of the difficulty. Civilization pays no attention to all this; it merely admonishes us that the harder it is to obey the precept the more meritorious it is to do so. But anyone who follows such a precept in present-day civilization only puts himself at a disadvantage *vis-a-vis* the person who diregards it. What a potent obstacle to civilization aggresiveness must be, if the defence against it can cause as much unhappiness as aggressiveness itself! 'Natural' ethics, as it is called, has nothing to offer here except the narcissistic satisfacation of being able to think oneself better than others. At this point the ethics based on religion introduces its promises of a better after-life. But so long as virtue is not rewarded here on earth, ethics will, I fancy, preach in vain. I to think it quite certain that a real change in the relations of human beings to possessions would be more help in this direction than any ethical commands, but the recognition of this fact among socialists has been obscured and made useless for practical purposes by a fresh idealistic misconception of human nature.

I believe the line of thought which seeks to trace in the phenomena of cultural development the part played by a super-ego promises still further discoveries. I hasten to come to a close. But there is one question which I can hardly evade. If the development of the civilization has such a far-reaching similarilty to the development of the individual and if it employes the same methods, may we not be justified in reaching the diagnosis that, under the influence of cultural urges, some civilizations, or some epochs of civilization–possibly the whole of mankind–have become 'neurotic'? An analytic dissection of cuh neuroses might lead to therapeutic recommendations which could lay claim to great practical interest. I would not say that an attempt of this kind to carry psycho-analysis over to the cultural community was absured to doomed to be fruitless. But we should have to be very cautious and not forget that, after all, we are only dealing with analyogies and that it is dangerous, not only with men but also with concepts, to tear them from the sphere in which they have originated and been evolved. Moreover, the diagnosis of communal neuroses is faced with a special difficulty. In an individual neurosis we take as our starting-point the contrast that distinguishes the patient from his environment, which is assumed to be 'normal'. For a group all of whose members are affected by one and the same disorder no such background could exist; it would have to be found elsewhere. And as regards the therapeutic application of our knowledge, what would be the use of the most correct analysis of social neuroses, since no one possesses authority to impose such a therapy upon the group? But in spite fo all these difficulties, we may expect that one day someone will venture to embark upon a pathology of cultural communities.

For a wide variety of reasons, it is very far from my intention to express an opinion upon the value of human civilization. I have endeavoured to guard myself against the enthusiastic prejudice which holds that our civlization is the most precious thing that we possess or could acquire and that its path will necessarily lead to heights of unimagined perfection. I can at least listen without indignation to the critic who is of the opnion that when one surveys the aims of cultural endeavour and the means it employs, one is bound to come to the conclusion that the whole effort is not worth the trouble, and that the outcome of it can only be a state of affairs which the individual will be unable to tolerate. My impartiality is made all the easier to me by my knowing very little about all these things. One thing only do I know for certain and that is that man's judgements of value follow directly his wishes for happiness–that, accordingly, they are an attempt to support his illusions with arguments. I should find it very understandable if someone were to point out the obligatory nature of the course of human civilization and were to say, for instance, that the tendencies to a restriction of sexual life or to the institution of a humanitarian ideal at the expense of natural selection were development trends which cannot be averted or turned aside and to which it is best for us to yield as though they were necessities of nature. I know, too, the objection that can be made against this, to the effect that in the history of mankind, trends such as these, which were considered unsurmountable, have often been thrown aside and replaced by other trends. Thus I have not the courage to rise up before my fellow-men as a prophet, and I bow to their reproach that I can offer them no consolation–for at bottom that is what they are all demanding–the wildest revolutionaries no less passionately than the most virtuous believers.

The fateful question for the human species seems to me to be whether and to what extent their cultural development will succeed in mastering the disturbance of their communal life by the human instinct of aggression and self-destruction. It may be that in this respect precisely the present time deserves a special interest. Men have gained control over the forces of nature to such an extent that with their help would have no diffculty in exterminating one another to the last man. They know this, and hence comes a large part of their current unrest, their unhappiness and their mood of anxiety. And now it is to be expected that the other of the two 'Heavenly Powers', eternal Eros, will make an effort to assert himself in the struggle with his equally immortal adversary.But who can foresee withwhat success and with what result?

Reference

1. The final sentence was added in 1931–when the menace of Hitler was already beginning to be apprarent.

Chapter-12

Religion, Class and Control

K. THOMPSON

Chapter-12

Theorertical introduction

It is generally agreed that the period of Engllish history from the middle of the eighteenth century to the middle of the nineteenth century was marked by considerable social upheaval and intense idological struggle. We have it on the authority of observers at the time that many workers who flocked, or were herded, into the growing towns experienced acute hardship and distress. It also saw the 'making of the working class', as E.P.Thompson put it, in which, as a result of their common experience 'in the years between 1780 and 1832 most English working people came to feel an identity of interests as between themselves, and as against their rulers and employers' —a class consciousness (Thompson, 1968, p.12). however, as Thompson suggests there were certain peculiarities about that consciousnes. Although their experiences were determined by the productive relations common to all wage-earners in a capitalist mode of production, the class consciousness of the English working class had its own peculiar characteristics. The way in which they interpreted their experience was affected by the cultural resources at their disposal and the social context in which they existed, with its various institutional structures. One of the most important features of English culture and social structure was its religious formation. In the feudal period the Church had been the dominant ideological institution and subseqent economic and poltical changes had been accompanied by ideological struggles couched in terms of religious beliefs, the stuggles were frequently overtly concerned with religious practices and organisation. It is not surprising, therefore, that the ideological struggles that accompanied the massive social changes entailed in capitalist industrialisation should manifest some of the same tendencies.

The problem of how to analyse the nature and effects of those ideological struggles, as they relate to religion, can be formulated in different ways. One problematic, which fits in with recent Marxist theories of ideology, but predates them and was shared by non-Marxists, such as the French historians who contrasted England with revolutionary France, poses questions about why working-class consciousness was not more often revolutionary consciousness. Answers tend to be sought in terms of the existence of structures, including structures of discourses and intellectual leadership, which impeded the development of such a consciousnes It will not be possible to arrive at a definitive answer to the question of why revolutionary consciousness did not become stronger or more widespread. however, it is possible to map out some of the key issues as they relate to the part that religion may have played in this connection, and to indicate some of the answers that have been suggested. The key issues are:

How important was religion in forming a non-revolutionary working class consciousness; and why did it take the form that it did ?

These issues can be broken down into a number of sub-questions and bypothetical answers:

1. Was there an affinity between pre-existing religious cultural elements and the new ideological currents that came to prominence during the Industrial Revolution, e.g. a reservoir of Protestant dissent that could be channelled in different directions ?

2. Was there an imposition on the working class of extraneous ideology emanating from the dominant class and transmitted through the agency of its intellectual leadership, e.g. the clergy, Sunday schools, and church building movments funded and encouraged by the state or members of the middle and upper classes?

3. Were there certain function that religion served for the working class in a period of disruption and hardship that might explain why religious solutions were adopted? Some of the suggested functions are: ' the opium of the people; (Marx); a compensation for those who suffer in this life through the promise of higher status in the spiritual realm (Weber); a transitional ideology helping the workers to adust to the

requirements of capitalist industrialisation or 'modernisation' by inculcating work-discipline (Weber); a form of community that eased the pallage from traditionally-based community (*Gemeinschaft*) to a more impersonal, rational and contractually-based social order (*Gesellschaft*) (Gillbert, 1976; and Semmel, 1974).

4. Did religion help to separate off from the working class its leading strata, the so-called 'aristocracy of labour; (Engels' term), those workers who, by virtue of their skill and relative independance, might have been the 'organic intellectuals' (Gramsci) capable of developing revolutionary working-class consciousness? Is it possible to go even further and find evidence that such strata were permeated by, and incorporated into, the ideology of the dominant class? (This 'dominant ideology thesis' and its relation to the notion of an 'aristocracy of labour' cannot be pursued in detail here, nor can we evaluate the evidence for its possible extensiveness, but some of the subsequent discussions of Methodism, sunday schools, and occupational community culture are relevant to it. For fuller discussion, see Abercrombie et al. 1980.)

5. What factors might have affected the degree of overlap between the culture of working-class commuities and the ideological content of those institutions in which the middle and upper classes performed a dominant leadership role, particularly religious institutions? Ideological contestation, as we will see, tended to be most acute where there was a strongly entrenched working-class culture based on a certain way of life, such as the mining and fishing villages and small towns in cornwall and similar areas, and the occupational communities of craftsmen in small workshops, where there were rituals and practices involving initiation and funeral rites, and patterns of mutual support, which made them resistant to extraneous ideological influences.

It is hoped that the following disusssion and the accompanying articles in this section, will help to clarify these issues, although we cannot hope to resolve them here. No overall theorisation of the issues will be attempted; indeed, it is doubtful whether an adequate general theory of ideology exists. Most current theories of ideology tend to be either extremly abstract (Thompson, 1978) or, where they are more concrete and specific, they are ill-suited to the task of ding justice to the historical specificity of religion as a cultural system in this earlier period. This is not surprising as the focus of recent theories of ideology has tended to be on the non-emergence of revolutionary working-class consciousness in *mature* capitalism, rather then in *emerging* industrial capitalism, However, some of the ideas and concepts deriving from these theories are potentially useful, particularly Gramsci's discussions of hegemony in terms of ideological leadership,' organic intellectuals', and cultures as multi-layered (including common sense notions, popular traditions, as well as various sorts of philosophies) (Gramsci,1971). These ideas find their nearest parallel in the sociology of religion in the work of Max Weber (Weber, 1965, and the article by Weber in this volume, pp.31-40). Weber can be criticised for not having developed a more dunamic view of the 'elective affinities' between ideologies and various social strata. The relationship appears rather passive, unlike Gramsci's picture of the ideological terrain as the site of contestation and struggle. However, Weber did sometimes show an awareness of this, as E.P.Thompson suggests in his account of Methodism and the making of the English working class, when he quotes Weber's statements that: Wherever modern capitalism has begun its work of increasing the produtivity of human labour by increasing its intensity, it has encountered the immensely stubborn resistance of ... pre-capitalist labour. (Thompson, 1968, p. 392)

If recent theories of ideology do not explain the specific cultural configuration in the period we are discussing, they do offer a better way of conceptualising that configuration than the older 'economistic' Marxist theory according to which religion was viewed as mere supersturcture, or a cultural 'transmission belt' for the interests of the dominant class. Gramsci rejected this principle of reduction' in analysing the relationship between class and ideology, in which an ideology would be reduced to, or belonged to, a certain class, and which had led to the assumption that the existence of a dominant class meant that other classes were automatically subject to, or incorporated into, a dominant ideology. Gramsci's guiding principle of 'articulation' envisaged a looser set of relationships in which there was no pure dominant ideology descending from above, nor a pure working-class ideology emanating from below, but rather complex forms of interaction of political, cultural and ideological negotiation within and between dominant groups (i.e.aristocracy and bourgeoisie) and various subordinate groups and classes.

On the whole, the following account of the issues will favoour this Gramscian view of the ideological terrain as the site of contestation and struggle in which religion can be seen to have provided the language of dissent and resistance for subordinate classes, as well as being a means by which the dominant class sought to establish and mintain hegemony. It follows from this that due weight will be given to the 'positive' features and functions of working-class religious life—the ways in which people actively created, adapted and used religion for their own needs. At the same time,we will consider some of the arguments for religion having acted as an agency of social control, whether through the splitting-off or incorporaton of working-class leaders, by acting as the 'opium of the people', or by functioning to instil a work-discipline or a transitional ideology in the passage from *Gemeinschaft* to *Gesellschaft* forms of social organisation.

The significance of the period from the latter part of the eighteenth century through the first few decades of the nineteenth centurym as far as religion and ideology are concerned, is that it was a period of intense contestation, This means that those involoved in religious movements and disputes will be found to have had an unusually well- developed awareness of the wider social relevance of their beliefs and practices, In these circumstances, even a narrow defination of ideology, such as that which designates it as the 'justificatory. apologetic' dimension of culture (cf. Geertz, in this volume,pp.82-3),would encompasss many of the most sailent ideological features of the religious situation. However, this narrow definition tends to spotlight only those aspects of religion which were most obviously in play as active elements in the ideological struggle along class lines, particularly in relation to the efforts of the governing classes to maintain social order and legitimate their authority. But a narrow view of ideology would miss some of the les obvious ideological elements of religious culture that were at issue in this period, and which helped to form the ideological complex that we associate with the Vivtorian moral ethos that became established from the middle of the nineteenth century onwards. We need a broad view of ideology that also directs our attention to those underlying structures of 'common sense' and 'presuppositions' by and through which people orientate themselves in their daily lives, and which make them accept such a way of life as natural. (Such a focus is not restricted to, although it gains much from, those who have developed rigorously 'structuralist' methods for analysing culture and ideology, e.g. Levi-Strauss and Althusser.) This broad view of ideowlogy, which in Gramsci's approach is combined with a sense of the dynamic character of the ideological terrain, is the one thaat is most likely to make sense of the ideological aspects of religion defined as a cultural system:

> A system of symbols which acts to establish powerful, pervasive, and long-lasting moods and motivations in men by formulating conceptions of a general order of existence and clothein these conceptions such an aura of factuality that the moods and motivations seem uniquely relistic.
> (Geertz, 1966.pp.3-4; and in this volume, p.67)

This broad definition of religion corresonds to the broad view of ideolgy, and its adoption has simiar consequences. For example, in the subsequent discusssion of religion in the period of capitalist industriallsation, it helps to determine whether or where we draw a line between religion and other elements of popular culture in working class communities, such as superstitions, tradional recreational activities, and the ritualised aspects of occupational and workplace cultures. On the whole, we will regard them as being closly involved with the more overtly religious elements and so part of the same idwological contestation. At times, the authorities will be seen to have had a similar recogition of their interconnectedness, viewing popular religious movments and other aspects of popular culture as posing the same threat. In other cases the ideological connotations of religion and popular culture were more subtle and less obviously reprsesntative of a stance towards the politicaleconomic order. This was so with respect to some of the more arcane theological disputes and the message of populaar hymns , not all of which conveyed the clear ideological message of those oft-quoted hymn lines :

> The rich man in his castle,
> The poor man at his gate,
> God made them high or lowly,
> And ordered their estate.

But quite often they did play some part in constituting the descourses that gave meaning to the social order, and which positioned people as 'subjects' within that order (cf. Althusser, 1969). There were real ideological implications in the disputes about whether 'Arminian' or 'Calvinist' doctrines shold prevail in Methodism, and about how people were categorised or positioned as 'subject' within this theological discourse - subjects like 'the saved', 'the elect', 'God's people', 'the damned' and 'the innocent'.

Historical background

The primary aim of this article is to explore and elucidate some of the intricate relations between ideology and social structure (partucularly social stratification) as exemplified by English religion berween 1740and 1850. This period marks the emergence and growht to maturity of industrial capitalism, and also the struggle of the Established Church (the church of England) to maintain and fulfil its role as the pre-eminent ideological institution cementing the social order—a role which it gradually and reluctantly relinquished to secular institutions such as the state systm of education. The 1740s saw the rise of Methodism, which seemed to present a challenge to the hegemonic position of the Established Church in the religious sphere as well as appearing to pose a threat to the established social order.We will examine the thesis put forward by the French historian, Elie Halevy, in 1906 (and subsequently readdressed by E.P. Thompson in The Making of the English working Classes, 1968), which maintains that, although Methodism may have appeared to pose a threat to the authorities

Methodism may have appeared to pose a threat to the authorities, it served to deflect or channel off any potential revolutionary impulses in the working class. The Church of England answered the challenges posed to it by its religious and secular rivals, and by social upheavals, in ways that came naturallly to an secular rivals, and by social upheavals, in ways that came naturally to an established church - it endeavoured to prove its usefulness to the state, and expected the state to fulfil its side of the partnerships in return. (For an account of the Church's espousal of this 'utilitarian' rationale, see K.A. Thompson, 1970.) We can mention three ways in which the Church attempted to make a contibution to cementing the social order in the face of external and internal threats: the fostering of nationlism during the FrenchRevolutionary and Napolenonic wars (1793-1815) (cf. Stafford, 1982); the church reforms and building drives that aimed to win the new urban working class (discussed in K.A Thompson, 1970); and the Sunday school movement, as a means of socialising working-class children into behaviour patterns appropriate to their future roles in a capitalist society (Laquwur, 1976; and in this volume, pp.183-203). However, although the church had some success in these respects, it was a very limited success. Nationalism was prominent during the period of the French threat, and church reform building movements increased the number of churches from 11,379 in 1801 to 14,077 in 1851 but the percentage of the population aged fifteen and over attending Easter communion dropped in this period, from 9.9 percent to 8.1 percent (Gilbert, 1976,p.28). The Census of 1851 showed that half of the 5-15 age group attended Sunday school, but the Church of England had only about 40 percent of the enrolments (Lequeur,1976). Laqueur makes a plausible case that the Nonconformist sunday schools may not have played such an important part in the process of indoctrination into bourgeois values, but rather expressed working class values and aspirations.

Overall, in the period of industrial and demographic expansion, 1740 to 1830, when the English population rose from about 5,500,000 to 13,200,000, the Church of England declined from a position in which it had nearly a monopoly of religious practice to one in which it almost became a minority religious establishment. By1831 there were only 605,000 Easter Day communicants (7.2 percent of the population aged 15 and over, compared with 535,000 in 1801), and clergy and church buildings had increased only marginally since 1740(Gilbert, 1976, 27-9). A massive church building drive was launched in the 1830s with support from the government, but the enormous increase in population to over 34 million by 1914 meant that the Church never really made up the ground lost betweeen 1740 and 1830 (see Table 1)

In the case og Methodism, there was a period of sustained rapid expansion from 1740 to 1840, followed by a period of slower and decelerating expansion untill 1906, and then continuing decline. There were also many schisms into small sects (see Table 2).

As for the success of Sunday schools, they made a slow start in the last two decades of the eighteenth century, and then their enrloments climbed steadily from 1800 to 1850, with some acceleration in the late 1820s and 1830s. After 1830, few working-class children could have escaped at least some exposure to sunday school (see Tables 3 and 4).

Many accounts of the social effects of religion in ninteenth-century Britain emphasise the stabilising effects, by which they mean it counteracted the disrruptive effects of capitalist industrialisation. Some accounts suggest that religion acted as a kind of social cement, binding otherwise divided social classes into a common set of beliefs and a religiously defined common identity. Another view is that religion served both to legitimate the superior position of the upper classes and to console the lower classes(acting like a drug - 'the opium of the people', as Marx called it). The hime missionary effort to build hundreds of new churches in working class areas, the Evangelical movement in the Church of England and the sunday school movement, have all been interpreted as conscious or unconscious attempts to provide a social cement, or to promote acquiescence to the status quo and consolation for the miseries of the lower classes. Even the growth of Methodism, which at first caused alarm and oppoition among the upper classes, has been viewed as an ideological distraction taking away working-

Table 1 The church of England

Churches, clergy, and Easter day communicants, 1801-1914

Year	Churches and chapels	Clergy	Easter Day communcants ('000s)	Easter Day communicant density
1801	11,379	-	535	9.9
1811	11,444	14,531	550	8.9
1821	11,558	-	570	7.9
1831	11,883	14,933	605	7.2
1841	12,668	15,730	755	7.9
1851	14,077	16,194	875	8.1
1861	15,522	17,966	995	8.3
1871	16,300	19,411	1,110	8.2
1881	16,956	20,341	1,225	7.9
1891	17,368	22,753	1,490	8.4
1901	-	23,670	1,945	9.4
1911	-	23,193	2,293	9.8
1914	-	-	2,226	9.2

Notes

1 In 1966 Anglican 'churches', 'clergy', and 'Easter Day communicants' numbered 17,761, 20,008, and 1,899,000 respectively. The 1966 Easter Day Communicant density index was 5.4.

2 The density index expresses Easter day communicant figures as a percentage of the population aged fifteen and over.

3 The figures on 'clergy' for 1811-41 include a few hundred Welsh clergy. Welsh clergy have been excluded from the subsequent figures. The increase of clergy in the 1840s consequently was greater than the series indicates.

(*Source*: Gilbert, 1976, p.28)

Table 2 Methodist membership in England, 1767-1914

A. Wesleyan membership, 1767-96

1767	22,410	1776	30,875	1791	56,605
1771	26,119	1781	37,131	1796	77,402
		1786	46,559		

B. Wesleyan, New Connexion, and total Methodist membership, 1801-1819

	W	NC	Total		W	NC	Total
1801	87,010	4,815	91,825	1816	181,631	8,146	189,777
1806	103,549	5,586	109,135	1819	184,998	9,672	194,670
1811	135,863	7,448	143,311				

C. Wesleyan, New Connexion, Primitive Methodist, Bible Christian, United Methodist Free Churches, and total methodist membership, 1821-1906

	W	NC	PM	BC	UMFC	Total
1821	188,668	10,404	16,394			215,466
1826	217,486	10,233	-	6,433		267,652
1831	232,883	11,433	37,216	6,650		288,182
1836	273,588	18,248	62,306	10,499		364,641
1841	305,682	20,506	75,967	11,353		435,591
1846	319,770	15,610	85,500	12,181		452,238
1851	285,000	16,962	106,074	13,324		490,000
1856	242,296	18,380	104,178	13,894		443,493
1861	291,288	22,732	127,772	16,866	52,970	513,628
1866	303,500	24,064	140,905	18,758	60,386	547,613
1871	319,495	22,870	148,597	18,050	61,924	570,936
1876	342,612	23,055	160,737	19,665	64,777	610,846
1881	349,695	25,797	168,807	21,209	65,067	630,575
1886	378,518	27,720	179,726	23,614	66,964	676,542
1891	387,779	28,756	180,518	25,769	67,200	690,022
1896	395,588	29,932	181,079	26,306	69,509	702,411
1901	412,194	32,324	187,260	28,315	72,568	732,668
1906	447,474	37,017	203,103	32,317	80,323	800,234

D. Wesleyan methodist Association and Wesleyan Reformers membership, 1837-1856

	WMA		WMA		WMA	WR
1837	21,262	1846	19,177	1856	18,136	46,609
1841	22,074	1851	20,557			

E. Wesleyan, Primitive methodist, United Methodist, and total Metodist Membership, 1911-19141

	W	PM	UM	Total
1911	436,356	202,479	144,888	783,723
1914	432,370	202,420	143,096	777,886

F. Total Methodist Membership as a percentage of the adult English population, 1801-1914

1801	1.6	1841	4.5	1881	4.0
1806	1.9	1846	4.3	1886	4.0
1811	2.3	1851	4.4	1891	3.8

1816	2.8	1856	3.8	1896	3.6
1821	2.9	1861	4.1	1901	3.5
1826	3.3	1866	4.2	1906	3.6
1831	3.4	1871	4.1	1911	3.3
1836	4.0	1876	4.1	1914	3.2

Notes

1 The *Total Methodist* Membership Series is based on an aggregration of the following connexional memberships: 1801-19, Wesleyan and New Connexion; 1821, Wesleyan, New Connexion, and Primitive Methodist; 1826-36, Wesleyan, New Connexion, and Primitive Methodist, and Bible Christian; 1836-56, Wesleyan, Methodist Association, and (1851 and 1856) the Wesleyan Reformers, 1861-1906, Wesleyan, New Connexion, Primitive Methodistm Bible Christian, and United Methodist Free Churches; 1911-14, Weslyan, Primitive Methodist, and United Methodist Church.

2 For the purpose of computing the density series of section F (above), 'Adult population' has been defined as the population aged fifteen years and over.

3 Wesleyan density in 1767 was around 0.5.

4 In 1968 membership of the Methodist Church in England was 603,100 and Methodist density was 1.7.Following the union of 1932 these figures represent a continuation of the Total Methodist Membership series.

(*Source:* Gilbert, 1976, pp.31-2)

Table 3 Numbers of Sunday schools built or founded 1780-185 distinguishing Anglican and Non- Anglican*

Years to:	Total no.	No. belonging to C. of E.	Percentage of total no. belonging to C. of E.
1801	2,290	1,282	56.4
1811	4,687	2,288	48.8
1821	8,236	3,766	45.7
1831	11,910	5,371	45.0
1841	17,168	7,815	45.0
1851	23,135	10,427	45.0

Table 4 Enrolment in English Sunday schools 1788-1850**

Years	Number	Percentage of populaton	Percentage of those age 5-15	Percentage of working class age 5-15
1788	59,980	-	-	-
1795	94,100	-	-	-
1801	206,100	2.5	10.3	13.8
1811	415,000	4.4	18.2	24.2
1818	452,325	4.2	17.6	23.4
1821	730,000	6.5	27.0	36.0
1831	1,096,000	8.4	37.2	49.6
1833	1,363,170	10.2	45.0	60.0
1841	1,679,000	11.4	49.8	66.4
1851	2,099,611	12.5	56.5	75.4

*Prepared from Census: Education 1852-53[1692]xc, Table 25. Those schools for which no date of founding or constructing of building is given, 1,071 Anglican, 420 Dissenting, were distributed equally over seven decades. There is no basis for a more sophisticated distribution of the undated schools.

**Numbers of 1788 and 1795 are. at best, educated guesses arrived at through the use of the following formula:

$$\text{no. in schools aided by the sundayschool society in 1788 and 1795} \times \frac{\text{no. of schools founded by 1801}}{\text{no. of schools aided by the Sunday School Society in 1801}}$$

(*Source:* Laqueur, 1976,p.44)

class revolutionary potential (Thompson,1968, and in this volume,pp. 154-82). on the basis of historical evidence, as we shall see, it is possible to make a case for each of these explanations having a certain amount of plausibility (exactly how plausible is less easily established). Howeveeer, a full picture of the social effects of religion in the nineteenth century must take account of evidence of religion operating in ways contrary to those encompassed by the 'social cement'and 'opium of the people' theories. In some respects religion exacerbated social divisions and deepened class conflict; indeed, the very phrase about religion being an opium of the people was first used by a clergyman, the Reverend charles Kingsley. It will be necessary, therefore, to examine ways in which religion furnished the language and beliefs for dissent and oppositon to the status quo. Also, it is possible to find evidence of a 'split consciousness' among subordinate classes, in that they seem to 'simultaneously produce their own view of the world and inhale the religious atmosphere produced by the dominant culture of the dominant class' (Turner, 1983, p.85). It may be that a better description would be that of an 'amalgam' rather than a 'split', as the culture of the lower classes in nineteenth-century Britain seems to have been a complicated mixture of traditional populaar beliefs practices and superstitions, elements of workplace culture and trades societies' rituals, and more orthodox Christian beliefs that they shared with other classes. This would correspond to Gramsci's view of ideological complexes.

We will endeavour to provide a sociaolgical analysis of religion in these various ideological complexes and their funtioning, whilst at the same time examining some of the evidence that historians have used to test what has been described as 'one of the most persistent, appealing, and useful hypotheses used to interpret English history in the eighteenth and nineteenth centuries', which runs as follows:

> On 24 May 1738 Wesley was converted. From that moment, so it is argued, a corrupt and lifeless Established Church was faced with the shock of the Methodist Revival. The Methodists, persecuted by mobs and forbidden to preach in many Anglican churches, were at length driven from the church of England.Their impact, however, continued, through their spiritual descendents, the Evangelicals.These Evangelicals (to continue the hypothesis) did not effect a takeover of the Church of England, but rather a takeover of the whole nation, imbuing it with their values and creating Victorianism. The methodists' main appeal was to the working classes. Besides accomplishing the civilization of a section of those classes, the Methodists imposed a degree of conservatism upon them which was providential, since the French Revolution and the industrial Revoulution together created uniquely powerful tensions which otherwise might have brought about the disintegration of society.
>
> (Armstrong,1973,p.7)

This is certainly a simplification of a complicated set of

religious developments and we will be looking at some of the wider social ramifications of religious beliefs and practices but Armstrong's formulation does provide a useful story-line. It received its classic statement in the form of the question posed by Halevy: 'Why was it that of all the countries of Europe England has been the most free from revolutions, violent crises and sudden change?' The answer, he believed, did not lie in England's political or economic institutions, but in English religion especially the effect of the Evangelical movement on the thinking of the potential leaders of a revolution:

> We have sought in vain to find the explanation by an analysis of her political institutions and economic organization. Her political institutions were such that society might easily have lapsed into anarchy had there existed in England a boourgeoisie animated by the spirit of revolution. And a system of economic production that was in fact totally without organization of any kind would have plunged the kingdom into violent revolution had the working classes found in the middle class leaders to provide it with a definite ideal, a creed, a practical programme. But the elite of the working class, the hard-working and capable bourgeois, had been imbued by the Evangelical movement with a spirit from which the established order had nothing to fear.
>
> (Halevy, 1938, Book 3, p.47)

Methodism and the working class

The Methodist Revival flourished at the same time as the Industrial Revolution and the French Revolution; consequently it its not surprising that there have been constant efforts to discern the connections. One of the first was by Robert Southey in the year of Peterloo,1819, who, while attacing the methodists for their irrationality and spititual tyranny, admitted that their conversions might have a great effect in improving the morality of individuals, and he commended Wesley's insistance on strict control over personal expenditure and the avoidance of personal indulgence. W.E.H.Lecky in his *History of England in the Eighteenth Century* (vol.3,Longmans, 1878), also criticised the Methodists' irrationalilty and spirtual tyranny, but argued that the new religious enthusiasm was one of the things that saved England from anything like the French Revolution. The thesis was elaborated by the French historian, E. Halevy in articles published in the *Revue de Paris* in 1906, and in his *History of the English People in the Nineteenth Century* (1913, English translation, 1924 Penguin edn 1938). The idea of Methodism as an antidote to revoution in Britain had already been promulgated by nineteenth-century French writers such as Taine and Guizot, and Halevy's thesis was in line with this French view (Semmel, 1971).

He also maintained that it was characteristic of social change in England that it took religious forms, and Nonconformism was a transitional phase for those who were upwardly socially mobile:

> Nonconformity ...tended to become a transitional creed, a stage in the history of an English family.The unskilled workman becomes in turn a skilled workman, an artisan, the head of a small business, a businessman possessed of a modest capital, and as he rises out of the barbarism in which the working clas was plunged he becomes a Nonconformist. If he himself rises still higher on the social ladder or if his children rise after his death, he or they go over to the Church of England.
> (Halevy, 1938,III, p.46)

Harold Perkin, in his Origins of Modern English Society 1780-1880 (1969), developed Halevy's obsevation on the connections between a person's rise in social status and his change in religion. In the birth of the modern class structure Perkin pictures religion as the 'midwife', in the sense that it enabled men to escape from dependence upon the gentry, and it gave them 'a model of class organization'.

E.P. Thompson's *The Making of the English Working Class* (1968) argues that Methodism had a disastrous effect on the English working class, for three reasons:

(i) working class radicalism was inhabited by the Methodist instistence on submissiveness;

(ii) Wesley's stress on the virtues of work, discipline and thrift played into the hands of the industrialists;

(iii) The Methodist concentration on the emotions had harmful psychological effects.

Methodism has been accused at various times of being both radical and conservative in its effects. Coinciding as it did with the French Revolution and the industrial Revolution, it seemed to many of its contemporaries that Methodism was a further threat to the established social and ideological order. Its teaching were radical in that they emphasised human sinfulness and the need for redemption, and the condemnation applied to all classes. In a more important sense, Methodism attacked the stuctures of society; it undermined the ideology inscribed in institutional practices:

> Visibly, the Methodist meeting—either outside or in one of the new chapels with the sexes segregated and seated on benches on the principle of first come, first seated—was in as sharp a contrast as could be imagined to the hierarchically ordered congregation at the parish church surrounded as it was with hatchments, memo-rials, and decorated pews. Less obviously, the attack on the parish was also an attack on the elaborate complex of property rights in which clergy and landowners shared.
> (Armstrong, op. cit.,p.113)

In its early years, Methodism was accused of all sorts of dangerous tendencies and the meetings were subject to attacks by gangs, which gave rise to riots. One bishop even accused the Methodists of administering drugs to people to induce hysteria (George Lavington, Bishop of Exeter, in his *Enthusiasm of Methodists and Papists compared,1749-51)*

The simple version of the historical hypothesis about the ideological functions of Methodism—that it imposed a degree of conservatism on the working class—is inadequate. It is important to take account of the quite different and varied functions that a religious ideology can serve. The strength of a highly developed and succesful ideology lies in its capacity to serve a multiplicity of functions and to have an affinity or congruity with a variety of aspects in the culture and experiences of the groups to whom it appeals. It is often the case that a sociologist or historian has emphasised one set of functions or aspects and ignored or downplayed other as a result of adopting a particular perspective, or as the result of a judgement about what was most important in terms of the scholar's own set of values. This has to be kept in mind when comparing different accounts of the functions of Methodism, as—for example—Gilbert (1976) and E.P.Thompson (1968). According to Gilbert, Thompson's account emphasises the repressive 'utility' of Methodism in inclucating a 'work discipline' rather than a more attractive observe aspect of its legitimation of self-improvement and economic endeavour. Thompson is accused of writing with some distaste for Methodist beliefs and values, evidently out of a conviction that the best they could offer was 'consolation' to those who felt' defeated and hopless'. Gilbert maintains that this was a minor function in the total ideological impact of Methodism; its most widespread appeal was to groups whose economic and social positions were improving and it echoed the aspirations rather than the despair of the working classes.

In fact, Thompson's approach is potentially more complicated than this summary might suggest. He sees Methodism as serving functions for both the 'exploiters' and the 'exploited' (Thompson, 1968, p.412). He gives three reasons for this: (1) it served the exploiters' interest in exercising social control through indoctrination of the workers, especially through the sundays schools; (2) it could 'offer to the uprooted and abandoned people of the Industrial Revolution some kind of community to replace the older community-patterns which were being displaced' (ibid., pp.416-17); (3) it offered compensation for disappointed this-worldly hopes, including political hopes, by emphasising the after life—it was the 'chiliasm of despair' (ibid.,p.419).On balance, however, Thompson's account emphasises the counter-revolutionary effects of Methodism, which is seen as serving the function of social control.

The issue of which of the ideological functions served by Methodism and Evangelicalism was the most important cannot be resolved by a simple appeal to neutral emirical evidence because such evidence is never completely independent of any conceptual structure. However, such evidence can clear away over-simplification and generalisations that are too broad. A comparison of the different accounts provided by Gilbert and Thompson reveals that certain functions telate to some groups of Methodist adherents but not others, and that this also varied from one period to another. For example, until the demoralising introduction of the powerloom had its impact on handloom weavers after the Napoleonic Wars, weavers joined Methodism in large numbers and found there an 'overall congruity' between the religious culture and the spirit of independance and self-reliance which characterised their socio-economic situation. As we will see, different ideological functions of Methodism might be emphasised depending on whether we concentrate on a 'social control' perspective or look at it in terms of the ways in which it served as an expression of working-class cultures and aspirations.Gilbert stresses the positive functions of the chapel communities, which were largely created and sustained by working-class lay members; whereas Thompson sees them more as instruments of the middle class for exercising social control and instilling discipline in the working class. The same contrast, between an imposed social control perspective and an approach which emphasises the ways in which working-class religion was an expression or translation in religious idiom of people's aspirations and communal values, occurs in accounts of the functions served by the Sunday school movement (in the exccerpt from Laqueur,1976, in this volume), and with regard to the relations between Methodism, popular beliefs and village culture (discussed in Rule, 1982).

In comparing the different accounts of the social functions of Methodism by Gilbert and Thompson, it is worth noting the differnt styles of the two accounts: Thompson builds up a poweful case emphasising the social control functions of Methodism and Evangelicalism—functions that mainly served the interests of the emerging system of industrial capitalism. Gilbert emphasises more strongly the functions that Methodism, Nonconformity and Evangelicalism served for certain sections of the working class in a period of transition. The point of thses remarks about the two accounts is not to suggest that one is right and the other is wrong—they both offer 'true' observations in terms of the theoretical perspective adopted for the task of guiding and interpreting observation. (Also, in many respects, the two approaches offer complementary insights.) The main point to be borne in mind when evaluating historical accounts such as those concerning the social functions or effects of Methodism is the need to discern the explicit and implicit theoretical perspectives used in producing theese accounts, which can help to explain why, on balance, they give different emphases to some facts and less to others.

'Social control' and 'social expression' might be seen as just two of the functional relationships between ideology and social classes or groups within the complex and dynamic field of ideology as mapped out by Gramsci.

Another functional relationship that has been posited between Methodism / Evangelicalism and both the working class and the bougeoisie, is that of providing a transitional ideology for integrating those classes into the capitalist industrial state, and for supplying an 'effective nourishing ground for English nationalism' (Semmel, 1974, p.80). According to Semmel, this was achieved through Evangelical Arminianism, a theological synthesis elaborated by Wesley and extended by his successors, 'uniting the emotional force of the quasi - mystical primitive christianity of the Reformation - with its powerful capacity to create "nes men" - with the "modernity" of Arminan doctrine... Evangelical Arminianism was the "ideology" of the Methodist Revolution' (Semmel, ibid.).

The modernity of Arminianism stemmed from the fact that it saw the relationship between Christ and his worshippers as akin to a commercial contract:

> Arminians saw Christ as having, by his sacrifice, both *purchased fovourable terms or conditions* for men and also as having restored to men a great part of their ability to fulfill these conditions of which they had been deprived by Adam's sin.God seemed as much bound by the contract, which offers a quid pro quo as was the individual worshipper ...In thus stipulating that salvation was dependent upon man's rational, responsible behaviour, the Arminans were

> asking for the kind of conduct which 'modern' political and economic life would find essential, and which, especially so far as the lower classes were conerned, was almost non-existent in the traditional order.
>
> (Semmel, op. cit.,p.12)

The genuis of wesley as an ideologist was that he managed to synthesise, or mediate between, different ideological streams and tendencies, and appeal to classes with seemingly different interests and cultures. In theological terms, 'Wesley appealed to both the Puritan sense of man's degenerate state, with its passionate plea for God's grace so essential to salvation, as well as to the Arminan insistence on personal responibility, on free will and good works' (Semmel, op.cit., p.13). In class terms, he not only united Puritanism and Arminianism into an instrument for the evangelisation of the growing industrial proletariat, but also inspired a simiar fusion by Anglican Evangelicals and Dissenters which permeated the bourgeoisie and even some of the aristocracy.

Sunday schools and social control

One of the main agencies of transmission of bourgeois values to the working class is reputed to have been the Sunday school movement, according to E.P.Thompson and other historians who adopt the Halevy thesis about the counter-revolutionary effects of religion in Britain. However, Laqueur (1976) provides a markedly different conclusion as a result of his study of the sunday school movement:

> The period 1780-1850 witnesseed the birth of a working-class culture that was deeply rooted in that ethic of education, religion and respectability which was embodied in the Sunday school. English working class politics lacked revolutionary ideology, a rhetoric of 1789, less because of religious education than because England did not experience a '1789'. And this latter fact is due to the stability of English society and the cohesion of its ruling class and not to the failure of ideology taken as an independent variable. The religious, educational and social institutions of the working class must be seen as significant cultural achiev-

ements in their own right and not merely as spurs or restraints in the development of revolutionary politics. Sunday schools were largely a creation of the community they served and 'helped to keep the soul alive in a population living under conditions that degrade the mind'.
(Laqueur, 1976,p. 245)

The issue as to whether the working class was successfully incorporated into a dominant, bourgeois ideology is not easily resolved, but it is certainly the case that the one area of high working-class involvement in religion, that of the Sunday school movement, does not provide unequivocal evidence of incorporation. Although E.P.Thompson is successful in showing that the midddle-class founders and management committees of Sunday schools often had that prpose in mind, Laqueur concludes that the working-class Sunday school teachers and parents did not share that intention. Many Nonconformist sunday schools seemed to have grown out of the demand from within the working class for basic education and the transmission to children of the values of the 'repectable' working class, or 'labour aristocracy'—industry, thrift, self-discipline, improvement, communalism and egalitarianism. Laqueur sees such Sunday schools as genuinely popular institutions that promoted working-class culture, and therfore akin to trade unions, friendly societies, co-operatives, building societies, saving banks, and various institutions for intellectual improvement. Certtainly the authorities in the church of England and in Wesleyan Methodism feared that the sunday schools could have such effects, and in the 1820s they prohibited the teaching of writing to sunday school pupils. The original Methodist emphasis, on the values of equality of all people before God and the community of believers within the church resonated with the democratic-egalitarian and communal-activist values of the working class, and were a source of acute tension within Wesleyanism as the reprisentatives of bourgeois values—the clergy and leading laymen—promoted centralisation, inegalitarianism, and support for the existing social order. This led to splits and some branches of Methodism, especially the Primitive Methodists, were closely connected with radical working-class movements and supported political action (Hobsbawm, 1957,1959).Even E.P. Thompson who paints a negative political picture of Methodism, admits that some Methodists did display confrontationist class-conscious, proletarian values in the early nineteenth century (Thompson, 1968, p.4.30)

The truth of the matter is that the evidence about working-class beliefs is somewhat sketchby and incomplets. There are few first-hand accounts of such beliefs and practices untill after the mid-nineteenth century and the spread of literacy. The amalgam of beliefs probably varried considerably betweeen areas, between sections of the working class, and depending on the degree of penetration of middle-class agencies of transmission of bourgeois values. Literacy and the printed woed provided the most potent agency for indoctrination into bourgeois values and for exercising social control. However, this should not be regarded as a straight forward, one way process; the working-class communities were not 'clay', open to the imprint of whatever values were pressed upon them, nor were values exclusively class related or derived. Firstlym as we have suggested with regard to sunday schools, the lerning and organisational abilities developed in the sunday schools could be used in working- class radicalism. Secondly, the actual content of the 'texts' used in the sunday school—scriptures and hymns—were open to a variety of interpretaions; they were not, after all, statements of bourgeois utilitarianism, but highly symbolic and potent images of various sorts. The political radicals wrote and thought in the metaphors of the Bible. As an opponent of Sunday schools and advocate of secular education put it in a report on the Kentish peasant risings, 'The narratives and lessons contained in the sacred writings may be turned, as they often have been, not merely into sources of error, but into authorities for wrong' (Liardet, 1839, quoted in Laqueur, 1976,p.244). The hymns of Wesley, which were widely loved and sung, even at Chartist and Luddite meetings, had more in common with Romanticism than with rational utilitarianism, as we will see in the next section. The third set of factors that need to be considered, which hindered or complicated the penetraion and indoctrination of working classs culture by more specifically bourgeois beliefs and values, relate to the pre-existing culture of working-class communities, whether at the workplace or in certain localities and occupations.

According to E.P. Thompson and others who judge religion to have been a counter-revolutionarry force, one of the most important means by which nineteenty-century religion functioned to exercise social control was through the Sunday school movement and the influence of certain dominant ideas purvayed through that movement and the influence of certain dominant ideas purveyed through that movement, which not only in fluenced chikdren but also—through them—the parents' generation. But Sunday school teaching was not a direct transmission of dominant bourgeois values. An important morif in the thought of the sunday school movement was a kind of Romanticism, a set of ideas concerned with childlike innocence, counerposed against adult sinfulness. One exp;anation for the popularity and success of the sunday school movement may lie in the content of its teaching and the character of the relations betweeen teachers and pupils. Laqeur argues that the content of the teaching, especially in Wesleyan and Evangelical sunday schools, tended to resolve the tension inherent in Protestant doctrines concerning the moral state of the child in favour of its innocence. Whereas strict Calvinist theology had proclaimed that each soul's fate was predestined from eternity, and some were reprobate from the womb, Wesleyan Methodism had elements of an Arminian theology which sometimes softenend that doctrine. It maintained that infants who died before they could choose redemption were destined for heaven because of their birtheright of innocence. Althoughthe hymns of John and Charles Wesley contained some of the usual Christian ambivalence about the moral state of the child, their metaphorical structure included the image of the innocent child. the hymn on the text, 'Suffer the little children to come unto me',proclaimed of children that they were formally born in sin:

> Born they are, like us, in sin
> Touch the unconscious lepers clean;
> Purchase of thy blood they are,
> Save them by Thy dying prayer.
> (quoted in Laqueur, 1976,p.13)

But a few lines later, under the text, 'For such is the kingdom of God' the hymn develops the metaphor of the soul regaining childlike innocence in order to enter paradise:

> Thy church is here with saints supplied
> Who childlike innocence regain;
> And every babe that ever dies
> Shall in thy heavently kingdom reign.
> (ibid., p.13)

Another famous example is to be found in the hymn for children,'Gentle jesus, meek and mind/ Look upon a little child', which continues,

> I shall live the simple life
> Free from sin's uneasy strife:
> Sweety ignorant of ill,
> Innocent and happy still.
>
> Keep me from the great offence,
> Guard my, helpless innocence,
> Hide me, from all evil hide,
> Self and stubbornness, and pride.

There was a new softness and sentimentality in the late eighteenth century and early nineteenth-century attitude towards children that suffused the sunday school movement. That is not to say there was none of the old calvinist theunder against immorality, disobedience and sin.There were also many arguments in favour of sunday schools which emphasised their utility for the purpose of maintaining social order and overcoming class divisions, as in the statement that they offered the hope and separated', the chain which once' united rich and poor', could some how be reforged (quote in Laqueur, op.cit.,p.7). But the sunday school movements cannot be un derstood solely in terms of its social utility; it shared with the high culture of romanticism a streak of anti-rationalism;' children because of there relative ignorance, their innocence and their simplicity were more likely to perceive religious reality and to accept the Holy Spirit than were adults' (Laqueur, p.15). Like Wordsworth, the sunday schools took as their dictum, 'the child is the father of the man'. The child not only epitomised the characteristics that would find favour in God's eyes, but he or she might also be the means of converting adults. This theme was put forward in one of the most widely read pieces of popular literature, Leigh Richmond's *The Dairyman's Daughter*, the sales of which exceeded half a million before 1850.

The character of the relations between sunday school teachers and pupils also differed from those that prevailed in other institutions, such as the factory or the day schools. One reason may have beeen that the teachers were much younger in the sunday schools—more like older brothers and sisters. Certainly the ideal of that relationship, as set forth in guides to sunday school teaching or organisation, stressed that the good teacher was 'affectionate in manner and mild in expression' and put for waed the model of the teacher as an older, wiser and steadier friend (see examples given in Laqueur, op.cit.,p.18). To a large extent the sunday school movement was staffed by the working class, even though it may have been encouraged and funded initially by middle-and upper -class patrons, who had in mind the need for social control and a disciplined workforce. If we simply take the statements of intention of these latter groups as a guide to the character of the sunday schools, then we could be misled. The sunday schools may have served some of the social functions the upper clases had in mind for them, but they also seved other functions for the working class. Many children learned to read in the Sunday schools, and they were communities in which poor children experienced pleasures, affection and kindness that were badly needed. To a certain degree the Sunday schools can be described as predominantly working-class institutions, staffed by members of the skilled or 'respectable sections of that class, who passed on some of the beefits they had gained from their relatively favoured positiones, such as the ability to read, instruction in cleanliness, and access to various social services and benefits organised by the Sunday school or the wider community. They had a collective-communalist orientation that was typically working class and therfore differed in practice from the values of bourgeois individualism.

Workplace and occupational culture

One of the problems that we face in evaluating the beliefs

and culture of the working class in the first half of the nineteenth century concerns the paucity of information about workplace culture. We know relatively more about those aspects of the affairs of the working class that were conducted in public, such as Chartism and the organised religious activities of the churches. The same cannot be said of workplace culture in that period. There is a good reason for this: studies of the workplace culture in that period (e.g. Behagg, 1982) suggest that the opacity and secrecy of workplace culture were part of a defensive reaction in which the workers sought to control their immediate working environment in the face of employers' attemps to 'improve' and 'reform' their morals and behaviour. Those urban missionaries who did manage to penetrate the workplace in places such as Birmingham found it contained many of the values and beliefs most calculated to undermine their efforts. One such missionary, Edward Derrington, drew attention in 1839 to the independence that the experience of work afforded to those who he had hoped would be pliable ex-sunday school scholars: ' the youths have at a very early age', he complained, 'been their own or nearly their own masters' (quoted in Behagg, op.cit., p.155). Such work experience threatened to undermine the missionaries' efforts to reform the workers' morals through involvement in 'rational recteation ' because the youths who started work at an early age tended, according to Derrington, to be 'the fighters - the pigeon flyers - dog fighters and gamblers' (quoted in Behagg, ibid.). Another missionary, Peter sebtree, expressed the same concern about a widow who had been left to run her husband's factory and who said 'that her children had been brought under the teaching of the Gospel among the Wesleyans, but now they were unhappily infidel having imbibed the notions from some of the workmen' (ibid.,p.156). Missionaries, such as William Jackson, who evangelised in Birmingham from 1842 untill 1847, feared to enter the factories, and when he did enter a nailer's workshop he was stopped and challenged to open debate by an 'infidel' workman(ibid.). His colleague Derrington's most abiding memory of such a visit was of 'an hour's close argument' with an 'infidel' navigator who 'eulogised Robert Owen as most benevolent man' (ibid.,p.157). The missionaries bemoaned the

fact that the infidel culture of the workplace and of the public house permeated into the homes, where the missionaries directed their efforts to converting the wives.
According to Behagg,

> The symbiosis of the workplace and the public house reprented, to the outsider, a culture that embraced not only drunkenness, violence and sensuality, but also radical politics, Owenite infidelity and, at times, an almost puritanical concept of moral justice. Once within either institution the intruders were confronted by an alternative set of values and beliefs that would intimidate them both physically and intellectually. It is argued here that in the first half of the nineteenth century the working class deliberately emphasized the distinct nature of their own culture, particularly the separateness of the workplace and their autonomous role within it in an attempt to retain some control over a work process that was undergoing structural change.
>
> (Behagg, 19852, pp.157-8)

Ritual and secrecy were two of the hallmarks of the trade societies, which is not surprising in view of the fact that trade unions were illegal from 1800 to 1824 and of only dubious legal status thereafter. The exclusivity and secrecy of the trade societies was exphasised by their rituals of initiation: oath-swearing, the wearing of surplices and the chanted liturgy of psalms and old Testament extracts. Similar rituals were to be found in groups as diverse as the leeds woolcombers, the London tailors, the West Country weavers and the Operative Stone Masons. Sometimes the trade societes would make a show of their exclusive and mysterious culture, as in their funeral processions. An account of a Typical trade society funeral in 1834 records that a Derby carpenter was accompanied to his last resting place by a hundred women in white robes and hoods, and the officers of more than eleven trade societies, similarly attired; at other funerals the robbed mourners carried a branch of ivy or bunch of thyme, which would be dropped on the coffin after the singing of the doxology (Behagg,p. 161). In such ways the workers gave witness to their 'mysterious brotherhood' and emphasised the life-long commitment undertaken at their initiation. The ceremonies expressed visually and in practice the ideological distinctiveness of the working community; the funerals, in particular, showed that the individual who respected collective values was, in turn, deserving of collective respect (Behagg,op.cit.).

Commentators who write from the angle of the study of working-class resistance to capitalist control and exploitation in the workplace tend to interpret these beliefs and practices as a cloak or shield to hide the worker's more 'important' activities from the employers and other aurhorities. As Behagg puts it:

> It was clearly the operation of the trade society, or where this did not exist the work group, within the workplace that were to be cloaked and hidden rather than the ceremonial itself. The actual rules of behaviour by which the workforce governed their own activites and attitudes at the place of work were largley unwritten and it is these rather than the elaborate initiation ritual that constitute the anonymous tradition of early English industrial relations. In order to control the work process, or rather to re-organize it, in a period of structural economec change, so that it answered the needs of capital rather than those of labour, the manufacturer had first to penetrate the collective culture of the workplace. This was a culture based upon asssumptions which he did not share, transmitted through face-to-face relàtionships in which he had no part. Penetration was made doubly difficult where collectivity was underpinned by mystification and...folk violence.
>
> (Behagg, 1982,pp.162-3)

This is to interpret these workplace rituals, cermonies and beliefs in a rather narrowly 'exclusivist' way. Although it is probably true that their secrecy and mysteriousness did serve the important function of preventing the manufacturer from penetrating and controlling the workplace, that was not their only function, nor can their character be understood and appreciated purely in terms of this function. In order to understand the character of these sub-cultures it is necessary to see how they articulated with other cultural layers, especially popular religion, superstition and folklore.

Popular culture and popular religion

Workplace culture did not come into existence to serve the function of withstanding capitalist control; it was part of a wider popular and traditional working-class culture that included old Testament and Christian elements, folk beliefs and rituals, superstitions and revelries. The historian Gareth Steadman Jones has pointed out that there is danger in making the concept of 'social control' central to accounts of developmnts in popular clture in the nineteenth century; it can lead us to view cultures too much in oppositional terms, in which one culture is on the defensive (tradional popular culture) and the other is on the offensive (the reforming cultures of evangelicals, Methodists, civil elites and capitalist employers, intent on imposing rational recreation on the working class as part of the process of incorporating it into the capitalist scheme of things). The 'social control' concept is suggestive of the attempted imposition of new forms of behaviour upon the working class by external forces. In some respects there were cultural opposittions: Methodism and teetotalism were opposed to the 'revelery' aspect of traditional popular culture. As Harrison has pointed out, it was over attempts to dominate popular leisure that the churches and the working class came most frequently into contact in the nineteenth century:

> Nineteenth century Christians deplored that recreational complex of behaviour which included gambling, adultery, drinking, cruel sports and sabbath breaking and blasphemy -all of which took place together at the race course, the drinking place, the theatre, the 'feast' and the 'fair'.
>
> (Harrison, 1966, p.2)

In other respects, however, there was less opposition and Methodism in particular merged with popular religion and superstition and other aspects of tradional popular culture. Indeed, the success of Methodism in some areas was due to the ease with which it could assimiate traditional forms of belief and action. In one of its most successful areas, among the miners and fishermen of Cornwall for example, Methodism did not so much replace folk beliefs as translate them into a religious idiom. The appeal of Methodism was not dissimilar to the appeal of witchcraft beliefs (discussed earlier in this book although mainly with respect to African examples) :

> Neither witchcraft nor spirit-agency as an explantion of events precludes commonsense empirical observation. Men die because they happen to be at a moment in time under a fall of rock. What needs explaining is why that man was in that place at that time. Witchcraft, as Max Gluckman has observed, explains that singularity of misfortune which the agnostic or scientific mind prefers to see as 'chance'. In modern British history no church of comparable weight has allowed a greater degree of comprehensiveness of frequency to divine or satanic intervention than did early Methodism. The idea of an omnipotent deity and malicious devil can explain singularity of misfortune as well as can witches or evil spirits. The retributive anger of God can explain the most widespread of disasters.
> (Rule, 1982,pp.63-4)

One of the reasons for John Wesley's success in appealing to the common people was probably that despite hes learning he was fascinated by, and in touch with, some of the ingredients of popular superstition and belief. as Armstrong puts it:

> Yet attempts to make Wesley a man representative of his time must fail. Conversion and assurance—his most obvious doctrines—were obvious throwbacks to the previous age. The practice of determinng a course of action by opening the Bible at random (which he took from the Moravians) was like wise out of tune with the eighteenth century. Witchcraft he would never reject, and he collected the most circumstantial accounts of witches. Before retailing a lengthy narrative of one Elizabeth Hobson in his Jounal for 25 May, 1768, he observed:
>
> It is true likewise, that the English in general and indeed most of the men of learning in Europe, have given up all accounts of witches and apparitions, as mere old wives'

> fables. I am sorry for it... The wisest and best men in all ages and nations ...well know that giving up witchcraft is, in effect, giving up the Bible.
> (Armstrong, 1973, p.82)

Conclusion

The case for the strong thesis that religion served a predominantly and crucially counter-revolutionary function in England during the period from the late eighteeenth century to the end of the nineteenth century has been examined with respect to two of its most important elements—the influence of Methodism, and Sunday schools. The discussion has centred on the cultural content of these two movements in relation to working class culture and its penetration or incorporation by bourgeois values. Although it is difficult to judge the degree of penetration or incorpoation achieved, partly because the evidence from first-hand accounts is limited, it has not been established that it was sufficient, of itself, to prevent a revolutionary class consviousness developing, At the most, the thesis could only be applied to the potential leaders of such a revolution (which is what Halevy's formulation of the thesis did imply), because it has been noted that the working- class involvement in organised religion, apart from sunday schools, was very low. Membership of Methodist sects ranged from 3.6 to 4.4 per cent of the English population throughout the nineteenth century; Church of England communications on Easter Day were in the range of 7.2 to 8.9 percent; and Roman Catholics attending mass were in the region of 4 percent as a result of Irish immigration after 1850 (Gilbert, 1976). In the rural areas, those members of the working class who were religious seem to have held an amalgam of beliefs that was completely antithetical to the bourgois values of industrialism, being made up of Christian elements intermixed with superstitions, magic and folkore (Obelkevich, 1976). This was also the case among Cornish miners and simiar occupational groups who were numerically prominent in Methodism (Rule, 1982), and even in the popular Methodism among factory operatives described by E.P. Thompson, not to mention some description of Wesley's own writing.

In so far as religious ideology did serve an anti-revolutionary function, it was probably in an indirect and diffuse way among the bourgeoisie itself. Although Halevy mentioned the working class in his thesis, it was the working-class elite and the bougeoisie, as the potential leaders of revolution who were described as having been 'imbued by the Evangelical movement with a spirit from which the established order had nothing to fear'. He was contrasting the situation in England with the revolutionary situation in France, where the blocked aspiration of the bourgeoisie led them to provide revolutionary leadership. In England, Evangelical ideology and organisational techniques enabled the bourgeoisie to succeed in their aspirations without having to lead the working class in a revolutionary direction. The stimulus of Wesleyan Methodism brought about a parallel Evangelical movement in the Church of England, and it was principally through the influence of this movement that the ruling clas became permeated with the distinctive ideological ethos that we call 'Victorianism', its political outcome was a programme of individual moral reform, not revolution or even collective social reform.

Rather than viewing religion in terms of whether it overwhelmingly served one function or another, or served the interests of one class or another, this account has suggested that religion should be viewed as part of a cultural system which is also an ideological terrain of contestation. We have spotlighted a number of functional relationships (or 'elective affinities' as Weber preferred to fall them) between ideological elements and social classes or groups, all occurring in the same period. It is a tribute to the richness of the symbolic sphere of which religion provides a preeminent example, that it defies analyses which are 'reductionist' or based on crudely mechanical models linking 'base' and 'superstructure'. A further corrective that emerges from consideration of specific examples of ideology such as Methodism and Evangelicalism, is to the theory that ideologies 'belong' to classes and are primarily used as instruments or 'transmisssion belts' to secure the interests of a class. This is not to say that groups do not seek to use ideologies for their purposes (the British govenment legislated to build churches, and benefactors founded Sunday schools, with such purposes in mind). But ideologies are fluid, dynamic and multi-functional: they overlap class cultures, are used for a variety of purposes, and have even more unintended than intended consequences. The English working class was not incorporated into the ideology of the dominant class; but that is not to say that it did not incorporate some of the elements of that ideology into its way of life. After all, the factory or coalmine formed part of that way of life alongside the chapel and Sunday school, and there was a cultural overlap in many instances, such as the inculcation of time-discipline and the notions of individual responsibility and contract. E.P. Thompson chose to interpret the ideological aspects of Methodism in terms or their part in providing the moral repression necessary for capitalist development. Semmel and Gilbert emphasise Methodism's function in creating a new type of man capable of bridging the gap between *Gemeinschaft* and *Fesellschaft* . Others have found this difficult to reconcile with the evidence of the active part played by Primitive Methodists, especially, in working-class politics and trade unionism. They would claim that a 'more balanced view' (Turner and Hil, 1975, p.160) would be that Methodism, through its class meetings and lay officials, found itself simutaneously 'producing men who revolted against the established order and also disowning them, if their activities seemed to imperil the religious society's existence' (Kent, 1966 ,p.137). Clearly a religion can produce all of these ideological effects, and much else.

Note

1 Arminius, a professor of theology at the University of Leiden, led a group of Protestants working in the commercial cities of Holland at the beginning of the seventeenth century, and put forward a new view of the relationship of God and man. In the Remonstrance of 1610, published the year after Arminius 'death, his followers proclaimed that because of Christ's sacrifice and atonement, *all men might* be saved, not merely a pre-ordained elect as Calvin had stipulated.

References

Abercrombie,N., Hill, S., and Turner, B.S.(1980) *The Dominant Ideology Thesis.* London, Allen and Unwin

Althusser, L.(1969) for Marx. Harmondsworth, Penguin.

Armstrong, A.(1973) *The Church of England, the Methodists and Society 1700- 1850.* University of London Press.

Behagg, C. (1982) 'Secrecy, ritual and folk violence: the opacity of the workplace in the first half of the nineteenth century', in Storch(ed.) *Popular Culture and Custom in Nineteenth Century England.* London, Croom Helm.

Gilbert, A.D. (1976) *Religion and Society in Industrial England,* ch.4, 'The functions of "church" and "chapel". 'London, Longman.

Gramsci, A. (1971) *Selections from the Prison Notebooks.* London, Lawrence and Wishart.

Halevy, E. (1938) *A History of the English People in the Nineteenth* Century, Penguin, 3 vols, edn, First English edn, pub, in London, by T. fisher, Unwin.

Harrison, B.(1966) 'Reliogion and recreation in nineteenth century England',

Papers presented to the Past and Present Confernce on Popular Religion, 9 July 1966.

Hobsbawm, E.J. (1967) 'Methodism and the threat of revolution in Britain' , in *Labouring Men: Studies in the History of Labour.* London, Weidenfeld and nicolson, 1964.

Kent, J. (1966) *The Age of Disunity.* London, Epworth.

Lequeur, T.W. (1976) *Religion and Respectability: Sunday Schools and Working Class Culture* 1780-1850, ch7, 'Sunday schools and social control' . New Haven, Conn., Yale University Press.

Obelkvich, J. (1976) *Religion and Rural Society: South Lindsay, 1825-1875.*

Oxford, University Press.

Perkin, H. (1969) *Origins of Modern English Society 1780-1880.* London.

Rule, J. (1982) 'Methodism, popular beliefs and village culture in Cornwall 1800-50', in Storch, R.D. (ed.) *Popular Culture and Custom In Nineteeenth Century England.* London, Croom Helm, pp.48-70.

Semmel, B. (ed.) (1971) *The Birth of Methodism.* University of Chicago Press.

Semmel, B. (1974) *The Methodist Revolution.* London, Heinemann.

Stafford, W. (1982) 'Religion and the doctrine of nationalism in England at the time of the French Revolution and Napoleonic wars', in S. Mews (ed.), *Religion and National Identity.* Oxford, Blackwell, pp. 381-98.

Thompson, E.P. (1968) *The Making of the English Working Class*, ch.11, 'The transforming power of the cross'. Harmondsworth, Penguin (first published 1963).

Thompson, E.P. (1978) *The Povery of theory.* London, Merlin Press.

Thompson, K.A. (1970) *Bureaucracy and church Reform: the Organizational Resoponse of the Church of England to social Chage 1800-1965.* Oxford, The Clarendon Press.

Turner, B.J. and Hill, M. (1975) 'Methodism and the piestist defination of politics: historical development and contemporary evidence', in M.Hill (ed.), *A Sociological Yearbook of Religions in Britain,* 8, London, SCM Press.

Turner, Bryan S. (1983) *Religion and Social Theory.* London, Heenemann Educational Books.

Weber, M. (1965) *The Sociology of Religion.* London, Methuen (first pulished In German, 1922).

Chapter-13

THE TRANSFORMING POWER OF THE CROSS

E.P. THOMPSON

Chapter-13

1. Moral machinery

Puritanism—Dissent—Nonconformity: the decline collapses into a surender. Dissent still carries the sound of resistance to Apollyon and the Whore of Babylon, Nonconformity is self-effacing and apologetic: it asks to be left alond. Mark Rutherford, one of the few men who understand the full desolation of the inner history of nineteenth-century Nonconformity - and who is yet, in himself, evidence of values that somehow survived - noted in his *Autobiography* the form of service customary in his youth:

> It generally began with a confession that we were all sinners, but no individual sins were ever confessed, and then ensued a kind of dialogue with God, very much resembling the speeches which in later years I have heard in the House of commons from the movers and seconders of addresses to the Crown at the opening of Parliament.

The example is taken from the Calvinistic Independents: but it will also serve excellently to describe the stance of Methodism before temporal authority. This surrender was implicit in Methodism before temporal authority. This surrender ws implicit in Methodism's origin in the toryismm of its founder and in his ambivalent attitude to the Established church. From the outset the Wesleyans fell ambiguously between Dissent and the Establishment, and did their utmost to make the worst of both worlds, serving as apologists for an authority in whose eyes they were an object of ridicule or condescension, but never of trust. After the French Revolution, successive annual Conferences were forever professing their submission and their zeal in combating the enemies of established order; drawing attention to their activity 'in raising the standard of public morals, and in promoting loyality in the middle ranks as well as subordination and industry in the lower orders of society'.[1] But Methodists were seldom admitted by the Establishment to ausience – and then only by the back door: never decorated with any of the honours of status: and if they had been mentioned in despatches it would probably have hindered the did of moral espionage which they were most fitted to undertake.

The wars saw a remarkable increase in the Methodist following.[2] They wittnessed also (Halevy tells us) 'an uninterrupted deeline of the revolutioary spirit 'among all the Nonconformist sects. Methdism is most remarkable during the War years for two things: first, its gains were greatest among the new industrial working class: secibd, the years after Wesley's death see the consolidation of a new bureaucracy of ministers who regarded it as their duty to manipulate the submissiveness of their followers and to discipline all deviant growths within the Church which could give offence to authority.

In this they were bery effective. For centuries the Established Church had preached to the poor the duties of obedience. But it was so distanced from them—and its distance was rarely grater than in this time of absenteeism and plural livings—that its homilies had ceased to have much effect. The deference of the countryside was rooted in bitter experience of the power of the squire rather than in any inward conviction. And there is little evidence that the evangelical movement within the Church met with much greater success: many of Hannah More's half penny tracts were left to littler the servants ' quarters of the great houses. But the Methodists—or many of them—were the poor many of their local preachers were humble men who found their figures of speech (as one said) 'behind my spinning -jenny'. And the great expansion after 1790 was in minnig and manufacturing districts. Alongside older salems and Bethels, NEw—brick Brunswick and Hanover chapels proclaimed the Methodist loyality. 'I hear great things of your amphitheatre in Liverpool,' one minister wrote to the Reverend Zabex Bunting in 1811:

> A man will need strong lungs to blow his words from one end of it to the other. In Bradford and in Keighlsy they are building chapels nearly as large as Carver Street Chapel in Sheffield. To what will Methodism come in a few years?[3]

Jabez Bunting, whose active ministry covers the full half-century, was the dominent figure of orthodox Wesleyabusn from the time of Luddism to the last years of the Chartist movement.

His father, a Manchester tailor, had beeen a 'thorough Radical' who 'warmly espoused the cause of the first French revolutionists', but who was not the less a Methodist for that.[4] But in the late 1790s, and after the secesssion of the Kilhamite New Connexion, a Group of younger minsters emerged, of whom Bunting was one, who were above all concerned to remove from Methodism the Jacobin taint. In 1812 Bunting earned distinction by disowning methodist Luddites; the next year, in Leeds, he counted 'several Tory magistrates of the old school, Church and King people, who, probabl, never crossed the threshold of a conventicle before, among his constant hearers'.[5] He and his fellow—ministers—one of the more obnoxious of whom was called the Reverend Edmund Grindrod—were above all organizers and administrators, busied with endless Connexional intrigues and a surfeit of disciplinary zeal. Wesley's dislike of the self- governing anarchy of Old Dissent wa continued by his successors, with authority vested in the Annual Conference (weighted down with ministers designated by Wesley himself) and its committee of privileges (1803). The Primitive Methodists were driven out because it was feared that their camp meetings might result in 'tumults' and serve as political precedents (as they did); the 'Tent Methodists' and Bible Christian, or Bryanites, were similarly disciplined; female preaching was prohibited; the powers of Conference and of circuit superintendents were strengthened/ Espionage into each other's moral failing was encouraged; discipline tightened up within the classes; and, after 1815, as many local preachers were expelled or struck off the 'plan' for political as for religious 'back - sliding'. Here we find an entry in the Halifax Local Preacher's Minute Book: 'Bro.M. charged with attending a political meeting when he should have been aat his class' (16 December 1816): there we find a correspondent writing in alarm from Newcastle to Bunting:

> ...a subject of painful and distressing concern that two of our local preachers (from North Shields) have attended the tremendous Radical Reform Meeting ... I hope no considerable portion of our brethren is found among the Radicals; but a small number of our leaders are among the most determinded friends to their spirit and design ... and some of the really pious, misguided sisterhood have helped

> to make their colours. On expostulation, I am glad to say, several members have quitted their classes (for they have adopted almost the whole methodist economy, the terms 'Class Leaders', 'Destrict Meetings', etc., being perfectly current among them). If men are to be drilled at Missionary and bibel meetings to face a multitde with recollection, and acquire facilities of address, and then begin to employ the mightly moral weapon thus gained to the endangering the very existance of the Government of the country, we may certainly begin to tremble ...

This was in 1819, the year of Peterloo. The response of the Methodist Committee of Privileges to the events of this year was to issue a circular which 'bears clear traces' of Bunting's compositon; expressing—

> strong and decided disapprobation of certain tumultuous assemblies which have lately been witnessed in several parts of the country; in which large masses of people have been irregularly collected (often under banners bearing the most shocking and impious inseriptions)...calculated, both from the infidel principles, the wiled and delusive political theories, and the violent and inflammatory declamations .... to bring all government into contempt, and to introduce universal disvontent, insubordination, and anarchy.[6]

Wesley at least had been a great-hearted warhorse; he had never spared himself ; he was an enthusiast who had stood up at the market-cross to be pelted. Bunting, with his 'solid, mathematical way of speaking', is a less admirable character. It was his own advice to 'adapt your principles to your exigencies'. ' In our family intercourse', a friend of his youthfuyl ministry informed his son:

> his conversation was uniformly serious and instructive. Like his ministry in the pupit, every word had its proper place, and every sentence might have been digested priviously ..... Sometimes your dear mother's uncontrollable wit suddenly distyrbed our gravity; but he was never seen otherwise than in his own proper character as a minister of the gospel of Christ.

Bunting's uncompromising Sabbatarianism stopped just short at the point of his own conveniece: ' he did not hesitate, in the necessary prosecution of his ministerial work, to employ beasts; though always with a self-imposed reserve...'With children it was another matter. We are often tempted to forgive Methodism some of its sins when we recollect that at least it gave to children and adults rudimentary education in its Sunday schools;and Bamford's happy picture is sometimes recalled, of the Middleton school in the late 1790s, attended by 'big collier lads and their sisters', and the children of weavers and labourers from Whittle, bowlee, Jumbo and the White mos. But it is exactly this picture, of the laxness of the early Methodists, which Bunting was unable to forgive.When, in his ministry at Sheffield in 1808, his eye fell upon children in Sunday school being taught to write, his indignation knew no bounds. Here was 'an awful abouse of the Sabbath'. There could be no question as to its theological impropriety—for children to learn to read the scriptures was a 'spitirual good' , whereas writing was a 'secular art 'from which 'temporal advantage' might accrue. Battle commenced in *Sheffield* (with the former 'Jacobin', James Montgomery, defending the children's cause in the Sheffield Iris), from which Bunting emerged victorious; it was renewed at Liverpool in the next year (1809) with the same result; and Bunting was in the forefront of a movement which succeeded, very largely, in extirpating this insidious 'violation' of the Lord's Day until the 1840s. This was, indeed, one of the ways in which Bunting won his national spurs.[7]

The spurs were needed, perhaps, to stick into the children's sides during the six days of the week. In Bunting and his fellows we seem to touch upon a deformity of the sensibility complementary to the deformities of the factory children whose labour they condoned. In all the copious correspondence of his early ministries in the industrial heartlands (Manchester, Liverpool, Sheffield, Halifax and Leeds, 1804-15), among endles petty connexional disputes, moralistic humbug, and pruient inquiries into the private conduct of young women, neither he nor his colleagues appeaar to have suffered a single qualm as to rhe consequences of industialism.[8] But the younger leaders of methodism were not only guilty of complicity in the fact of child labour by default. They weakended the poor from within, by adding to them the active ingredient of submission; and they fostered within the Methodist Church those elements most suited to make up the psychic component of the work discipline of which the manufacturers stood most in need .

As early as 1787, the firest Robert Peel write : "I have left most of my works in Lancashire under the management of Methodists, and they serve me excellently well.'[9] Weber and Tawney have so thoroughly anatomized the interpenetraion of the capitalist mode of production and the Puritan ethic that it would seem that there can be little to add. Methodism may be seen as a simple extension of this ethic in a changing social milieu; and an 'economist' argument lies to hand, in the fact that Methodism, in Bunting's day, proved to be exceptionally well adapted, by virtue of its elevation of the values of discipline and of order as well as its moral opacity, both to self made mill - owners and manufacturers and to foremen, overlookers, and sub-managerial groups, And this argument —that Methodism served as ideological self-justification for the master—manufacturers and for their satellites—contains an important part of the truth. So much John Wesley—in an often - quoted passage—both foresaw and deplored:

> ...religion must necessarily produce both industry and frugality, and these cannot but produce riches. But as riches invrease, so will pride, anger, and love of the world .... How then is it possible that Methodism, that is a religion of the heart, though it flourishes now as a green bay tree, should continue in this state? For the Methodists in every place grow diligent and frugal; consequently they increase in goods. Hence they proportionately increase in pride, in anger, in the desire of the flash, the desire of the eyes, and the pride of life. so, although the form of religion remains, the spirit is swiftly vanishing away.

Many a Methodist mill-owner - and, indeed, bunting himself —might serveas confirmation of this in the early nineteenth century.[10] And yet the argument falters at a critical point. For it is exactly at this time that Methodism obtained its greatest success in serving simultaneously as the religion of the industrial bour-geoisie (although here it shared the field with other Nonconformist sects) and of wide sections of the proletariat. Nor can there be any doubt as to the deep-rooted allegiance of many working- class communities (equally among miners, weavers, factory workers, seamen, potters and rural labourers) to the Methodist Church. How was it possible for Methodism to perform, with such remakable vigour, this double service?

This is a problem to which neither Weber nor Tawney addressed themselves. Both were mainly preoccupied with Puritanism in the sixteenth and seventeenth centuries, and with the genesis of commercial capitalism; both addressed themselves, in the main, to the psychic and social development of the middle class, the former stressing the Puritan concept of a 'calling' , the latter the values of freedom, self discipline, individualism and acquisitiveness. But it is intrinsic to both arguments that puritanism contributed to the psychic energy and social coherence of middle- class group which felt themselves to be 'called' or 'elected' and which were engaged (with some success) in acquisitive pursuits. How then should such a religion appeal to the forming proletariat in a period of exceptional hardship, whose multitudes did not dispose them to any sense of group calling, whose experience at work and in their communities favoured collectivst rather than individualist values, and whose frugality, discipline or acquisitive virtues brought profit to their masters rather than success to themselves?

Both Weber and Tawney, it is true, adduce powerful reasons as to the utility, from the point of view of the employers, of the extension of Puritan or pseudo-Puritan values to the working class. Tawney anatomized the 'New Medicine for Poverty', with its denunciation of sloth and improvidence in the labourer, and its convenient belief that—if success was a sign of election—poverty was itself evidence of spiritual turpitude.[11] Weber placed more emphasis on the question which, for the working class, is crucial: work- discipline. Wherever modrn capitalism has begun its work of increasing the productivity of human labour by increasing its intensity, 'wrote Weber, 'it has encountered the immensely stubborn resistance of... prevapitalistic labour.'

> The capitalistic economy of the present day is an immense cosmos into which the individual is born, and which presents

> itself to him.... as an unalterable order of things in which he must live. It forces the individual, in so far as he involved in the system of market relationships, to conform to capitalistic rules of action.

But, as industrial capitalism emerged, these rules of action appeared as unnaturral and hateful restraints: the peasant, the rural labourer in the unenclosed village, even the urban artisan or apprentice, did not measure the return of labour exclusively in money-earnings, and they rebelled against the notion of week after week of disciplined labour. In the way of life which Weber describes (unsatisfactorily) as 'traditionalism', 'a man does not "by nature" wish to earn more and more money, but simply to live as he is accustomed to live and to earn as much as is necessary for that purpose'. Even piece-rates and other incentives lose deffectiveness at a certain point if there is no inner compulsion; when enough is earned the peasant leaves industry and returns to his village, the artisan goes on a dunken spree. But at the same time, the opposite discipline of low wages is ineffective in work where skill, attentiveness or responsibility is required. What is required—here Fromm amplifies Weber's argument —is an 'inner compulsion ' which would prove ' effective in harnessing all energies to work than any outer compulsion can ever be' :

> Against external compulsion there is always a certain amount of rebelliousness which hampers the effectiveness of work or makes people unfit for any differentiated task requiring intelligence, initiative and responsbility..... Undoubtedly capitalism could not have been developed had not the greatest part of man's energy been channelled in the direction of work.

The labourer must be turned 'into his own slave driver'.[12]

The ingredients of this compusion were not new. [13]Weber has noted the difficulties experienced by employers in the 'Putting -Out' industries—notably weaving—in the seventeenth century, as a result of the irregular working habits (drunkenness, embezzlement of yarn and so on) of the workers. It was in the West of England woollen industry—at Kidderminster—that the Presbyterian divine, Richard Baxter, effected by his ministry a notable change in labour relations; and many elements of the Methodist work-discipline may be found fully-formed in his *Christian Directory* of 1673.[14] Similar difficulties were encountered by mineowners and northern woollen and cotton manufacturers throughout the eighteenth century. Colliers generally received a monthly pay; it was complained that 'they are naturally turbulent, passionate, and rude in manners and character'.

> Their gains are large and uncertain, and their employment is a species of task work, the profit of which can very rerely be previously ascertained. This circumstance gives them the wasteful habits of a gamester.....
>
> Another trait in the character of a collier, is his predilection to change of situation... Annual changes are almost as common with the pitman as the return of the seasons...Whatever favours he may have received, he is disposed to consider them all cancelled by the refusal of a single request.[15]

The weaver-smallholder was notorious for dropping his work in the event of any farming emergency; mosst eighteenth -century workers glasdly exchanged their employments for a month of harvesting; meny of the adult operatives in the early cotton mills were 'of loose and wandering habits, and seldom remained long in the establishment'.[16] A few of the managerial problems in the early enterprises are suggested by the list of fines at Wedgwood's Etruria works:

> ....Any workman striking or likewise abusing an overlooker to lose his place. Any workman conveying ale or liquor into the manufactory in working hours, forfeit 2/-
>
> Any person playing at fives against any of the walls where there are windows,
>
> forfeit 2/-...[17]

Whether his workers were employed in a factory or in their own homes, the master-manufacturer of the Industrial Revolution was obsessed with these problems of discipline. The out-workers required (from the employers' point of view) education in 'methodical' habits, punctilious attention to instructions, fulfilment of contracts to time, and in the sinfulnesss of exbezzling materials. By the 1820s (we are told by a contemporary) 'the great mass of Weavers' were 'deeply imbued with the doctrines of Methodism'. Some of the self-made men, who were now their employers, were Methodists or Dissenters whose frugality—as Wesley had foreseen —had produced riches. They would tend to favour fellow -religionists, finding in them a 'guarantee for good conduct' and 'a consciousnes of the value of character'.[18] The 'artisan' traditions of the weavers, with their emphasis on the balues of independence, had already prepared them for some variant of Puritan faith.[19] What of the factory operatives?

It is in Dr Andrew Ure's *Philosophy of Maufactures* (1835) - a book which, with its Satanic advocacy, much influenced Engels and Marx—that we find a complete anticipation of the 'economist' case for the function of religion as a work -discipline. The term Factory, for ure:

> involves the idea of a vast automaton, composed of various mechanical and intellectual organs, acting in uninterrupted concert for the production of a common object, all of them being subordinated to self-regulated moving force.

'The main difficulty' of the factory system was not so much techonological but in the distriution of the different members of the appartus into one cooperative body' , and, above all, 'in training human beings to renounce their desultory habits of work, and to identify themselves with the unvarying regularity of the complex automation' :

> To devise and administer a succesful code of factory discipline, suited to the necessities of factory diligence, was the Herculean enterprise, the noble achievement of Arkwright. Even at the present day, when the system is perfectly organized, and its labour lighterened to the utmost, it is found nearly imossible to convert persons past the age of puberty, whether drawn from rural or from handicraft occupation, into useful factory hands. After struggling for a while to conquer their listless or restive habits, habits, they either renounce the employment spontaneously, or are dismissed by the overlookers on account of inattention.

'It required, in fact, a man of a Napoleonic nerve and ambition, to subdue the refractory tempers of work-people accustomed to irregular paroxysms of diligence....Such was Arkwright.' Moreover, the more skilled a workman, the more intractable to discipline he became, 'the more self-willed and ... the less fit a component of a mechanical system, in which, by occasional irregularities, he may do great damage to the whole'. Thus the manufacturers aimed at withdrawing any process which required 'peculiar dexterity and steadiness of hand ... from the cunning workman' and placing it in charge of a 'mechanism, so self-refulating, that a child may superintend it '. 'The grand object therefore of the modern manufacturer is through the union of capital and science, to reduce the task of his work-people to the exercise of vigilance and dexterity, - faculties .... speedily brought to perfection in the young.'[20]

For the children, the discipline of the overlooker and of the machinery might suffice; but for those 'past the age of puberty' inner compulsions were required. Hence it followed that Ure devoted a section of his book to the 'Moral Economy of the Factory System', and a special chapter to reliion. The unredeemed operative was a terrible creature in Ure's sight; a prey to 'artful demagogues';chronically given to secret cables and combinations; capable of any atrocity against his masters. The high wages of cotton-spinners enabled them 'to pamper themselves into nervous ailmentss by a diet too rich and exciting for their indoor occupaitons':

> Manufactures naturally condense a vast population with in a narrow circuit; they afford every facility for secret cabel ...; they communicate intelligence and energy to the vulgar mind; they supply in their liberal wages the pecuniary sinews of contention ...

In such circums6tances, Sunday scools presented a 'sublime spectacle' The committee of a stockport Sunday school, erected in 1805, congratulated itselfupon the 'decoum' preseved in the town, in 1832, at a time of 'political excitement' elsewhere : 'it is hardly possible to approach the town .... without encountering one or more of these quier fortresses, which a wise benevolence has erected against the encroachments of vice and ignorance'.

And Ure drew from this a moral, not only as to general poltical subordination, but as to behaviour in the factory itself:

> The neglect of moral discipline may be readily detected in any establishment by practised eye, in the disorder of the gereral system, the irregularities of the individual machines,the waste of time and material....

Mere wage -payment could never secure 'Zealous services'. The employer who neglected moral considerations and was himself 'a stranger to the self-denying graces of the Gospel'—

> Knows himself to be entitled to nothing but eye-sevice, and will therefore exercise the most irksome vigilance, but in vain, to prevent his being overreached by his operatives - the whole of whom, by natural instinct as it were, conspire against such a master. Whatever pains he may take, he can never command superior workmanship ...
>
> It is, therfore, excessively the interest of every mill-owner to *organize his moral machinery on equally sound principles with his mechanical, for otherwise he will* never command the steady hands, watchful eyes, and prompt cooperation, essential to excellence of product .... There is, in fact, no case to which the Gospel truth, 'Godliness is great gain,' is more applicable than to the administration of an extensive factory.[21]

The argument is thus complete. The factory system demands a transformation of human nature, the 'working paroxysms' of the artisan or outworker must be methodized untill the man is adapted to the discipline of the machine.[22] But how are these disciplinary virtues to be inculcated in those whose Goklines (unless they become overlookers) is unlikely to bring any temporal gain? It can only be by inculcating 'the first and great lesson ... that man must expect his chief happiness, not in the present, but in a future state'. Work must be undertaken as a *'Pure act of virtue* ... inspired by the love of a transcendent Being, operating .... on our will and affections' :

> Where then shall mankind find this transforming power? -in the cross of Christ. It is the sacrifice which removes the guilt of sin: it is the motive which removes love of sin: it

> mortifies sin by showing its turpitude to be indelible except by such an awful expiation; it atones for disobedience; it purchases strength for obedience; it purchases strength for obedience; it makes obedience practicable; it makes it acceptable; it makes it in a manner unavoidable, for it constrains to it; it is, finally, not only the motive to obedience, but the pattern of it.[23]

Ure, then, is the Richard Baxter of Cottonopolis. But we may descend, at this point, from his transcendental heights to consider, more briefly, mundane matters of theology. It is evident that there was, in 1800, casuistry enough in the theology of all the available English churches to reinforce the manufacturer's own sense of moral self-esteem. Wheather he held an heriarchic faith, or felt himself to be elected, or saw in his succes the evidence of grace or godliness, he felt few promptings to exchange his residence beside the mill at Bradford for a monastic cell on Bardsey Island. But Methodist theology, by virtue of its promiscuous opportunism, was better suited than any other to serve as the religion of a proletariat whose memberes had not the least reason, in social experience, to feel themselves to be 'elected '. In his theology , Wesley appears to have dispensed with the best and selevted unhesitatingly the worse elements of Puritanism: if in class terms Methodism was hermaphroditic, in doctrinal terms it was a mule. We have already noted Methodism's rupture with the intellectual and democratic traditions of Old Dissent.But Luther's doctrines of submission to authority might have served as the text for any Wesleyan Conference in the years after 1789:

> Even if those in authority are evil or without fait, nevertheless the authority and its power is good and from God ....
>
> God would prefer to suffer the government to exist, no matter how evil, rather than allow the rabble to riot, no matter how justified they are in doing so...

(Jabez Bunting, however, unlike Luther, could niever have admitted the notion that the rabble could ever be 'instified'.) The general Lutheran bias of Wesleyanism has often been noted.[24] Wesley's espousal of the doctrine of the university of grace was incompatible with the Calvinist notion of 'election'. If grace was universal, sin was universal too. Any man who came to a conviction of sin might be visited by grace and know himself to be ransomed by Christ's blood. Thus for it is a doctrine of spititual egalitarianism : there is at least equality of opportunity in sin and grace for rich and poor. And as a religion of 'the heart' rather than of the intellect, the simplest and least educated might hope to attain towards grace. In this sense, Methodism dropped all doctrinal and social barriers and opened its doors wide to the working class. And this reminds us that Lutheranism was also a religion of the poor; and that, as munzer proclaimed and as Luther learned to his cost, spiritual egalitarianism had a tendency to break its banks and flow into temporal channels, bringing thereby a perpetual tension into Luthran creeds which Methodism also reproduced.

But Christ's ransom was only provisional. Wesley's doctrine here was not settled. He toyed with the notion of grace being perpetual , once it had visited the penitent; and thus a dejected form of Calvinism (the 'elected' being now the 'saved') re-entered by the back door. But as the eighteenth century wore on the doctrine of justification by faith hardened—perhaps because it ws so evident that mutitudes of those 'saved' in the revivalist campaigns slid back to their old ways after years or only months. Thus it became doctrine that forgiveness of sin lasted only so long as the penitent weent and sinne no more. The brotherhood and sisterhood who were 'saved' were in a state of conditional, provisory election. It was always possible to 'backslide'; and in view of human frailty this was, in the eyes of God and of Javez Bunting, more than likely. Moreover, Bunting was at pains to point out God's view that—

> Sin .... is not changed in its nature, so as to be made less'exceedingly sinful' .... by the pardon of the sinner. The penalty is remittred; and the obligation to suffer that penalty is dissoved; but it is still naturally due, though graciously remitted. Hence appears the propriety and the duty of continuing to confess and lament even pardoned sin. Though released from its penal cosequences by an act of divine elemency, we should still remember, that the dust of self -

abasement is our proper place before God ....[25]

But there are further complexities to the doctrine. It would be presumptuous to suppose that a man might save himself by an act of his own will. The saving was the prerogative of God, and all that a man could do was to prepare himself, by utter abasement, for redemption. Once convinced of grace, however, and once thoroughly introduced to the Methodist brotherhood, 'backsliding' was no light matter to a working man or woman. It might mean expulsion from the only community- group which they knew in the indudtrial wilderness; and it meant the everpresesnt fear as to an eternity of lurid punishment to come:

> There is a dreadful hell
> And everlasting pains,
> Where sinners Must with devils dwell
> In darkness, fire and chains

How, then to keep grace? Not by good works, since Wesley had elevated faith above works: 'You have notheing to do but save souls. 'Works were the snares of pride and the best works were mingled with the dross of sin; although—by another opportunist feint—works might be a *sign of grace*. (A vestigial Calvinism here for the mill-owners and shopkeepeers.) Since this world is the ante-room to eternity, such temporal things as wealth and poverty matter very little: the rich might show the evidence of grace by serving the Church (notably, by building chapels for their own workpeople). The poor were fortunate in being less tempted by 'the desire of the flesh, the desire of the eyes, and the pride of life'. They were more likely to remain graced, not because of their 'calling', but because they faced fewer temptations to backslide.

Three obvious means of maintaining grace presented themselves. First, through service to the Church itself, as a class leader, local preacher, or in more humble capacities. Second, through the cultivation of one's own soul, in religious exercises, tract-reading, but—above all—in attemps to reproduce the emotional convulsions of conversion, conviction of sin, penitenc, and visitation by grace. Third, through a methodical discipline in every aspect of life. Above all, in labour itself (which, being humble and unpleasent, should not be confused with good works), undertaken for no ulterior motives but (as Dr Ure has it) as 'a pure act of viryue' there is an evident sign of grace. Moreover, God's curse over Adam, when expelled from the Garden of Eden, provided irrefutable doctrinal support as to the blessednes of hard labour, poverty, and sorrow 'all the days of thy life'.

We can now see the extraordinary correspondence between the virtues which Methodism inculcated in the working class and the desiderata of middle-class Utilitarianism.[26] Dr Ure indivates the point of junction, in his advice to the mill-owner 'to organize his moral machinery on equally sound principles with his mechanical'. From this aspecct, Methodism was the desolate inner landscape of Utilitarianism in an era of transition to the work-descipline of industrial capitalism. As the 'working paroxysms' of the hand -worker are methodized and his unworkful impulses are brought under control, so his emotional and spiritual paroxysms increase. The abject confessional tracts are the other side of the dehumanized prose style of Edwin Chadwick and Dr Kay. The 'march of intellect' and the repression of the heart go together.

But it was Wesley's claim that Methodim was, above all things, a 'religion of the heart'. It was in its 'enthusiasm' and emotional transports that it differed most evidently from the older Puritan sects.[27] We might note some of the approval stages in religious experience, taken from a characteristic tract which describes the conversion of a sailor, Joshua Marsden, in the 1790s. These tracts normally follow a conventional pattern. First, ther are descriptions of a sinful youth: swearing, gaming, drunkenness, idleness, sexual looseness or merely 'desire of the flesh'.[28] There follows either some dramatic experience which makes the sinner mindful of death (miraculous cure in mortal illness, shipwreck or death of wife or children); or some chance-hap encounter with God's word, where the sinner comes to jeer but remains to learn the way to salvation. Our sailor had all these experiences. A shipwreck left him 'Trembling with horror upon the verge both of the watery and fiery gulph... the ghosts of his past sins stalked before him in ghastly forms,. A severe illness 'sent him often weeping and broken-hearted to a throne of grace', 'consumed and burned up sensual desires', and 'showed the awfulness of dying without an interest in Christ'. Invited by a friend to a

Methodist class meeting, 'his heart was melted into a child -like weeping frame.... Tears trickled down his cheeks like rivulets. 'There follows the long ordeal of intercession for forgivenesss and of wrestling with temptations to relapse into the former life of sin. Only grace can unloose 'the seven seals with which ignorance, pride, unbelief, enmity, self-will, lust and covetousnes bind the sinner's beart'. Again and again the penitent in his 'novitiate' succembs to obscurely-indicated 'temptations'.[29]

> In spite of all, he was sometimes borne away by the violence and impetuosity of temptation, which brought upon him all the anguish of a broken spirit. After being overtaken with sin he would redouble his prayers .... Sometimes the fear of dying in an unpardoned state greatly agitated his mind, and prevented his falling asleep for fear of awakening in the eternal world.

When the 'desire of the flesh' is to some degree humbled, the 'Enemy' places more subtle spiritual temptations in the penitent's path. Chief among these are any disposition which leads to 'hardness of the heart' – levity, pride, but above all the temptation to 'buy salvation ' by good works rather thatn waiting with patience to 'receive it as the free gift of God, through the infinite merits of the bleeding Reconciler'. The doctrine of good works is 'this Hebrew, this Popish doctrine of human merit'. Thus 'hadness of the heart' consists in any character-trait which resists utter submission:

> God ... before he can justify us freely ....ust wither our gourd, blast the flower of proud hope, take away the prop of self-dependence, strip us of the gaudy covering of christless righteousness, stop the boasting of pharasaical self-sufficiencey, and bring the guilty, abased, ashamed, blushing, selg-despairing sinner, to the foot of the Cross.

At this point of abasement, 'all his prospects appeared like a waste howling wilderness'. But 'the time of deliverance was now at hand'. At a love-feast in the Methodist chapel, the penitent knelt in the pew 'and, in an agony of soul, began to wrestle with God'. Although 'the enemy raged and rolled upon him like a flood'.

> Some of the leaders, with some pious females, came into

> the gallery, and united in interceding for him at a throne of grace : the more they prayed, the more his distress and burthern increased, till finally he was nearly spent, and sweat ran off him .... and he lay on the floor of the pew with little power to move. This, however, was the moment of deliverance ... He felt what no tongue can ever describe; a something seemed to rest upon him like the presence of God that went through his whole frame; he sprang on his feet, and felt he could lay upon Christ by faith.

From this time forward the 'burthen of sin fell off'. 'The new creation was manifested by new moral beauties—love, joy, hope, peace, filial fear, delight in Jesus, tender confidence, desire after close communion, and fuller conformity.... Anew kingdom of righteousness was planted in the heart.' God's glory became 'the end of each action'. But salvation was conditional; the convictin of grace coexisted with the knowledge that man 'is a poor, blind, fallen, wretched, miserable and (without divine grace) helpless sinner'.[30]

Our sinner has now been'translated from the power of Satan to the kingdom and image of God's dear Son'. And we may see here in its lurid figurative expression the psychic ordeal in which the character-structure of the rebellious pre-industrial labourer or artisan was violently recast into that of the submissive indutrial worker. Her, indeed, is Ure's 'transformming power'. It is a phenomenon, almost diabolic in its penetrat in into the very sources of human personality, directed towards the repression of emotional and spiritual energies. But 'repression' is misleading word; these energies were not so much inhibited as displaced from expression in personal and in social life, and confiscated for the service of the Church. The box-like, blackening chapels stood in the industrial districts like great traps for the human psyche. Within the Church itself ther was a constant emotional drama of backsliders, confessions, forays against Satan, lost sheep; one suspects that the pious sisterhood, in particular, found in this one of the great 'consolations' of religion. For the more intellectual ther was the spiritual drama of :

> trials temptations, heart sinkings, doubts, struggles, heaviness, manifestation, victories, coldness, wanderings,

> besetments, deliverances, helps, hopes, answers to prayer, interpositions, reliefs, complaints ... workings of the heart, actings of faith, leadings through the mazes of dark dispensations ... fiery trials, and succour in the sinking moment.[31]

But what must be stressed is the *intermittent character* of Wesleyan emotionalism. Nothing was more oftsen remarked by contemporaries of the workaday Methodist character, or of Mehtodist home-life, than its methodical, disciplined and repressed disposition. It is the paradox of a 'religion of the heart' that it should be notorious for the inhibition of all spontaneity. Methodism sanctioned 'workings of the heart' only upon the occasions of the Church; Methodists wrote hymns but no secular poetry of note; the idea of a passionate Methodist lover in these years is ludicrous. ('Avoid all manner of passions', advisted Wesley.) The word is unpleasant; but it is difficult not to see in Methodism in these years a rutualized form of psychic masturbation. Energies and emotions which were dangerous to social order, or which were merely unproductive (in Dr Ure's sense) were released in the harmless form of sporadic love-feast, watch-nights, band-meetings or revivalist campaigns. At these lovefeasts, after hymns and the ceremonial breaking of cake or water- biscuit, the preacher then spode, in a raw emotional manner, of his spiritual experiences, temptations and contests with sin:

> While the preacher is thus engaged, sighs, groans, devout aspirtation, and ... ejaculations of prayer or praise, are issuing from the audience in every direction.

In the tension which succeeded, individual members of the congregation then rose to their feet and made their intimate confessions of sin or temptation, often of a sexual implication. An observer noted the 'bashfulness, and evident signs of inward agitation, which some of the younger part of the females have betrayed, justs before they have risen to speak'.[32]

The Methodists made of religion (wrote Southey) 'a thing of sensation and passion, craving perpetually for sympathy and stimulants'.[33] These Sabbath orgasms of feeling made more possible the single-minded week day direction of these energies to the consummation of productive labour. Moreover, since salvation was never assured, and temptations lurked on every side, there was a constant inner goading to 'sober and industrious' behaviour— the visible sign of grace— every hour of the day and everey day of the year. Not only 'the sack' but also the flames of hell might be the consequence of indiscipline at work. God was the most vigilant overlooke of all. Even above the chimney breast 'Thou God Seest Me ' was hung. The Mehtodist was taught not only to 'bear his Cross' of poverty and humiliation' the crucifixion was (as Ure saw) the very pattern of his obedience: 'True followers of our bleeding Lamb, Now on Thy daily cross we die...[34] Work was the Cross from which the 'transformed' industrial worker hung.

But so drastic a redirection of impulses could not be effected without a central disorganization of the human personality. We can see why Hazlitt described the Mehodists as 'a collection of religious invalids'.[35] If Wesley took from Luther his authoritarianism, from Calvinism and from the English Puritan divines of the seventeenth century Methodism took over the joylessness: a methodical discipline of life 'combined with the strict avoidance of all spontaneous enjoyments'. [36]From both it took over the almost-Manichaean sense of guilt at man's depravity. And, as gratuitous additions, The Weleys absorbed and passed on through their hymn and writings the strange phenomenon of early eighteenth-century necrophily and the perverse imagery which is the least pleasent side of the Moravian tradition. Weber has noted the commexion between sexual repression and work-discipline in the teachings of such divines as Baxter:

> The sexual asceerticism of Puritanism differs only in degree, not in fundamental principle, from that of monasticism; and on account of the Puritan conception of marriage, its practical influence is more far-reaching than that of the latter. For sexual intercourse is permitted, even within marriage, only as the means willed by God for the increase of His glory according to the commandment, 'Be fruitful and mutiply. 'Along with a moderate vegetable diet and cold bath, the same prescription is given for all sexual

> temptations as is used against religious doubts and a sense of moral unworthiness: 'Work hard in your calling.'[37]

Methodism is permeated with teaching as to th sinfulness of sexuality, and as to the exteme sinfulness of the sexual orans. These —and especially the male sexual organs (since it became invresingly the convention that women could not feel the 'lust of the flesh')—were the visible fleshly citadels of Satan, the source of perpetual temptation and of countless highly unmethodical and (unless for deliberate and Godly procreation) unproductive impulses.[38] But the obsessional Methodist concern with sexuality reveals itself in the perverted eroticism of Methodist imagery. We have already noted, in John Nelson's conversion, the identification of Satan with the phallus.God is usually a simple father image, vengeful, authoritarian and prohibitive, to whom Christ must intercede, the sacrificial Lamb 'still bleeding and imploring Grace. For every Soul of Man'. But the association of feminine—or, more frequenly, ambivalent—sexual imagery with Christ is more perplexing and unpleasent.

Here we are faced with layer upon layer of conflicting symbolism. Christ, the personification of 'Love' to whom the great bulk of Wesleyan hymns are addressed, is by turns maternal, Oedipal, sexual and sadomasochistic. The extraordinary assimilation of wounds and sexual imagery in the Moravian tradition has often been noted. Man as a sinful 'worm' must find 'Lodging, Bed and Board in the Lamb's Wounds'. But the sexual imagery is easily transferred to imagery of the womb. The 'dearest little opening of the sacred, precious and thousand times beautiful little side' is also the refuge from sin in which 'the Regenerate rests and breathes':

> There in one Side-hole's joy divine,
> I want to spend my life in three...
> There in one Side-hole's joy divine,
> I'll spend all future Days of mine.
> Yes, yes, I will for ever sit
> There,where thy Side was split.[39]

Sexual and 'womb-regressive' imagery appears here to be assimilated. But, after the Wesleys broke with the Moravian brethren, the language of their hymns and the persistent accusation of Antinomian heresy among Moravian communities had become a public scandal. In the hymns of John and Charles Wesley overt sexual imagery was consviously reressed, and gave way to imagery of the womb and the bowels:

Come, O my guilty brethren, come,
Groaning beeath your load of sin!
His bleeding heart shall make you room,
His open side shall take you in ....

This imagery, however, is subordinated to the overpowering sacrificial imagery of blood, a if the underground traditions of Mithratic blood sacrifice which troubled the early Christian Church suddenly gushed up in the language of eighteenth-century Methodist hymnody. Here is Christ's bleeding love', the blood of the sacrificial Lamb in which sinners must bathe, the association of sacrifice with the peniten's guilt. Here is the 'fountain that 'gushes from His side, / Open'd that all may enter in':

Still the fountain of Thy blood
Stands for sinners open'd wide;
Now, even now, my Lord and God,
Iwash me Thy side.

And sacrificial, masochistic, and erotic language all find a common nexus in the same blood-symbolism:

We thirst to drink Thy precious blood,
We languish in Thy wounds to rest,
And hunger for immortal food
And long on all Thy love to feast.

The union with Christ's love, especially in the eucharistic 'marriage feast' (which the Church collectively 'offers herslf to God' by offering to God the Body of Christ'),[40] unites the feelinga of self-mortification, the yearning for the oblivion of the womb, and tormented sexual desire, 'harbour'd in the Saviour's breast':

Tis there I would always abide,
And never a moment depart,
Conceal'd in the cleft of Thy side,
Eternally held in Thy heart.[41]

It is difficult to conceive of more essential disorganization of human life, a pollution of the sources of spontaneity bound to reflect itself in every aspect of personality. Since joy was associated with sin and guilt, and pain (Christ's wounds) with goodness and love, so every impulse became twisted into the reverse, and it became natural to suppose that man or child only found grace in God's eyes when performing painful, laborious or self-denying tasks. To labour and to sorrow was to find pleasure, and mascohism was 'Love'.

This strange imagery was perpetuated during the years of the Industrial Revolution, not only in Methodist hymnody but also in the rhetoric of sermons and confession. Nor did it pass unnoticed. 'The Deity is personifiedand embodied in the grossest of images, 'Leigh Hunt commented in an essay 'On the Indecencies and Profane Rapture of Mehtodism'. 'If God must be addresed in the language of earthly affection, why not address him as a parent rather than a lover?'[42] But by the end of the eighteenth century, the Methodist tradition was undergoing a deslate change. The negation or sublimation of love was tending towards the cult of its opposite: death. Charles Wesley himself had written more than one hymn which presages this change:

> Ah, lovely Appearance of Death!
> No Sight upon Earth is so fair.
> Not all the gay pageants that breathe
> Can with a dead Body compare.

The Methodist tradition here is ambivalent. On the one hand, Mehtodist Preachers perfected techniques to arouse paroxysms of fear of death and of the unlimited pains of Hell. Children from the age that they could speak, wer terrified with images of everlasting punishment for the slightest misbehaviour. Their nights were made lurid by Foxe's Book of Martyrs and similar reading.[43] But at the same time, those who could read were deluged throughout the early nineteenth century, with the tracts which celebrated 'Holy Dying'. No Methodist or evangelical magazine, for the mature or for children, was complete without its deathbed scene in which (as Leigh Hunt also noted) death was often anticipated in the langauge of bride or bridegroom impatient for the wedding-night. Death was the only goal which might be desired without guilt, the reward of peace after a lifetime of suffering and labour.

So much of the history of Methodism has, in recent years, been written by apologists or by fair-minded secularist trying to make allowances for a movement which they cannot understand, thatone notes with a sense of shock Lecky's judgement at the end of the nineteenth century:

> A more appalling system of religious terrorism, one more fitted to unhinge a tottering and to darken and to darken and embitter a sensitive nature, has seldom existed.[44]

Over the Industrial Revolution there brooded the figure of the Reverend Jabez Branderham (almost certainly modelled upon Jabez Bunting) who appears in Lockwood's grim nightmare at the opening of *Wuthering Heights*: 'good God ! what a sermon; divided into *four hundred nd ninety parts* ... and each discussing a seprate sin ! It is against this all-enveloping ' Thou Shalt Not!', which permeated all religious persuasions in varying degree in these years, that we can appreciate at its full height the stature of William Blade. IIt was in 1818 that he emerged from his densely allegorical prophetic books into a last phase of gnomic clarity in *The Everlasting Gospel.* Here he reasserted the Values, the almost-Antinomian affirmation of the joy of sexuality, and the affirmation of innocence, which were present in his earlier song. Almost every line may be seen as a declaration of 'mental war' against Methodism and Evangelicalism.[45] Their 'Vision of Christ' Was his vision's greatest Enemy'. Above all, Blake drew his bow at the teaching of humility and submision. It was this nay-saying humility which 'does the Sun and Moon blot out', 'Distorts the Heavens from Pole',

> Rooting over with thorns and stems
> The buried Soul and all its Gems.

2. The chiliasm of despair

The utility of Methodism as a work-discipline is evident. What is less easy to understand is why so many working people were willing to submit to this form of psychic exploitation. How was it that methodism could perform with such success this dual role as the religion of both the expoiters and the expoited?

During the years 1790-1830[46] three reasons may be adduced: direct indoctrination, the Methodist community-sense, and the psychic consequence of the counter-revolution.'

The first reason—indoctrination—cannot be overstated. The evangelical Sunday schools were ever-active, although it is difficult to know how far their activities may be rightly designated as 'educational'. The Wesleyans had inherited from their founder a peculiarly strong conviction as to the aboriginal sinfulness of the child; and this expressed—in Wesley's case—with a corce which might have made some Jesuits blench:

> Break their wills betimes. Begin this work befor they can run alone, before they can speak plain, perhaps before they can speak at all. Whatever pains its costs, break the will if you would not damn the child. Let a child from a year old be taught to fear the rod and to cry softly; from that age make him do as he is bid, if you whip him ten times running to effect it ... Break his will now, and his soul shall live, and he will probably bless you to all eternity.[47]

At Wesley's Kingswood School only severely workful 'recreations' were allowed—chopping wood, digging and the like —since games and play were 'unworthy of a Christian child'. ('I will kill or cure,' said Wesley, who rarely said things he did not mean: 'I will have one or the other—a Christian school, or none at all.') A brief glance at the 'educational' materials in common use in Sunday schools in the first decades of the nineteenth century exposes their true purpose. The Wesleys' lurid hymns, employed in the adult services, were replaced by Isaac Watts' Divine *Songs of Children*, or moralistic variants by later writers. Toddlers were taught to sing that they were 'By nature and by practice too, A wretched slave to sin. 'The All-seeing God's 'piercing eye' looked upon their most 'secret actions':

> There's not a sin that we commit,
> Nor wicked word we say,
> But in thy dreadful book 'tis writ,
> Against the judgement-day.

A characteristic moral story of the time exemplifies the general tendency of this 'teaching'.[48] John Wise is the son of 'a very poor man. who had many children, and could scarce get bread for them all by hard labour. He had to work with all his might each day in the week, and lived on oatcake, and oatmeal boiled up with water.' His father, notithstanding, was a good 'prayerful' man, repeatedly giving thanks for his blessings: for example, 'Some of us might have died, but we are all in the land of the living. 'John mother taught him Watts' hymn of the work-discplined sun:

When from the chambers of the east
His morning race begins,
He never tires, nor stops to rest,
But round the world he shines,
So, like the sun, would I fulfil
The duties of this day,
Begin my work betimes, and still
March on my heavenly way.

John's parents teach him the sanctity of the Sabbath, and deliver various homilies on duty, obedience and industry. Then comes the awful story of Betty, John's wicked sister, who goes for a wolk on Sunday, and comes back wet and muddy, having lost a shoe. Her father rebukes her, and reads to the family Moses' decre that the man who gathered sticks on the Sabbath should be stoned to death. Betty's sin is much worse than this man's, but this time she is pardoned. But worse sins follow: some children play truant from Sunday school and play football instead! The next Sunday the children are admonished, and told the story of the fortytwo children who mocked the aged Elisha and who were torn in pieces, at the behest of a merciful God. The infants then carol another of Watts' hymns:

When children in their wanton play,
Serv'd old Elisha so;
And bid the prophet go his way,
'Go up, thou bald-head, go:
GOD quickly stopt their wicked breath,
And sent two raging bears,
That tore them limb from limb to death,
With blood, and groans, and tears.

In the end, the piety of John and of his father are rewarded by an inheritance from a stranger, deeply moved by their patience and submission to poverty.

One might laugh; but the psychological atrocities committed upon children were terribly real to them. One may doubt the emphasis placed by a recent writer upon the repressive effect of Puritan infant—binding (in tight swaddling cloths and anal training, although the point cannot be dismissed.[49] But despite all the platitudes repeated in most textbooks as to the 'educational initiatives' of the Churches at this time, the Sunday schools were a dreadful exchange even for village dame's schools. Eighteenth-century provision for the education of the poor—inadequate and patchy as it was—was nevertheless provision for education, in some sort, even if (as with Shenstone's schoolmistress) it was little more than naming the flowers and herbs. In the counter-revolutionary years this was poisoned by the dominant attitude of the Evangelicals, that the function of education began and ended with the 'moral rescue' of the children of the poor.[50] Not only was the teaching of writing discouraged, but very many Sunday school scholars left the schools unable to read, and in view of the parts of the Old Testament thought most edifying this at least was a blessing. Others gained little more than the little girl who told one of the Commissioners on Child Labour in the Mines: ' if I died a good girl I should go the heaven—if I were bad I should have to be burned in brimstone and fire: they told me that at school yesterday, I did not know it before'.[51] Long before the age of puberty the child was subject at Sunday school and at home (if his parents were pious) to the worst kind of emotional bullying to confess his sins and come to a sense of salvation; and many, like young Thomas Cooper, went 'into secret places twenty times a day, to pray for pardon....'[52]

Lecky's epithet, 'religious terrosrism', is in fact by no means an excessive term to aply to a society which provided no alternative educaional arrangement for the children of the poor —at least until the Lancastrian charity school movement, in which the notion of 'moral rescue' was modified by genuine educational intentions and by the utilitarian concern for equipping children for industrial occupations.[53] But—and here we come to our second reason—we should beware of giving too bleak and too unqualified a picture of the evangelical chuches from the evidence of Sunday school primers, or from the dogmas of such men as Bunting.

What the orthodox Methodist minister intended is one thing; what actually happened in many communities may be another. The old 'Arminian' Methodists had a more humane attitude to Sunday school teaching; the methodists of the New Connexion were always more intellectual in their approach than those of the Wesleyan orthodoxy; we have noted that James Montgomery (of the *Sheffield Iris*) led the fight among the Sheffield Non-conformists to retain the teaching of writing in the Sunday school syllabus. The lay teachers, who volunteered their services, were less likely to be doctrinaire; and there was a continuous tension which could at times produce unlikely result. 'Even our Sunday Schools', a Bolton minister wrote to the Duke of Portland in 1798:

> may become in some Instances the Seminaries of Faction We have discovered one if not two who have taken the Oaths of United Englishmen, who are acting in the capacity of S. Schoolmasters *gratis* ...[54]

The 'quiet fortress' of the Stockport Sunday schools, which Dr Ure so commended in the 1830s, nevertheless had been besieged with a vengeance (and to some degree actually displaced) between 1817 and 1820, when the Reverend Joseph Harrison and the Stockport Politcal Union sponsored a Radical Sunday School movement which must have been staffed, in part by former teachers and scholars of the orthodox schools.[55]

And this should be seen, not only in the schools, but also in relation to the general influence of the Methodist churches. As a dogma Methodism appears as a pitiless ideology of work. In practice, this dogma was in varying degrees softened, humanized, or modified by the needs, values and patterns of social relationship of the community with in which it was placed. The Church, after all, was more than a building, and more than the sermons and instructions of its minister. It was embodied also in the class meetings: the sewing groups: the money-raising activities: the local preachers who tramped several miles after work to attend small functions at outlying hamlets which the minister might rarely visit. The picture of the fellowship of the Methodists which is commonly presented is too euphoric; it has been emphasized to the point whree all other characteristics of the Church have been forgotten.[56] But it remains both true and important that Methodism, with its open chapel doors, did offer to the uprooted and abandoned people ot the Industrial Revolution some kind of community to replace the older community- patterns which were being displaced. As an unestablished (although undemocratic) Church, ther was a sense in which working people could make it their own; and the more closely knit the community in which Mehtodism took root (the mining, fishing or weaving village) the more this was so.

Indeed, for many people in these years the Methodist 'ticket' of churchmembership acquires a fetishistic impotance; for the migrant worker it could be the ticket of entry into a new community when he moved from town to town. Within this religious community there was (as we have seen its own drama , its own degrees of status and importance, its own gossip, and a good deal of mutual aid. There was even a slight degree of social mobility, although few of the clergy came from proletarian homes. Men and women felt themselves to have some place in an otherwise hostile world when within the Church. They obtained recogniton, peerhaps for their sobriety, or chastity, or piety. And there were other home, to which we shall return . The Puritan character-structure, moreover, was not something which could be confiscated solely for the service same dedication which enabled men to serve in these roles, will be seen in the men who officered trade unions and Hampden Clubs, educated themselves far into the night, and had the responsibility to conduct working-class organizations. In analysing the ideology of Methodism, we have presented an intellectualized picture. In the fluency of social life, plain common sense, compassion, the obstinate vitality of older community traditions, all mingle to soften its forbidding outlines.

There is a third reason, however, why working people were exceptionally exposed to the penetration of Methodism during the years of the Napoleonic Wars. It is, perhaps, the most interesting reason of all, but it has been scarcely noticed. It may best be approached by recalling the hysterical aspect of Methodist and Baptist revivalism, and of the smaller sects. During the worst years of the Industrial Revolution, real opiates were used quite widely in the manufacturing districts. And Charles Kingsley's epithet, 'the opium of the masses,' reminds us that many working people turned to religion as a 'consolation', even though the dreams inspired by Methodist doctrine were scarcely happy. The methods of the revivalist preavhers were noted for their emotional violence; the tense opening, the vivid descriptions of sudden death and catastrophe, the unspecific thetoric on the enormity of sin, the dramatic offer of redemption. And the open-air crowds and early congregations of Methodism were also noted for the violence of their 'enthusiasm' - swooning groaning, crying out , weeping and falling into paroxysms. Southey, indeed, suggested that revivalism was akin to Mesmerism: Wesley 'had produced a new disease, and he accounted for it by a theological theory instead of a physival one'.[57] Sometimes these symptoms took the form of violent mass hysteria, as in the incident at Bristol recorded in Wesley's Journal in March 1788 when a 'vehement noise .... shot like lightning through the whole congregation':

> The terror and confusion was inexpressible. You might have imagined it was a city taken by storm. The people rushed upon each other with the utmost violence, the benches were broken in pieces, and nine tenthes of the congregation appeared to be struck with the same panic.

At Chapel-en-le-Frith, he recorded in 1786, this hysteria had already become habit-forming:

> Some of them, perhaps many, scream all together as loud as they possibly can. Some of them use improper, yea, indecent expressions in prayer. Several drop down as dead, and are as still as a corpse, but in a while they start up and cry, Glory glory ....

Such excesses of hysteria Wesley condemned, as 'bringing the real work into contempt'.[58] But throughout the Industrial Revolution more muted forms of hysteria were intrinsic to Methodist revivalism. Tight communities, miners, hill-farmers or weaverss, might at first resist the campaign of field-preaching and prayer-meeting among them; then there might be a little moving among the dry bones'; and then 'the fore broke out; and it was just as when the whins on a common are set on fire, – it blazed gloriously'.[59]

The example is taken from propaganda in West Riding weaving villages in 1799-1801, when whole communities declared themselves—at least temporarily—saved'. And it is rarely noted that not only did the war years see the greatest expansion of Methodism, notably in the northern working class, but that this was also accompanied by renewed evidence of hysteria. For example, in the years 1805-6, when numbers flocked to the Methodists in Bradford, 'no sooner, in many cases, was the text announced, than the cries of persons in distress so interrupted the preacher, that the service .... was at once exchange for one of general and earnest inercession'.[60] 'Three fell while I was speaking, a preacher of the Bible Christian in Devon noted complacently in his diary in 1816: 'We prayed and soon some more fell; I think six found peace.' The ministrations of this sect among the moorland farmers and labourers were often accompanied by agonies, prostrations, 'shouts of praise', and 'loud and piteous cries of penitents'.[61]

Methodism may have inhinited revolution; but we can affirm with certainty that its rapid growth during the Wars was a component of the psychic processes of counter-revolution. There is a sense in which any religion which places great emphasis on the after-life is the chiliasm of the defeated and the hopeless. ' The utopian vision aroused a contrary vision. The chiliastic optimism of the revolutionaries ultimately gave birth to the formation of the conservative atttitude of resignation.....' —the words of Karl Mannheim's describing another movement. And he also gives us a clue to the nature of the psychic process:

> Chiliasm has always accompnied revolutionary outbursts and given them their spirit. When this spirit ebbs and deserts these movements, there remain behind in the world a naked mass-frenzy and a despiritualized fury.[62]

Since, in England of the 1790s, the revolutionary impulse was stifled before it reched the point of 'outburst', so also when the spiri6t ebbed, the reaction does not fall to the point of fren. And yet there are many phenomena in these decades which can scarcely be explained in any other way. Authentic millennarialism ends in the late-1790s, with the defeat of English Jacobinism, the onset of the of the Wars, and the confining of Richard Brothers in a mad-house. But a number of sects of 'New Jerusalemites' prospered in the next fifteen years.[63] Prophet after prophet arose, like Ebenzer Aldred, a Unitarian minister in an isolated village in the Derbyshire Peak (Hucklow):

> There he lived in a kind of solitude, became dreamy and wild; laid hold on the prophecies; saw napoleon in the Book of Revelation: at last fancied himself the Prophet who, standing neither on land nor water, was to proclaim the destruction of a great city.....

and, colthed in a white garment, his grey hair floiwing down his shoulders, sailed in a boat on the Thames, distributing boolkets and prophesying doom.[64] Radical, mystic and militarist contested for the robes of Revelation: the lost tribes of Israel were discovered in Birmingham and Wapping: and 'evidence' was found that 'the British Empire is the peculiar possession of Messiah, and his promised haval dominion'.[65]

But the most startling evidence of a 'despiritualized fury' is to be found in the movements surrounding—and outliving—the greatest prophetess of all, Joanna Southcott. It was in 1801 that her first cranky prophetic booklet was published, The Strange Effects of Faith. And the gereral climate of expectant frenzy is shown by the rapidity. With which the reputation of the Devon farmer's daughter and domestic servant swept the country [...]

The Methodists, of course, had many advantages over the Southcottians : organizational stability, money the benign attitude of the authorities. What members they lost to the cult were probably soon regained. but this does not mean that we can dismiss the cult as a mere 'freak', irrelevant to the stolid lines of social growth. On the contrary, we should see the 'Johannas' and the methodist revival of these years as intimate relations. The wars were the heyday of the itinerant lay preachers, with their 'pious ejaculations, celestial groans, angelic swoonings'[66] – the 'downright balderdash' which so much enraged Cobbett:

> Their heavenly gifts, their calls, their inspirations their feelings of grace at work within them, and the rest of their canting gibberish, are a gross and outrageous insult to

> common sense, and a great scandal to the country. It is in vain that we boast of our enlightened state, while a sect like this is invreasing daily.[67]

As orthodox Wesleyanism throve, so also did breakaway groups of 'Ranters'—the Welsh 'Jumpers' (cousins to the American 'Shakers'), the Primitive Methodists, the 'Tent Methodists', the 'Magic Methodists' of Delemere Forest, who fell into trances or 'visions', the Bryanites or Bible Christians, the 'Quaker Methodists' of Warrington and the 'Independent Methodist' of Macclesfield. Through the streets of war- time and post war England went the revivalist missionaries, crying out: 'Turn to the Lord and seek salvation!'

One is struck not only by the sene of disequilibrium, but also by the *impermanence* of the phenomenon of Mehodist conversion. Rising graphs of Church membership are misleading; what we have, rather, is a revivalist pulsation, or an oscillation between periods of hope and periods of despair and spiritual anguish. After 1795 the poor had once again entered into the Valley of Humiliation. But they entered it unwillingly, with many backward looks; and whenever hope revived, religious revivalism was set aside, only to reappear with renewed fervour upon the ruins of the political messianism which had been overthrown. In this sense, the great Methodist recruitment between 1790 and 1830 may be seen as the chiliasm of despair.

This is not the customery reading of the period; and it is offered as an hypothesis, demanding closer investigation. On the eve of the French Revolution the Methodists claimed about 60,000 adherents in Great Britain. This indicated little more than footholds in all but a few of the industrial districts. Thereafter the figures claimed advance like this: 1800, 90,619; 1810, 137,997; 1820, 191, 217; 1830, 248, 592.[68] Years especially notable for revivalist recruitment were 1797-1800, 1805-7, 1813-18, 1823-4, 1831-4. These years are so close to those of maximum political awareness and activity that Dr Hobsbawm is justified in directing attention to the 'marked parallelism between the movements of religious, social and political consciousness'.[69] But while the relationship between political and religious excitement is obviously intimate, the nature of the relationship remains obscure

: the conclusion that 'Methodism advanced when Radicalism advanced and not when it grew weaker' does not necessarily follow.[70] On the contrary, it is possible that religious revivalism took over just at the point where 'political' of temporal aspirations met with defeat [...]

References

1. Cited in E.Halevy, *A History of the English People in 1815*, penguin edn, BK3, III,p.53. For accounts of Methodism's political stance during these years, see E.R. Taylor, *Methodism and Politics*, 1791-1850; and R.F. Wearmouth *Methodism and the Working Class Movements of England*, 1800-1850(1937), especially the chapters on 'The Methodist Loyalty' and ' The Methodist Neutrality'. See also J.L. and B. Hammond, *The Town labourer*, London, Longman & Green, 1917, Ch.13, 'The Defences of the Poor'.

2. See below,p.179.

3. T.P. Bunting, *Life of Jabz* Bunting, D.D. (1887), p.338.

4. *Ibid*., p.11. It is intersting to note that Oaster's father, a Leeds clothier was also a Methodism and a 'Tom Painite'. In his maturity, Oastler's opinion of Methodism was scarcely more complimentry than that of Cobbett.

5. J.Wray, 'Methodism in Leeds', Leeds Reference Library.

6. T.B. Bunting, *op. cit*., pp.527-8.

7. *Ibid*. , pp.295-7,312-14, 322-3; Bamford, Early *Days, pp*. 100-101. It is fair to note that the Established Church and other Nonconformist sects also forbade the teaching of writing on Sundays.

8. The only humanitarian cause to which Methodist like Bunting gave consistent support was Anti-Slavery agitation; but as the years go by, and the issue is trotted out again and again, one comes to suspect that it was less a vestigial social conscience than a desire to disarm criticism which propped this banner up.

9. L. Tyerman, *John Wesley (1870)*,III,p.499,See also J. Sutcliffe, *A Review of Methodism* (York, 1805), p.37.

10.See W.J.Warner, The *Wesleyan Movement in the Industrial Revolution, 1930,* 168-80.

11. R.H. Tawney, *Religion and the Rise of Capitalism*, 1926, Penguin edn.,pp.227ff.

12. Max Weber, *The Protestant Ethic and the Spirit of Capitalism,* Allen and Unwin, 1930, esp. pp. 54, 60-67, 160-61, 178; E.From, *The Fear of Freedom* ((1960 edn), p.80.

13. Nor is this work -disvipline in any sense limited to Methodism .We are discussing Methodism here as the leading example of developments which belong also to the history of Evangelicism and of most nonconformist sects during the Industrail Revolution.

14. Weber, op.cit., pp.66-7,282; Tawney, op. cit., pp.198ff. Baxter's Writings were favoured reading among the early Methodist, and were much reprinted in the early decades of the nineteenth century.

15. *Report of the society for Bettering the Condition of the poor,* I (1798), pp.238ff.; account of the Duke of Bridgewater;s colliers (near Manchester). The Duke's colliers were regarded as 'more moral than most, and 'some of the duke's agents are men of a religious cast, and have established Sunday schools...'

16. A. Redford, *The Economic History of England*, 2nd edn. 1960, pp. 19-20. As late as the 1830s Samuel Greg was complaining of 'that restless and migratory spirit which is one of the peculiar characteristics of the manufacturing poplation'.

17. V. W. Bladen, 'The Potteries in the Industrial Revolution', *Econ. Journal* (Supplement), 1926-9,p.130. See also M. McKendrick, 'Josiah Wedgwood and Factory Discipline', *Hist. Journal*, IV,I, 1961, p.30. It was Wedgewood's aim to 'make such *Machines of the Men* as cannot err'.

18. R. Guest, *A Compendious History of the Cotton Manufacture* (1823), pp.38,43.

19 In the seventeenth century the Puritan sects had a large weaver following, but—except in the West of England □ this traditional had little life in the early eighteenth century.

20. A. Ure, *The Philosophy of Manufactures,* 1835, pp.13-21. Cf. also p.23: 'It is in fact the constant aim and tendency of every improvement in machinery to supersede human labour altogether, or to diminish its cost, by substituting the industry of women and children for that of men; or that of ordinary labourers, for trained artisans.' As an expression of the mill-owners' intentions this is interesting, and relevant to the textile indutries; but as an expression of the 'law' of capitalist development, Marx and Engels perhaps gave Ure's claims too much credence.

21. Ibid., III, Chs.1 and 3. Thompson's italics.

22. Cf. D.H. Lawrence in *The Rainbow :* 'They believe that they must alter themselves to fit the pits and the place, rather than alter the pits and the place to fit themselves. It is easier.'

23. Ure, op. cit., pp.423-5.

24. Weber, in his brief discussion of Methodism in *The Protestant Ethic and The Spirit of Capitalism,* exaggerates the Calvinist elements in its theology, and therby fails to see its special adaptability as a religion of the proletariat. He thus presses too far the sense of a 'calling' among the Wesleyans, especially when he seeks to apply it to the 'calling' of the working man, a doctrine which has less significance in England than those of submission and obedience.

25. Jabez Bunting, *Sermon on Justification by Faith* (Leeds, 1813), p.11. Bunting's imagery reminds one that in January of this same year (1813) some Luddites had suffered the full 'penal consequences' on the gallows, while others had their penalty 'graciously remitted' to fourteeen years transportation.

26. Weber and Tawney, of course direct attention to the parallel development of Puritan and Utilitarian dogmas: cf. Tawney, op.cit., p.219: 'Some of the links in the Utilitarian coat of mail were forged ... by the Puritan divines of the seventeenth century. 'It was Methodism, however, which forged the last links of the Utilitarian chains riverted upon the proletariat.

27. Excepting, of course, the Baptists—notably in Wales.

28. For an example, taken from this tract, see Thompson (1968),

p.62.

29 . The language often suggests that the objective component of the 'sin' was masturbation. And this might well be deduced from three facts: (1) The introversial nature of penitent self-absorption. (2) The obsessional Methodist teaching as to the sinfulnes of the sexual organs. (3) The fact that the children of Methodists were expected to come to a sense of sin at about the age of puberty. See G.R. Taylor, *The Angel -Makers* (1958), p.326 for the increase in literature on the subject in these year.

30. Joshua Marsden, *Sketches of the Early Life of a Sailor* (an autobiography in the third person) (Hull, n.d.), *passim*

31. *Sketches of the Early Life of a Sailor,pp. 104,111.*

32. Josephes Nightingale, *Portraiture of Methodism* (1807), pp. 203ff.

33. R. Southey, *Life of Wesley and Rise and progress of Methodism* (1890 edn), 381ff.

34. J.E.Rattenbury, *The Eucharistic Hymns of hohn and Charles Weley* (1948),p.240:

We cast our sins into that fire
Which did thy sacrifice consume,
And every base and vain desire
To daily crucifixion doom.

35. W. Hazlit, 'On the Causes of Methodism', *'The Round Table (1817), Works,* IV, pp.57ff.

36. Weber, *op.cit., p.53.*

37. Ibid., pp.158-9.

38. Only an appreciation of the degree to which this obsession came to permeate English culture—andin particular working class culture—can lead to an understaning of why Lawrence was impelle to write *Lady Chatterley's Lover.*

39. See R.A. Knox, *Enthusiasm* (Oxford, 1950), pp.408-17, G.R. Taylor, op. cit., pp. 166-7.

40. J.E.Rattenbury,op.cit., p.132.

41. Ibid ., pp.109-11, 202-4, 224-34; and J.E.Rattenbury, *The*

Evangelical Doctrines of Charles Wesley's Hymns (1941), p. 184. This subject is due for renewed and more expert attention. Mr. G.R. Taylor's study of *The Angel Makers* is suggestive, but hjis attemp to find a 'sexual ' explanation of historical change in patrist and matrist child - orientations is pressed to point of absurdity.

42. The Editor of the Examiner [Leigh Hunt], *An Attempt to Show the Folly and Danger of Mehodism* (1809), esp.pp.54-64, 89-97. The language also laid the Methodists open to charges that love-feasts, watch-nights, and revivalist fervour became occasions for promiscuous sexual intercourse. Among sober critics, Nightingale discounted these accusations, Leigh Hunt supported them, Southey reserved judgement. See such *canaille* as A Professor, Confessions of a Methodist (1810).

43. Cf. W.E. H. Lecky, *History of England in the Eighteenth Century* (1891 edn), II, p.585: 'The ghastly images [the Mehtodist preachers] continually evoked poisioned their imaginations, haunted them in every hour of weakness or depression, discoloured all their judgements of the world, and added a tenfold horror to the darkness of the grave.'

44. W. E. H. Lecky, *History of the English people in the 18th century, 1891,*III,pp. 77-8.

45. Cf. Wilberforce, *A Practical View of Christianity, p.437;* 'Remember that we are all fallen creatures, borm in sin, and naturally depraved, Christianity recognizes no *innocence or goodness of heart.'*

46. These years cover the period of the rise and dominance of Jabez Bunting and his circle. After 1830 liberalizing tendencies can be sen at work within the Methodist Connexion; and although Bunting fought a determined rearguard action, by the 1840s Methodism entered a new and somewhat softened stage. On the other hand, some second or third generation mill-owners and employers left the Methodists for the respectability of the Established Church. On the other hand, Mehtodists appears as the authentic outlook of some in the small shopkeeper and clerical and sub-managerial groups, in which a muted radiscalism is joined to the ideology of 'self-help'. See E. R. Taylor, op. cit., chs.5, 6,

and W.J. Warner, op. cit. pp. 122-35.

47. R.Southey, *Life of Wesley and the Rise of Methodism,*1890 edn., p.561. We can see, for example from Bamford's memoirs of the 1790s, and from Thomas Copper's *Life* (when as a Methodist schoolmaster in the 1820s he regarded it as a sign of grace that he should not strike his pupils) that Wesley's teachings were humanized by many of his late eighteenth-century and early nineteeenth-century followers. But see the orthodox utilitarian advocacy of Jabez Bunting in *Sermon on a great work described* (1805).

48. *The History* of *John Wise, a Poor Boy* : I*ntended for the Instruction of Children* [Halifax, 1810].

49. G. R. Taylor, op. cit.

50. Cf. Raymond Williams, *The Long Revolution* (1961) pp. 1356.

51. Cited in J.L. and B.Hammond, *Lord Shaftesbury* (Penguin edn), p.74.

52. T. Cooper, *Life,*p.37.

53. Those writer today who rightly expose the human depreciation resulting from the commercial abuse of the media of communication, seem to me to have matters out of proportion when they overlook the extent and character of mass indoctrination in earlier periods.

54. Rev. Thomas Bancroft, 12 February 1798, P. C. A. 152.

55. See D. Read, *Peterloo* (Manchester, 1957), pp. 51ff., and below, p.788.

56. The sense of fellowship in the early years of the Church is expressed sympathetically in L. F. Church is expressed sympathetifally in L.F. Church, *The Early Methodist People (19...?).* See also , of course, Dr. Wearmouth's book, among many others.

57. Southey, op.cit., pp. 382ff.

58. See the discussion of the 'enthusiasm' in R. A. Knox, op. cit., pp.520-35.

59. F. A. West, *Memoirs of Jonathan Saville* (Halifax, 1844).

60. W. M. Stamp, *Historical Notes of* Wesleyan *Methodism in Bradford* (1841), p.85.

61. F. W. Bourne, *The Bible Christians* (1905).pp.36-42.

62. K. Mannheim, *Ideology and Utopia* (1960 edn),pp. 192-6.

63. In march 1801, Earl Fitzwilliam was enquiring into the activities of the followers of Brothers in Bradford, led by Zacchaus Robinson, a weaver, who 'was for many years a strong Methodist, & what is here called a Class Leader'. Fitsz william Papers, F.45(a).

64. T. A. Ward, op.cit., pp. 188-9; Eben-Eser, The Little Book (1811).

65. R. Wedgwood, *The Book of Remembrance (1814)*

66. Halifax Theatre Royal playbil, 1793.

67. *Political Register,* 12 June 1813.

68. Census of Religious Worship, England and Wales, 1851 (1853), p.lxxviii. Orthodox Wesleyan circuits with over 1,000 membersub 1815 were claimed to be: London, Bristol, Redruth, St Ives, Birmingham, Burslem, Macclesfield, Manchester, Bolton, Liverpool, Colne, Nottingham, Sheffield, Leeds, Birstal, Bradford, Halifax, Isle of Man, Sunderland, Wakefield, Dewsbury, Epworth, York, Hull, Darlington, Barnard Castle, Newcastle, Shields. See M.E. Edwards, 'The Social and Political Influence of Methodism In the Napoleonic Period' (London Ph.D. Thesis, 1934).p.244.

69 . *Primitive Rebels,* 1959, pp. 129-30.

70. See E. J. Hobsbawm, 'Methodism and the Threat of Revolution,' *history today (1957), VII,p.124.*

Chapter-14

SUNDAY SCHOOLS AND SOCIAL CONTROL

T. W. LAQUEUR

Chapter-14

Introduction

Modern historians who investigate the social role of Sunday schools agree on two propositions. First, that the schools were agencies of the upper and middle classes which were imposed on the 'lower orders' or the working clas. Second, that thay were an important agency in suppressing, with a minimum of coercion, traditional lower-class patterns of behaviour which were replacced with conduct more suited to an industrial society. Both points appear in numerous guises and with varying degrees of specificity.

The workingclasses, argues J.F.C.Harrison, 'had no alternative but to accept the instruction offered in middle-class day and Sunday schools'. The breakdown of the old popular culture and its supersession by formal literary instruction based on the three Rs was the conscious aim of middle-class educationalists who provided these schools.[1] Based on the theories of Weber and his successors, historians have sought and found in evangelical religion the source of all those pers-onal traits and values suited to and indutrial society.[2] One scholar discusses Sunday schools in the company of 'vatious other schemes which were used to discipline the lower orders'.[3] Another cites both charity and Sunday schools as 'the principal channels through which the upper and middle classes sought to impose their social ideas upon the working class' while the latter schools, he argues, were 'even more explicitly geared to manning the growing industries than the former'.[4] E.P. Thompson singles out the Sunday school as one of the insti-tutions created by the middle class in order to wean the working classes from their pre-indutrial rhythms of work and play and to inculcate in them the 'time thrift' necessary in an industrial society. The military rules of behaviour, the insistence on regularity and punctuality of attendance, and undisguised indoc-trination are adduced to support the views of some contemporaries that Sunday schools constituted 'a spectacle of order and regularity' which as a

Gloucester manufacturer put it, 'made children more tractable and obedient, less quarrelsome and revengeful'. 'Once within the schools gates', Thompson argues, 'the child enterd the new universe of disciplined time' leaving behind pre-industrial sloth for modern industry.[5]

His Making of the English Working Class develops and extends these themes. Here too it is argued that: 'The pressures towards discipline and order extended from the factory, on one hand, the Sunday school, on the other, into every aspect of life: leisure, personal relationships, speech,manner.'[6] Methodism between 1790 and 1830 acted at the same time as the ideology of the oppressed and the oppressor. Of the three reasons given for this curious state of affairs—direct indoctriantion, the Methodist community sense, and the psychic consequences of counter-revolution—he argues that 'the first reason—indovtrination—cannot be overstated'. Furthermore, the Evang-elical Sunday school is identified as the main agency of this indoctrination.[7] According to Thompson, these schools acted upon Wesley's doctrines of the aboriginal sinfulness of the child; they practised a kind of religious terrorism on the young, convincing them of their spiritual unworthiness and offering hard work, adherence to duty and submission to the wishes of their betters as a kind of exculpatory act. Far worse than being merely agencies of moral rescue, Sunday schools weak-ened the wills and corrupted the souls of their inmates, making them the victims of an objectively hostile ideology.[8]

Thompson's view of the Sunday school must be considered in the context of his general thesis. 'And class', he argues, 'happens when some men, as a result of common experiences (inherited or shared), feel and articulate the identity of their interests as between themselves, and as against other men whose interests are different from (and usually opposed to) theirs.'[9] Between 1780 and 1832 a working class in this sense came into being; in these decades',most English working people came to feel an identity of interests as between themselves, and as against their rulers and employers'.[10] If this model is true, the bourgeois values and precepts of the Sunday school, indeed the institution itself, ought to have become increasingly repugnant to the working classes during the industrial revolution.

Furhtermore, the richly varied radical working-class culture which Thompson describes presumably ought to have been significantly different from the culture of the Sunday school.

But neither of these things happened. Indeed, the interpretation of Sunday schools developed most fully in the *Making of the English Working Class* is insufficiently subtle to encompass the facts. It is difficult to maintain in any literal sense that Sunday schools constituted an imposition by the middle upon the working class. Many of those active in founding Sunday schools in both the eighteenth and nineteenth centuries were from the working class. The teachers were almost all from the same social strata as those they taught; after 1810 some sixty percent of all teachers had been students themselves. Even in those schools where the managers were manufacturers or shopkeepers, teachers played an impotant part in deciding the internal policies of the school. While early Sunday schools in both towns and villages were often financed by the dominant social class, the change in the early nineteenth century away from subsriptions to annual sermons as a priary source of funds meant that the community at large played a more sign-ificant part in underwriting the schools.

Fund-raising sermons were a popular and important element of working class community life, reported alike in the *Manchester Guardian* and the *Northen Star*. Indeed, Sunday schools were accepted, patronized, and occasionally idealized precisely because they grew out of the working class as a means of fulfilling the real and percieved needs of the comm-unity. Any analysis of Sunday schools as an agency of social control or as an institution through which certain norms and values were transmitted must take these facts into account. Therefore, a model which regards Sunday schools primarily as a weapon in an alleged bougeois assault on working-class culture simply will not do.The schools were effective in large measure because they worked freom within and because they were not merely organs of middle-class propaganda.

Sunday schools and the aims of the middle class

In order to put the question of indoctrination in context, it is important to note that Sunday schools represented the first step in the increased specialization of educational activities during the late eighteenth and nineteenth centuries. Children were taken from, or sent buy, their parents each Sunday to a school whose function was to do what the parent, or perhaps the isolated clergyman, could not do. But the emergence of children, even tempoarily, from the educational nexus of family relationships had enormous political and social ramification which were not lost on contemporaries.

Sunday schools were advocated by the eighteenth-century Evangelicals and some of their successors as a means of removing children from the corrupt influence of the parent to a morally and politically more salutary atmospher. 'The children of the poor, by being drawn out of their obscurity into notice and protection are humanized and civilized,'argued a friend of Hannah More.[11] Teachers must begin their work by 'unlearning the children much of what they have been taught' because 'being from the lowest order of prople they have not been taught to associate happiness with virtue'.[12] Mrs Trimmer told potential subscribers to her school that the immoralities of the poor, which 'keep their employers in a constant state of suspicion and uneasiness', would be a thing of the past now that the 'education of poor children is no longer entirely left to their ignorant and corrupt parents'. Only good could result from the fact that 'it has in many places become a public business'.[13] Most bluntly put, Sunddy school managers could 'at all times exercise authority under a conciliating title, and, while they patronize the children, can insensibly control the conduct of the parents'.[14]

There is little doubt, moreover, that some Sumday schools intended to play their part in restraining political radicalism among the working class, Those founded by the London based, Evangelical dominated, Sunday School Society or by committees of notables in the provinces were a fundamentally conservative response to what was perceived to be a moral and political crisis. Education generally, and the Sunday school in particular, was welcomed as a means of bringing religion to the lower orders which would, it was thought, elevate them above the mire of sin and deprivation into which they had fallen, and thereby assure the harmony and continuity of an heirarchic sociey of orders. Only as much learning as was necessary to achieve this end was to be offered in Sunday school, and indeed the public was invited to contribute to the project under the assurance that their funds would be used to ensure social stablity.[15]

Sermon after sermon, appeal after appeal, emphasized the value of the new institution in restraining the lower orders and maintaining the relationship between the clases which appeared so threatened by the revoloutions in France. Mrs Trimmer vouched for the political safety of her schools by incl-uding in ger guide for genteel patrons a list of 'virtues' which the children were to learn. Among them were civility and gratitude.

> If you are civil you will behave with respect to ladies and gentlemen. you will say, Sir, or Madam, when you speak to them; you will rise from your seat when they come into a room where you are sitting; you will make a coutsey to them when you meet them ... If you have gratitude in your mind you will think your self much obliged to those who subscribe to the school; and you will take care to improve in every respect, that their money and advice may not be thrown away upon you.[16]

A Baptist preachernoted that: 'Christian knowledge has a tendency to establish the peace of society by teaching each individual to fill up that place which Providence has assigned him', and furthermore that a well instructed Christian peasantruy will constitute the support and happiness of the nation."[17] The horrors of the French Rebolution could only be prevented in England, argued an anonymous member of the SPCK, if the poorer classes were preserved from the doctrine, preached among them by evil and designing men, that all men were created equal. Sunday schools, he said, were of particular importance because the impress on the poor 'while still youg and tender the duty of behaving lowly and revrently to all their betters... and to fear God and honour the King'.[18]

Most public declaration of educations of policy in the late eighteenth century espoused the conservative doctrines of a Sarah Trimmer, a hannah More, or a Jonas Hanway. Whether or not Sunday schools in fact inculcated meekness and submi-ssion, it remains true that many of their early supporters wan-ted them to teach ' a superstitious veneration for the church of

England, and to bow to every man in a handsome coat'.

There is also evidence that Sunday schools were occasi-onally used as centers for middle-class propaganda during the nineteenth century. One witness before Sadler's Commitee, for example, claimed that during the spinners' turn-out some two or three years earlier manufacturers had come to the Sunday schools of Manchester to tell children that it was a sin to withstand their employeres, that they ought to be subject to them, and that they would be well advised to go back to work. Other instances might be cited, according to this informant.[20] A dresser in Robinson's mill, Stockport, told another committee that the schools of Stockport were controlled by manufacturers, were subservient to their interests, and served as an outlet for tracts and lectures pleading the factory owners' case. His denunciations were taken seriously enough to prompt rebuttals from the incumbent of St Thomas and the overlooker in the mill where the witness, Joseph Sadler, had been employed.[21] Radicals and Chartists on occasion made similar assertions and not without some justification. Indeed some factory owners did require their hands to attend a Sunday school, though not necessarily one provided by the employer.

Finally, the politically charged, overtly conservative children's literature of the 1780s adn 1790s continued to be distributed by Sunday schools well into the nineteenth century. All of the evidence so far presented seeem to constitute an overwhelming indictment of the Sunday school as na agency of class repression. But there is also considerable, and in the end convincing, evidence on the other side.

The decline of the educative family and the removal of the child from the home into the school is in itself a politically neutral occurrrence.[22] The Sunday school was, as has been shown, tightly integrated into the working-class community. When children left the home and entered the very different atmoshphere of the school they came into contact with the most literate of their class and imbibed the values of artisan respectability taught there. Though the potential for interge-nerational change was great it was not of a kind generally repugnant to working-class parents.

It must also be remembered that the most restrictive

definitions of Sunday school educaion were made as pre-emptive counter-arguments in debate with still more reactionary views. The character modelled on the Author in Hannah More's story of the founding of a Sunday school only adcaned the view that her proposed school would he limited to teaching the poor to read the Bible, a book which could only lead to the increased obedience and industry of servants, when the farmer being solicited for funds objected that teaching the poor to read was the surest road to national disaster.[23] The Rev. Johnson Grant's caution to Sunday school scholares to regard all printed work with caution and his conviction that education could only lead to religion and this to loyality seem less offensive when read beside an ultra-reactionary critique of his words. Sunday schools, noted one such article, had turned out fanatical teachers who led disputations, encouraged scepticism, infidelity and the anti-Christ. 'Those taught to read, to write, to reason', this review concludes, 'we see now grasping with eager curiosity every pernicious treatise within reach.'[24] Evidence of their activities and other publications suggest in fact that when the Sheffield Sunday School Union advertised itself as creating a society with 'each in his station under the final influence of religion' or the Stockport Sunday School devoted most of its 1819 report to recounting its battles against those who would attack Britain's matchless Constitution', both institutions were defending themselves against real or imagined threats from the Right rather than expressing the views which activated them during calmer times.[25]

Moreover, by the 1820s a new and more progressive conception of Sunday school education had come into being. The doctrine of self-help and advancement through merit replaced those older views of woirking class educaion as an exercise in the creation of deference. Already in 1794 The Baptist Daniel Turner was pointing out that some of 'the richest jewels of society' had been found among the poor whose advancement should be encouraged through educaion; the Rev. T. Wood recommended Sunday schools to his fellow Wesleyans by recalling the poverty-to greatness tradition in English history, and suggesting that the schools would 'excite in some of the children strong desires after further attainments'.[26] The advancement of science and learning that would result from mass education became a common theme. Cardinal Wolsey and Shakespeare were favorite subjects for Sunday school stories because of their rise from poverty to greatness, and stories of lesser men—Sunday scholars who learned the three Rs well enough to become prosperous merchants—abound.[27] There were, of course, still sermons and tracts which wished for the restoration of the old order with its patriarchal benevolence of rich to poor and which valued Sunday schools because of their role in maintaining the social order.[28] But by the late 1840s even the Church of England's Sunday school magazine could praise teaching in its schools as a step in the process of self-culture and self-improvement; and a widely read children's magazine of evangelical Dissent could include in each of its issues a story of 'Pursuit of knowledge under Difficulties'.[29] Indeed, by the mid-Victorian era the early nineteenth century Sunday school was almost a symbol of working-class advancement thro-ugh self-help. Tens of thousands of men had achieved prominence based on their Sunday school education, declared A.J.Mundella. 'From the kinds of qulifi-cations which will be required in the leading men of another generation or two', according to a sabbatarian tract, 'it is not too hazardous to say, that many of the children of our Sunday schools will become the rulers or the parents of the rulers of the destinies of the world'.[30] Local school histories proudly proclaimed the success of their alumni; Bradwell Methodist Chapel, for example, produced Ralph Benjamin Somerset, fellow of Trinty College, Cambridge, Thomas Morton, a quartermaster in India, and the owner of a large works in Stocksbridge who in turn employed three other ex-Sunday school men in imp-ortant positions.[31]

But quite apart from its ideological bent, the coercive and propagandistic powers of the Sunday school were severely limited. Since they met on only one day a week they could not, like the public schools of the aristocracy or the less great boa-rding schools of the bourgeoisie, organize all aspects of their students' lives. As one commentator noted sadly, 'For one day, partially spent in the company of the pios, the children are exposed, during six, to all the moral contagion and impurity of their own dwellings and neighbourhoods.'[32] Furthermore, competition for students between rival religious bodies made coercion impossible in the long run. It must be admitted, however, that there is some evidence of Anglican use of compulsion in the 1780s and 1790s which in many ways resembled the Church's efforts to control Methodism throughout the eighteenth century. In those decades, the Anglican clergy, for fear of losing what hold it had on the populace, sometimes used more than superior teaching to prise children from Dissenting schools. It was alleged thta they threatened on occasion to withhold relief and exclude families from parish charities; on occasion they even carried out their threats. There was a widely publicized case in Oxfordshire of over twenty families being excluded from the Christmas feast because they refused to send their children to the Anglican school.[33] A fierce controversy in Warwickshire developed into a full scale pamphleteering war in the best eighteenth century tradition when a Presbyterian minister and his allies accused the Angl-ican rector and his curate of first bribing and later threa-tening with loss of employment and eviction certain families who would not send their children to the Church Sunday school. On the other hand, the Dissenters made cash payments to their scholars, which might be regarded as bribes but which they justified on the grounds that the pittance involved was merly compensation for the social services lost by failure to attend the parish institution.[34] As late as 1811 Anglican authorities sought to harrass a Dissenting Sunday school in Portsmouth by bringing a prosecution under the Conventicle Act.[35] But, with only a handful of exceptions the market in Sunday school education was relatively free after the turn of the century.

As noted earlier, factory owners occasionally enforced Sunday school attendance. On me employee of the Strutt's mill even had his quarterly gift money stopped for not doing so.[36] But the extreme rarity of such instances, the absence of complaints about them from the working people, and the efforts schools made to attract children suggest that by and large attendance was a matter of choice and of compulsion. There may have been a few cases in which parent were not actually compelled to send their children to a school on the mill groudns but would lose respect if they did not do so. But again the great majority of schools were not attached to a mill or workplace and moral pressure would have been far more difficult to exercise in the pluralist religious envionment which characterized even small communities. Because of this pluralism, raw coercive power played little part in the world of Sunday schools. It is, of course, possible that those who managed Sunday schools exercised a measure of control over children and their parents by excluding, or threatening to exclude, radicals and malcontents from the services and the society of the school. But this kind of control is rare indeed; by and large the Sunday school did not interfere with the political lives of scholars or teachers.

The Stockport Sunday School provides a good case in point. The town in which it was situated lay at the centre of radical activity during both the Peterloo and Chartist period and was decidedly industrial. More than any other school in England this one was the creature of the manufacturing interests. Modern historians use its annual reports again and again as evidence for the repressive nature of Sunday schools.[37] Although its teachers came almost entirely from the working classes and although in their quarterly meeting they exercised some measure of control over the school's internal affairs, the relation of the school with the community were in the hands of a board of managers composed entirely of industrialists.[38] They were by no means all Tories; in fact, most probably supported the 1832 Reform Act, repeal of the corn laws, and other Whig-radical measures. Nevertheless they were opposed to Chartism, trade-union activity, and any other form of independent working-class redicalism. If the Sunday schools of England exercised a powerful control over working-class behaviour through their powers of exclusion, the Stockport School, therefore, ought to exhibit this facet of social manipulation to the fullest. It does not. In the history of the school from 1792 to 1850 there was only one case of expulsion as a result of internal subversion, namely, an attempt by working-class teachers to assume some of the powers of the middle -class committee [...]

The managers certainly distributed tracts whose message, insofar as it was political, advocated quiescence and maintenance of the *Status quo;* they quite probably delivered the occasional lecture to the same effect; they used a crown and sceptre resting on a Bible as an illustration at the beginning of many of their annual reports. But by and large politics were not central to the life of the school. Except during the years 1818-20 the managers were content to leave the worldly convictions of students and teachers outsider their sphere of interest. In a town which was at the centre of radical politics for most of the first half of the century the working classes seemed oblivious to the politics of those who financed the schools. So far as the middle-class board of managers was concerned they were content to let sleeping dogs lie and to get on with the recreational, religious and educational work of the Sunday school [...]

The inculcation of values: lectures, sermons and patriotic exercises

If the coercive powers of the Sunday school were limited, so also was the time spent on direct propaganda, and the means available. It is true that Sunday schools might have exercised indirect influence on the political attitudes of children through efforts to form their habits of work and play, both of which are discussed below. The more direct methods, however, were limited to three. Through sermons and lectures, through partici-pation in patriotic festivals and moset importantly through the literature they distributed, Sunday school could work on the minds of students to inculcate values which sustained the *status quo*. Sermons and lectures, however, had severe limit-ations in this regard. Only about twenty per cent of each day was available for direct propaganda by a school's managers; the remainder of the time was spent in the classroom engaged in religious or educational exercises having no direct political importance [...]

Viewed as instruments of bourgeois control the annual encounters with the aristocracy and occasional participation in patriotic exercises were not very important, They were often not organized by the bourgeoisie and in any case were too ephemeral and infrequent to have a major impact. However, they were an important reflection of the relationship of the working clas to society and of the subtle ways that clas tied itself to the social order.

The inculcation of values : literature, politics, and virtue

A far more significant vehicle of propaganda was the vast body of literature with which the working-class child was bombarded.

It can be divided into three categories: tracts and reward books given to scholars in school; magazines and periodicals published by denominational or Church organizations, by private individuals, or by Sunday school associations; and finally the textbooks which formed the main body of reading material for the boys and girls during schools hours. The literature in the first category is so enormous in scope and number of titles that a proper analysis would be a research project in its own right.[39] They range from the most blatantly propagandist and counter-revolutionary tracts to fanciful accounts of heaven and hell to 'books... such as relate to Natural History, to Biography, to Travels and Voyages, to the History of England, and even to metaphysics', all of which , one reactionary noted, 'are scarcely publications *fit* for the lowest order of Society'.[40] [...]

The literature discussed so far constituted the great bulk of the reading material associated with English Sunday schools during the period 1780-1850. It was first of all religious. Secondly, it formed part of the working-class culture of self-improvement with its concern for history, the natural sciences, and 'useful' knowledge. Thirdly, it dwelt on a morality advocating honesty and kindness while condemning sabbath breaking, disrespect to parents, lying and similar offences. Direct political propaganda as evidenced in the tracts of Hannah More or in some of the production of the SPCK was rare. The religious content of working-class political life and the aspiration toward respectability, of which self improvement was a part, may indeed have limited the revolutionary potential in English society during the period being considered. But it was through such channels, and not through coercion or propaganda, that Sunday schools played a political role. They did, however, promote certain values often associated with industrial society.

The inculcation of values : literature and work discipline

On paper, the ideal Sunday school child was certain to grow up into the ideal capitalist man or woman. The perfect scholar was imbued with the puritan ethic:

> ...of temper sweet and mild
> No angry passions e're were seen

In this engaging child.

She very soon could knit and sew
And help her mother too
For Hannah would not waste her time
As idle children do

Each sabbath morn she rose betimes
And dressed her clean and neat
Nor ever utter'd naughty words,
Or loitered in the street.

She knew that God would never love
Girls that are bold and rude
And therefore little Hannah prayed
That he would make her good.[41]

He, or she, went around reciting deities like:

In books, or work, or healthful play
Let my first years be passed
Thaat I may give for every day
Some good account at last.[42]

In short he or she was hard working, clean, conscious of the value of time, obedient, and (although not stated in these rhymes) thrifty as well. Indeed it has been argued that Sunday schools were middle-class agencies designed to inculcate just these virtues, that they were part of an assault on the pre-indutrial personality. In support of this view, it could be poointed out, for example, thtat Sunday schools, particularly in industrial cities, were often founded and financially supported by the manufacturing class; that when asked their views some factory owners remarked that the discipline and instruction of the Sunday school caused the children so educated to be 'more orderly and subordinate than others', 'more tractable, better behaved', 'improved in their general conduct and habits of cleanliness' and taken as a whole, more moral and manageable.[43] The aesthetic vision of the Sunday school and the factory during the nineteenth century were also remarkably similar. Ure talks of the 'sublime spectacle of witnessing crowds of factory children arraged in Sunday school' or of '1,500 boys, and as many girls regularly seated upon benches, the one set on the right side, the other on the left'.[44] Seventeen thousand children atending the Halifax Sunday School Jubilee were described in the official report as 'an invading and well disciplined army—well clad and cheerful'.[45] For some, the spectacle of tens of thousands of spindles turning through the motion of the same drive shaft was not dissimilar to thousands of children following the orders of one individual. But from the facts that the virtues favoured in Sunday schools were those characteristic of the entrepreneurial bourgeoisie, that this class on occasion praised and supported Sunday schools, and that on some occasions certain observers saw a similarity between the schools and new forms of industrial oraganisation it does not follow that Sunday schools were agents of the middle classe for imposing suitable character traits on children of their employees.

Two questions remain. To what extent can the puritan ethic in this period be seen as a form of bourgeois ideology? Secondly, in what ways, and how successfully, did Sunday schools propagate or instil this ethic? both these question must be answered in the context of the facts presented in Chapter Two. Sunday schools were by no means a simple outgrowth of the factory system or even of industrialism. In 1818, Wiltshire, Dorest, Buckinghamshire and Bedfordshire ranked fourth, fifthe, sixth and seventh respectively among counties in percerntage of their population enrolled in Sunday school. Bedfordshire stood first in 1851, with almost a fifth of the populaion enrolled, while Huntingdonshire, Rutland, Cornwall and Buckinghamshire were all in the top one quarter of counties based on *per capita* enrolment. Sunday schools began at a time when the factory system had scarcely gained a foothold and grew to contain millions of children before the factory became the dominant organization of production. They were as much a rural as an urban phenomenon, as much part of an agrarian as of an industrial economy. Furthermore, as has been noted already in this chapter, Sunday school teachers were predom-inantly working class, funds often came from the working-class community, and indeed the lower orders responded as eagerly to the philanthropic surge of the late eighteenth century as did other strata of society. The great majority of Sunday schools were then neither the direct product of industrialism nor of the middle class.

Nevertheless they undoubtedly taught the work ethic that is so often associated with the bourgeoisie. Although texts were primarily religious diligence, cleanliness, punctuality, thrift and obedience were all pressed on students [...]

It would be a mistake, however, to conflate these precepts or ideals into a distinct bourgeois ideolog. Indeed, the puritan ethic found some of its most vehement supporters among the leaders of a nascent working class [....]

It is scarcely surprising that working-class leaders should have adopted so readily the ethic traditionally associated with the entrepreneuial middle class; the personality traits of the successful political leader, journalist, or trade-union militant. It was as important for the *Northern Star* as for *The Times or Guardian* that its copy be handed in on time, that its distributors pick up their bundles regularly, and that payments be reliable.[46] A congruence between the fundamental values of the middle and 'respectable' working classes is thus natural and not difficult to understand.

The inculcation of values: school organization and work discipline

In real life, however, practice is more important than preaching; and the decisive role of the Sunday school in the develoment of personality had less to do with what was taught than with how things were taught, with the structural and operaional organization of the institution. The structure of authority, the discipline of time and place, to a lesser extent the organization of teaching the rules governing appearance, and the system of rewards and punishments all arose out of the school *qua* school. Though they may have had, and in some cases did have, almost obsessional ideological justification as well, this was largely window dressing on a reality determined by the nature of the institution.[47] A consideration of these features will allow us to understand how they acted to encouage inner drives and outward behaviour appropriate to an industrial society.

In the same way that the authority relationship in the family appear as a small-scale version of these relationships in an organic society, the nature of power in the Sunday school was based on reason rather than on deference; on a rule book rather than longstanding tradition. In contrast with the far smaller charity schools, many of these schools issued rule books or sheets setting out in writing the privileges and obliga-tions of various categories of personnel. Some were quite short, the size of a broadsheet, and were read out to the assembled students and teachers once each month in order to remind everyone of the nature of the social system in which they were participating. Other sets of rules were extraordinarily extensive, going on for over fifty pages and defining in the minutest detail the power relationships that governed the school. Perhaps the Napoleonic Wars inspired the military langusage in which they were couched: superintendents are colonels, inspectors are majors, teachers are captains, monitors are sergeants, and the best students in each classs are the corporals.[48] The set of rules from which this is drawn resembles nothing so much as Ambrose Crowley's reglations for the operation and management of his iron works. In the Sunday school as in the liberal state or the large firm, obedience is given to a person not because of who he or she is but because of the position they fil with in a system of law. Furthermore, both the teaching and the structure of the Sundaly school emphasized that it was rational to act according to these laws. In secular affairs this rationality might imply that one ought not to engage in trade-union activity because it was against the immutable laws of political economy to do so; alternatively, of course, it might encourage working class trade-union or political activism on different but equally rational grounds [....]

It would be misleading to argue that Sunday schools had a uniform system of teaching or of rewards and punishments. The author of a teacher's manual running to over 350 pages gave up in despair trying to describe the range of rewards and censures, claiming that another book of equal length would be required to do the job.[49] One basic generalization, however, can be made. This is that there was great reluctance in Sunday schools to exercise severs discipline and that stress was always more on rewards than on punishments. The result was that the apparent rigidity of the rules in theory was greatly softened by the unwillingness to enforce them in practice by a system of penalties. Whether the reasons for this laxity were pedagogical theory, theological scruples or a fear of losing pupils does not affect the result. Almost from the beginning of Sunday schools, corporal punishment was condemned as inappropriate for the sabbath; similarly any form of punishment arising out of anger or impatience on the part of the teacher was condemned, That hated figure, the wicked and quick tempered day schoolmaster of working-class autobiographies occurs with extreme rarity in remembrances of Sunday school. The pioneerdays when Raikes could burn the fingers of a student on a stove, the managers of a midland school hoist a student up in a basket, or force a child to hold a Bible at arm's length for hours on end were looked back on, after the turn of the century, as regrettable instances of a benighted era. Punishments which induced a sense of shame in scholars were more common. Students might be forced to wear a sign saying 'LATE' or SWORE' or 'UNRULY'; they might be made to sit on a form in the centre of the room; or they could be threatened with public expulsion during which they would be subjected to a stern lecture and then escorted to the door by a cadre of their former schoolmates.[50] But this too was frowned upon in more enlightened circles, both Anglican and Dissenting. If virtue had to be rewarded at all—and there was some controversy about this—then these rewards should consist of books and tracts or of tickets which could be exchanged for such reading material; punishment should consist of confiscation of rewards or of withholding them altogether. As this view of punishment became more widely accepted, however, it forced managers to give little gifts to all students so that there would be something that could be taken away in case of improper behaviour. Although there is no way of knowing precisely how various schools operated their reward systems, the inspection of a large number of anniversary accounts leaves the impression that most children on the annual or quarterly feast day were likely to receive something or other. So, as an analogue of the world at large, this aspect of the Sunday school was probably not very effective.

Several other factors softened the impact of the teaching regime and overall discipline in creating suiable work habits. First, while the Sunday school as a whole was a large complex organization, each class was far smaller than that of the modern school. Ten students per teacher was an average, with many groups as small as five or six.[51] A child's experience of the school was therefore less of the large and ordered world of the school at large and more of the less regulated and more family -like atmosphere of the small class. Furthermore, although teachers were expected to follow a definite regime of instruction, ensuring that each student learned systematically and was accordingly tested on what he or she was meant to learn a number of factors made the teacher more like a parent than an impartial mentor. The most basic of these was the ambiguity of goals in the Sunday school; secular learning which could be tested and even objective biblical knowledge were only one part of the task. Conversion a sense of seriousness, and love of God were far more important, at least in the eyes of those who wrote about schools. Teachers were therefore encouraged to develop a highly personal relationship with the children in their class, to get to know their homes, and most importantly to let love and kindness guide their dealings with their classes.[52] This of course conflicted with the far more impersonal role assigned to the instructor in his or her role as purveyor of knowledge alone. For example students who read poorly were nevertheless encouraged so that they would not come to dislike Bible reading; teachers were praised who, though deficient in learning, were highly religious; and the specific relationship a child had toward his parents, arising from the Evangelical ideal of the home, was taken as a model at least as often as the universalistic model of the pupil-teacher relationship in a modern school.

All these features of the school worked against the inculcation of suitable work discipline. They mitigated the rational, orderly, impersonal aspect of the Sunday school and indeed account for the widespread acceptance of the independent schools by communites which at the same time rejected those of the National and the British and Foreign Societies. On the other hand, the Sunday school was far more a part of the industrial world or large-scale enterprise than of the artisan—workshop era . If there was a certain mechanistic quality about their discipline and an aggressive commitment to the puritan virtues, it was not because of the school's specific relationship with factory owners or other managers of large-scale enterprise. It was because both the school and the factory were part of the same stage of historical development in which it was, and is, more difficult to maintain humansitic values.[53]

The inculcation of values : Sunday schools and the use of leisure

The role of Sunday schools in transforming working-class leisure was far more profound and pervasive than their part in political propaganda and repression. Their very being was dependent on the existence of leisure; they constituted an alternative way of spending Sunday and had to compete with other activities for the time of children who worked during the week. The child who spent his or her day in Sunday school was therefore taken out of the street or field, away from football, dice, hoopspinning, or simply noisily playing about. The schools also sounded the alarm against leisure activities which, though not directly injurious to the cause of sabbath education, offended the aesthetic sensbilities, the ideas of what constituted civilized behaviour, or simply the practical economic or political judgements of those who managed or taught in them. In place of the proscribed amusements, the Sunday school offered the 'rational pastimes', the outings, walks, railroad excursion, the teas and meeting which formed the core of respectable working-class leisure until the growth of large-scale public entertainment in the late nineteenth and early twentieth century. Neither in its negative nor its poitive modes can the Sunday school hbe regarded simply as an agent of the bougeoisie molding a recalcitrant working class into conformity with alien values. A certain puritanism, a passive if not an active rejection of the 'picarsque hedonism' of the lower orders in the eighteenth century, was too much a part of radical working-class culture in the nineteenth century for so unambiguous a class interpretation to be balid. Nevertheless, the ascendency of bourgeois sesibilities—the decline of bear-, bull-, and badger-baiting, the end of the old style pugilism, the growth of the temperance movement, the decline of public violence, and not least the establishment of the Evangelical sabbath—were all part of the cultural underpinnings of the new industrial society which Sunday Schools helped to esablish [...]

Undoubtedly, some of those who founded and worked for Sunday schools sought to control working-class leisure in order to control crime in general, and most particularly that crime committed in violation of the sabbath. But others, the great majority of the working men and women who taught in the schools, did so because they believed that leisure on the sabbath and at other free times should be well spent, either in preparing for the next life or in improving oneself for a happier and more prosperous earthly existence. For them the remaking of patterns of leisure was part of the culture of self-help, self-improvement, and, above all, respectability.

Sunday schools waged their battle for the control of children's leisure in three ways. First, Through education as itself a morally regenerative enterprise; second, through the support of temperance and other reform campaigns; and third, through the provision of counter- recreation. Like religion, educaion was thought to have a transforming effect on all it touched. The recreations of the educated man, the man who could use his mind, would not be those of the ignorant; education changed man the beast to man the angel, or so it was thought. Rational amusement, made possible by literacy, was therfore touted from the pulpit and in the bougeois and the working-class press [...]

Sunday schools were thus undoubtedly advocates of refinement and respectability. It is more difficult, however, to determind if they were therefore on the side of the middle classes against the working classes, or the side of counter-revolution against revolution. There were compelling tactical as well as ideological reasons that kept organized working-class politics out of the politics of moral reform,. But the vices condemned by the Sunday school were almost as often condemned in the working class press and in the writing of impotant spokesmen. A certain puritanism pervaded many of these writings, which suggests that the division in society between the decadent, pleasure-seeking and idle classes on the one hand and the upright, serious and hard-working classes on the other was as important in the minds of their authors as the imputed antagonism between a middle and a working class [...][54]

Of course, Sunday schooles cannot be adduced to explain the general decline of fairs and wakes. Their demise was part of the slow death, already well under way in the eighteenth century, of the traditional order. Some festivals, like the London fairs, were suppressed by the magistracy; others, like the Cotswold games, were prohibited by acts of Parliament, a victim of overlarge crowds and new sensibilities. Religion generally and Sunday schools in particular were only one of the forces making for the new attitudes which rejected old pastimes.[55] Nevertheless, for three reasons the school were instrumental in the process of reforming working-class leisure. They were part of a larger, systemic transformation of pre-industrial to industrial society. They offered a relatively refined form of leisure activity which many working-class men and women already embraced, at least for their children if not for themselves. And finally, their efforts by and large grew out of the community they sought to influence rather than being imposed on it from the outside.

But by helping to form cultural linages bewween classes Sunday schools contributed to the stability of Victorian society and the success of a capialists economy [...]

Conclusions

The repressive, middle-class dominated Sunday school of Hannah More or Williams Fox was a rarity by the early nineteenth century. Within two decades of their founding Sunday schools had become one strand of a uniquely working-class cultural constellation. In their literature and the teaching they stessed moral and ethical as against overt social or political values. Honesty, orderliness, punctuality, hard work and refinement of manners and morals may all have been congruent with the industrial system and thus in the interest of the bourgeoisie but they were not therefore middle-class values. The great divisions in early nineteenth century society were not between the middle and the working classes but between the idle and the non-idle classes, between the rough and the respectable, between the religious and the non-religious. All of those division ran across class lines. The puritan ethic was therfore not the monopoly of the owners of capital; it was the ideology of those who worked as against those who did not. Sunday schools were effective in the transmission of certain values precisely because these values were those of the working-class men and women who taught in and supported the schools.

Furthermore, the life of the Sunday school mirrored an aspect of working - class life which has received short shrift from historians. In it the comparative strength of cohesive over disintegrative forces in society were reflected. The five years between 1838 and 1843 saw not only the publication of the People's Charter, the Newport risings and the plug Riots but also a parade in Bolton of 12,000 working-class children celebrating the Queen's coronation.[56] In 1841 as Chartist agitation was growing,1500 children in blackburn marched out of the town on Easter Monday for a day of pleasure. 'Masters and servants, parents and children were united in the most innocent sports' under the sponsorship of the Sunday school.[57] The 'Age of the Chartists' witnessed scenes like that of the banker Joseph Gurney standing on the platform in Norwich waving to 5,000 Sunday school scholars as their train left the station. The children responded by singing 'The Fine Old English Gentleman' to the music of the band.[58]

References

1. J. F. C. Harrison *Learning and Living*. 1790-1960, (1960) 40.

2. See for example Reinhard Bendix *Work and Authority in Industry* (New York, 1956), 65-8.

3. Maurice Quinlan *Victorian Prelude* (New York, 1941) 44 and generally 44-50.

4. M. W. Flinn 'Social Theory and the Industrial Revolution', in Tom Burns and S. B. Saul, eds. *Social Change and Economic Change* (1967) 14 and 17.

5. E. P. Thompson 'Time Work Discipline and Industrial Capitalism ' *Past and Present* no. 38 (1967) 84.

6. Thompson *Making of the English Working Class (1963) p.401.*

7. *Ibid.* p.375.

8. Thompson *Making of the English Working Class* (1963) pp.50, 361, and particularly pp. 375-83; a similar interpretation of the social role of religion in general and of

Sunday schools in particular is given in Harold Silver *The Concept of Popular Education* (1965) 36-40 and Sydney Pollard *The Genesis of Modern Management* (1965, Penguin ed. 1968) 228-31, 243.

9. Thompson *Making*... p.9.

10. Ibid. p.11.

11. George Horne DD *Sunday Schools Recommended: A Sermon* (Oxford, 1786)11.

12. Rev. Thomas Stevenson *The Difficulties and Encouragements attending the communication of religious instruction to the children of the poor : A semon deliverd April 11,*1814 (1814) 20.

13. Trimmer *The Oeconomy of Charity (1781) pp.26-8.*

14. [Rev. Richard Raikers] Considerations on the Alliance between Christianity and Commerce Applied to the Present State of this Country (1806) 56.

15. See Chapter 5, pp. 125-7: Silver *Popular Education* ... gives the most comprehensive review of Evangelical attitudes towards education.

16. Sarah Trimmer *The Oeconomy of Charity* vol 1 (2 vol. 1801 edn.) 321-2

17. J.Liddon *General Religious Instrucion of the poor* (1792)13 and16.

18. *Introductory Address to the Public on the Importance of Sunday Schools at the Present Time* (Canterbury, 1800) 23.

19. William Godwin *An Enquiry Concerning Political Justice* vol.2 (1798 ed.) 299.

20. *Report from the Select Committee on the Bill to Regulate the Labour of Children in the Mills & Factories of the United Kingdom :* Together with minutes of Evidence 1831-32 (706) xv. pp.327 ff.

21. First *Report of the Factory Commissioners* 1833 (450)xx, D2 114.

22. See F. Musgrove 'The Decline of the Educative Family'

Universities Quarterly vol. 14(1959-60) 377-404.

23. 'The Sunday School'in Hannah *More Works* vol.4 (new ed., part) 1818)376-9.

24. Johnson Grant *The Abuses and Advantages of Sunday Schools: a Sermon preached at Ormskirk, Nov.3. 1799* ...(1800) and *Anti Jacobin Review* vol.7 (1800) 214-17.

25. 'Report of the Sheffield Sunday School Union' quoted in John Salt, 'Early Sheffield Sunday Schools and their Educaional Importance' *Trans.of the Hunter Archaeological Society, vol.9,* part 3 (1967) 183; Report *of the Stockport Sunday School*(1819) 5-13 and particularly 12.

26. Turner *Hints on religious education (1794)* second sermon; Rev. T. Wood *Thoughts on Sunday Schools: Importance of Knowledge to the Lower Classes of Society (1815) 8.*

27. See for example SS Teachers' Magazine (1839) 135.

28. See for example 'Sermon for Sunday Schools on Prov. xxii,6' reprinted in *Christian Remembrancer* vol.14 (1832) 623-8; the Weslyan could always be counted on for right wing views; see for example the quotation from 'Report of the Wesleyan Methodist Sunday Schools of Lincoln' on Rex Russell *Sunday Schools in Lindsey* (Lincoln, 1965) 17; or another report in Scruton *Sketches of Old Bradford p.103.*

29. C. of E. SS Quarterly Magzine (1848-49)274; The Teachers' Offering or Sunday School Monthly Visitor (1850).

30. *Prize Essays (1849) 26-27.*

31. Seth Evans *Methodism in Bradwell* 89; or for example, Anon. *Founded upon a rock : A Chronicle of Wesleyan Methodism in Betty Brow (1897) 17.*

32. A. H. Davis *Religious Instruction (1826)*p.11.

33. *Evangelical Magazine* vol.30(1822)71.

34. For the Dissenting case of this wide-ranging controversy see Rev. William Field *A Letter addressed to the inhabitants of Warwick in answer to the charges against the dissenters (Birmingham,1791) and A second letter in reply to remarks ... of the Rev. the Vicar and the Curate of St. Nicholas upon the*

first letter (Birmingham, 1791); Rev. Benjamin Carpenter *A letter to the Rev. R. Foley, rector of Old Swinford in answer to chares brought against the dissenters in Stourbridge .... To which is added an account of the proceedings at Lye-wasteby J. Scott (1795); see* particulary the section by Scott, pp.39 ff.; for the Anglican case see Rev. Robert Miller and Rev. Hugh Laughterne *Remarks upon a letter to the printer of the Birmingham Gazette ... and also upon a letter ... to the inhabitants of Warwick ... by W. Field (Warwick, 1798).*

35. *Evangelical Magazine* vol. 19 (1811) 356-8. For full account see the trial report re-printed from the *Times* (7 August 1811) in *Philanthropist* No.4 (1811) 388-91.

36. R. S. Fitton and A.P. Wadsworth, *The Strutts and the Arkwrights 1758-1830 (Menchester, 1958), pp.256-7.*

37. See note 8 p.188.

38. Names were secured from the *Annual Reports* and occupations determined from commercial directories. All board members are traceable for 1800, 1820, and 1840.

39. See Chapter 4, pp.113-19 for a discussion of the scope and volume of publishing for Sunday school audiences.

40. R. Lloyd MA *A letter to a Member of Parliament (in these days of infidelity and sedition) showing the serious and dangerous of British and Foreign Schools (1819).*

41. *The Sunday School Scholar's Gift, or a present for a good child* (Wellington, 1814).

42. *Teachers' Offeringvol.4* (1844) *270;* it is prefaced by 'Be industrious . It is a discredit to be idle; children's time is valuable; always be doing something; let every young child take for his motto.

43. *Reports from each of the four Factory Inspectors on the effects on the Educational Provisions of theFactories Act; together with joint reports 1839(42)* xlii, pp.11, 29 and 7.

44. Andrew Ure *The philosphy of Manufactures* (1835) 408 and 411.

45. *SS Teachers' Magazine (1841) 665.*

46. Most issues of the *Northern Star* for example carried a 'notes from the editor' section which *inter alia* contained pleas to contributors asking that they hand in their copy on time, to distributors complaining about tardy or altogether neglect pick-ups, etc.

47. The model in this section is derived, in part, from Talcott Parsons 'The School as a Social System : Some of its functions in American Society' originally published in the *Harvard Educational Review* vol.24 (fall 1959) 297-318 and reprinted in A. H. halsey *et al.*, eds. *Education, Economy, and Society: A Reader in the Sociology of Education* (New York, 1961) 435-55. Parsons' insights are elaborated in Robert Dreeben *On What is Learned in School* (Reading, Mass., 1968) which provides most of the theoretical framework employed here.

48. *Rules and Regulation of the Sunday School held in the Wesleyan Methodist Chapel, Spring Gardens, Doncaster* (Doncaster, 1815) 41.

49. R. N. Collins *The Teachers' Companion designed to exhibit the principles of Sunday School Instruction and discipline* (1840) 196. He then proceeds to discuss the question for the next 58 pages.

50. J. H. Harris, ed. *Robert Raikes,* (1887), *Centenary Volume of the Bank Str. Sunday School, Manchester* (1907); Collins *Teacher's Companion ...* p.271; Pratt *Black Country Methodism* p.172.

51. See Chapter 4, pp. 108-10.

52. See Chapter 1, pp.17,18; 'treat them (students) like your family' advises the *Evangelical Review* (1812) 174.

53. This paragraph is based partly on the formulation of the relationship between schools and society in Ivan Illich *Deschooling Society* (1972).

54. See Brian Harrison *Drink and the Victorians* (1971),p.33 and his 'Religion and Recreation in Nineteenth Century England' *Past and Present* no. 38 (1967) 105-25, esp. 121-2, for a similar hypothesis with respect to moral-reform

movements.

55. See further, Robert W.Malcolmson *Popular Recreation in English Society,* 1700-1850 (1973).

56. Rothwell *Memorials* ... p.163.

57. *Sunday School Magazine* (1841) 146.

58. *SS Teacher's Magazine* (1846) 394-6.

Chapter-15

Sociology and the Study of Religion

Chapter-15

Sociology as a social science is based on the recognition that uniformities reveal themselves in human behavior, which are not to be completely understood in terms of either the psychology of the individual actors or the ideas and values of a given cultural tradition. This recognition points to the existence of social structures and social processes which are neither reducible to individual psychology nor to be explained as the effects of ideas. That relatively autonomous level of social phenomena provides the context of relationships within which human action takes place and as such exercises independent causal influence on such action. Sociology is the disciplined and systematic study of this level of social structure and social process both in itself and in relation to individual motivation and the ideas and values of the culture.[1] Hence sociology is closely related to psychology and to the study of culture, but it is also related to history, with which it shares important common interests. It is not true to say that sociology studies historical phenomena "from the outside." Sociology is concerned both with the inner content of ideas and values and with the previous course of historical development of the phenomena it studies, but that interest is restricted by its concentration on analysis, understanding, and prediction in terms of social structure and social process.[2] Hence sociology is one discipline among many requisite to the study of religion, but it is one whose contribution is of considerable Importance.

The sociology of religion is the study of religion in relation to social structure and process, both those involved in the relation between religion and the general society and those internal to the religious organization and institution. There has developed in the present century a sizable and respectable body of ideas which provide a conceptual frame of reference and a vocabulary of analysis useful to sociologists in the study of religion. Al-

From an Invtiational Conference on the Study of Religion, October 23-25. 1964 (New Haven: 1965) by permission of The Society for Religion in Higher Education.

though neither the theoretical implications nor the research potentialities of these ideas have been developed fully,[3] such a body of theory in this sense does exist. In the years since World War II there has been a renewal of interest in the study of religion on the part of sociologists—an interest reflected in an increasing number of empirical studies, an increase in textbooks on the sociology of religion for the college level and to some extent in the composition of sociology faculties.

This body of ideas which comprise a theoretical structure for the sociology of religion, although still left in a relatively undeveloped state, is, in fact, quite impressive. It derives from a number of significant figures and traditions in the social sciences: Malinowski and the cultural anthropologists,[4] Durkheim and his successors,[5] Ernst Troeltsch,[6] Max Weber,[7] and later Joachim Wach[8] and Talcott Parsons, who has done much to make explicit the relation of the ideas of his predecessors to sociological theory generally.[9] There has also been some influence from Karl Marx and the Marxists[10] and from economic historians such as R. H. Tawney and Amintore Fanfani.[11] The contributions of these men and the scholarly and scientific traditions they represent do not permit lengthy presentation and criticism in the scope of this chapter. Instead we shall describe two common theoretical contexts in which religion is studied by contemporary sociologists—contexts constructed largely on the insights and contributions of these men.

Functional Theory: Traditional Religion and the Stable Society

We shall begin with functional theory, which rests primarily on the insights of Durkheim and the cultural anthropologists. Functional theory is based (in its concern with religion) primarily on studies made on small-scale nonliterate societies and may with some justice be accused of overemphasizing the traditional and conservative aspects of religion in its relationship to the general society. Nevertheless, it raises and provides useful answers to fundamental questions and thereby contributes to sociology an overall frame of reference and an approach to the study of religious phenomena. Functional theory conceives of societies as "social systems"; that is, as ongoings equilibriums of social institutions. which pattern human activity on the basis of a normative consensus—of shared norms held by the actors them selves to be legitimate and binding on them. The social system itself is composed of subsystems, of institutional complexes. which are interdependent with another and with the social system as a whole. Such a point of view rules out the search for simplified cause-and-effect relationships and introduces instead a concern with multiple causation and reverse "feedback" relationship of effects on causes in the systemic whole.[12] Changes anywhere in the system affect other institutional complexes and are affected by events in the other institutional complexes in reaction to the change.

Religion is looked upon as one kind, although in certain ways a unique kind, of institutional behavior existing, in a state of interdependence with other institutions and the society as a wholer. It is a postulate of functional theory that all forms of institutionalized behavior have a function in relation to the maintenance of the social system, although that function may be manifest or latent, obvious or subtle, intended and recognized or unintended and unrecognized by the actors involved.[13] Hence there arises the functional question with respect to religion: what is the contribution of religion to the maintenance of the social system?

Functional theory also views culture as a more or less system- body of knowledge and lóre, and values and beliefs, transmitted and developed from generation to generation, which provides orientation, in terms of both cognition and evaluation, to the participants in a society or social system. It is an ideational system whose elements may be implicit or explicit, possessing some kind of meaningful integration, though not necessarily on the model of Western rationality. It is integrated with the social system in that it enters into the definitions of means and ends, presriptions and proscriptions, which define the roles in which society's members act out the events of their lives and insofar as it affects, through the training and education of the young, the motivations and aspirations of individuals. It is the creation of men, emerging together with stable social, forms, from human activity under the conditions and demands of the environment. It presents a fabric of meaning to the members of the society and, once established, exhibits a partial autonomy and, by defining the meaning of events, affects future human action. Religion is seen as an important aspect of this cultural phenomenon Functional theory would accept the definition. of Wendell T. Bush that "religions is a very important of the world of imagination that functions socially, and its verbal expressions represent only a small fraction of it."[14]

Contemporary sociology further recognizes that while men share ideas and values and act in socially structured context subject to the manifest and latent forces of social control, nevertheless it is the individual human being who acts, and feels, and thinks, and not some hypostatized entity such as a group mind or a cultural or historical tendency. Hence sociology accepts the contributions of dynamic psychology and thereby often considerably enriches the insights of its founders. For example, Max Weber's interest in religion as an independent causal factor in human history, particularly in connection with the origin and development of capitalism, when supplemented by a sophisticated concern with its psychological implications, leads to the study of the ways in which societies may or may not develop in their members attitudes toward work and achievement of farreaching consequences."

Culture, social system, and personality are seen as three aspects of a complex social phenomenon whose effects are observed in human behavior. The functional question is raised necessarily in relation to all three. What is the effect of religion and of religious institutions on the ongoing system of social relations, on the maintenance of the culture, and on the functioning of personality? This question expresses the basic frame of reference in which sociology studies the phenomenon of religion and its role in human life. It obviously does not exhaust the human significance of religion, but it does raise an important question concerning it. Within its broad context narrower, more specific questions can be asked as the basis of empirical research.

Functional theory distinguishes two types of needs and propensities to act as characterizing man in society. He must act in a practical manner so as to ensure his survival in a given environment and a human society with its culture is seen as the unit of survival, sometimes requiring the nonsurvival of some of its members to assure its own. Human activity must to some degree be instrumental and adaptive in an active or passive sense, promoting mastery over or at least permitting adjustment to the environing conditions. Men also have expressive needs—needs to act out emotions and to enter relationships. In the course of their problem-solving activities they develop relationships and rituals which acquire value in their own right.[16] Here, too, the functional question arises: What is the significance of religion in terms of these adaptive and expressive needs and in terms of supporting the social contexts which render life orderly and meaningful?

In this general functional context, religion is seen as something that transcends empirical, adaptive expenence and allows and patterns the expression of important expressive needs. Human being in all societies,including the technologically advanced societies of the West, confront problems and dilemmas which cannot be handled in terms of empirical knowledge alone. Moreover, the ways in which problems are solved by men—for example, the development of a system of economic or political institutions—involve a patterning of relationships which inflict deprivation and cause frustration to some and often to many of the participants. Institutional patterns involve consensually validated allocations of power, resources, functions, facilities and rewards, both material and nonmaterial and such patterned allocation inevitably involves both discipline and deprivation and, consequently, frustration. Since such frustration is involved in society's functioning, it usually presents individuals with sutuations heyond their capacities to change. Hence some way must be provided to ensure human acceptance of and adjustment to them.

Most important of these aleatory and frustrating elements in the human situations which transcend human control are those involved in what has been called the "uncertainty context" and the "impossibility context." The former refers to the unhappy fact that all human ventures, however well palnned and executed, are liable to disappointment and that such ventures often involve an extremely high investment of human interest and human emotion. "The best laid schemes o' mice and men gang aft a-gley." The latter refers to the equally unhappy fact that not everything men desire can be realized here on earth in their lifetimes and that the aspirations men set their hearts upon are often beyond human capacities.

There is a strategic importance in the way in which the uncertainty and impossibility contexts bring men beyond the everyday life of the workaday world. The problems and dilemmas involved bring men not simply *beyond* the skills and capacities of their cultural milieu but also *beyond* the established and defined situation of everyday social behavior and cultural definitions of goals and norms. The inherent element of contingency in the humansituation bringsmen to a confrontation with sutuations in which human knowledge and social forms display a total insufficency for providing either means of solution or "mechanisms" for adjustrnentarid acceptance. They provide men with "breaking points" in the socially structured and culturally defined world of mundane existence. As "breaking beyond" the everyday, they raise questions which can find an answer only in some kind of "beyond" itself.

If these questions are not answered, the worth of everyday activity itself and the value of institutionalized goals and norms are called into question. It is at these breaking points that what Max Weber has called the "problem of meaning" arises in a sharp and poignant form. Suffering and death, disappointment and deprivation, frustration and oppression, what in theglogy is called the "problem of evil," arises as a fundamental existential problem in the lives of men and threatens the stability of human societies. These problems and dilemmas, are inherently involved in man's attempt to handle his environment and in the social contexts he evolves as the framework for for such activity. They must be made to make sense, and ways of adjusting to the tragic realities must be provided. Man must achieve a means security in a fundamentally inscrutable world which is characterized by a large measure of contingency and often condemns him to injury and pain.Unless this is provided, human morale for everyday activity founders and the acceptance of the normative consensus on which society rests is undermined.

If man can go beyond the appearances and make a relationship with some ground of experience and existence, however variously conceived and given symbolic form in various cultures, and if a larger view can be formulated transcending the empirical experience of the "here and now"—a view in which the evil events and experiences can be seen as making sense—and further, if the norms of society which are a cause of frustration can be seen as justified in terms of such a larger view and in relation to such a ground, contingency can be borne frustration and misfortune accepted. All is not in pieces, and all coherence is not gone, and the "her and now" becomes meaningful by being seen in the context of a larger *beyond.*

Moreover, functional theory sees that "beyond" not simply as transcending everyday existence in a cognitive sense but as possessing a specific quality radically differentiating it from the world of everydayness. It is perceived by men as "sacred" and therefore as eliciting from men an attitude and response of intense respect. Durkheim's treatment of the sacred, which paralleled in important respects that of Rudolph Otto,distinguishes it as radically heterogeneous from the profane sphere of experience and characterized as nonutilitarian, ambiguous, being both propitious and threatening, as involving forces and powers deeper than the appearances of things as in supower and seriousness, as evoking awe and respect, and as strength-giving and demanding to those who enter into relationship with it. Thus religion provider an answer to contingency by allowing the worshiper to make a relationship with a more powerful, sacred ground of experience and Justifies norms that frustrate men by sacralizing them. Functional theory also calls attention to man's attempt not only to enter into relation to the sacred but also to manipulate these forces and powers through magic. In discussing ritual and rite involved in these two forms of human commerce with the sacred, Malinowski points out that the regligious rite is an acting out of attitudes for their own sake, while magic is an attempt to manipulate the sacred forces for empirical ends. Both are, however, characterized by the qualities of the sacred suggested above.[17] Durkheim has emphasized the way in which the performance of the religious rite reasserts the sanctity of the norms and reestablishes the solidarity of the group;[18]

Malinowski, the way the performance of magic supplements the limitations of empirical skills in situations of danger and threat and thereby supports human morale in situations in which it might otherwise fail.

Thus functional theory sees religion as meeting the problem of meaning at the breaking points of human experience where a transcendental referent becomes necessary. It sanctifies the norms of society and thereby makes an important contribution to the maintenance of social control and of order in society. Kingsley Davis has summarized this functionalist point of view with brevity and succinctness:

> Religion, then, does four things that help to maintain the dominance of sentiment over organic desire, of group ends over private interest. First, it offers, through its system of supernatural belief, an explanation of group ends and a justification of their primacy. Second, it provides, through its collective ritual, a means for the constant renewal of the common sentiments. Third, it furnishes, through its sacred objects, a concrete reference for the values and rallying point for all persons who share the same values. Fourth, it provides an unlimited and insuperable source of rewards and punishments–rewards for good conduct, punishment for bad. In these ways religion makes a unique and indispensable contribution to social integration.[10]

Religion contributes not only to the integration of society and culture but to humanpersonality as well. It provides the necessary answer to the ultimate question of meaning: it integrates the individual into a meaningful realm by placing him in relation to the sacred and into his group by its ritual reassertion of its values and norms. It thereby enlarges his significance for himself. It provides him with mechanisms for adjustment to loss and frustration and reconciles him to the difficulties and tragedies involved in the uncertainty and impossibility contexts. Davis summarizes this aspect of religion's function as well Religion, by providing

> goals beyond this world serves to compensate people for the frustrations they invariably experience in striving to reach socially valuable ends. It replaces a possibly dangerous

> aggression with a benevolent faith in the unseen. . . . Religion thus gives release from sorrow and fear. . . . Ritual means are freely provided for wiping away guilt, so that one can count on divine grace.[20]

I have presented functional theory in some detail because it represents the theoretical basis of most sociological approaches to the study of religion. Moreover, it is the conceptual framework in which college textbooks in sociology and anthropology typically present religion as a social phenomenon. Most important, it contains certain important insights for the study of religion. Its posing of the functional question in the context of society, culture, and personality actually opens up a vast area for empirical research. It represents a great advance on those theories in the social sciences at the turn of the century which tended to view religion as a survival of superstition or as the ignorance and error of backwar people and treated all human activity not based on technological or economic rationality as of negative significance for the progress of human societies.[21] Yet functional theory as formulated in our texte and even in theoretical works exhibits a number of serious shortcomings. Commenting on Davis' summary of functional theory, Charles Y. Glock has justly stated:

> These propositions are drawn primarily from studies of religion in nonliterate societies and, in large part, from studies of a generation or more ago. Since these studies were made, there have been frequent attacks on their inability to account fully for the place of religion in modern, complex, and changing societies. The task of elaborating them to increase their applicability to modern society, however, has been almost wholly neglected.[22]

Moreover, based on observation of traditional societies, functional theory tends to focus attention on the conservative function of religion and neglects the role of religion in innovation and even in revolution. Also, while its general propositions on the function of religion are useful and suggestive, there has been insufficient attention to delineating the degree of contribution to integration of a particular religion or of particular types of religion and an almost total neglect of the importance of religion surrogates (functional equivalents of religion) which in the secularized societies of the West today perform many of the functions of religion in the past. These present a most varied array, from political ideology to medical psychiatry. The rate of secularization in our day, not only in the West but in the developing countries, makes this a most significant oversight.[23]

Moreover, an overemphasis on function has tended to keep some sociologists from paying sufficent attention to the effect on the development of religious institutions of the doctrines implicit in the original religious experience of the founders. Such a tendency tends to keep the sociological perspective removed from internal problems of religious organization and to militate agains the development of an internal functionalism of religious institutions themselves.[24]

The Developmental Point of View

Functional theory in the form stated above, however, does not exhaust the theoretical resources of the sociology of religion. Turning to the works of Ernst Troeltsch and Max Weber, we find a body of ideas of considerable utility to empirical study in the religious field. Max Weber, in his treatment of charisma, introduces a way of looking at religious movements which enables us to follow their.direction of development sensitized to its, strategic crises and moments. Charisma is for Weber a characteristic of spontaneous leaders which exhibits unusualness, spontaneity, and creativity and often a character bearing marked resemblance to the sacred and the holy as discussed by Durkheim and Otto. Religious movements (and other movements as well, many of which may be functional equivalents of religious movements) are seen beginning with a charismatic leader, who stands to some degree outside tradition and the established social structures of the time and whose message in some way offers innovation and novelty, and the circle of disciples which he succeeds in drawing about him. While Weber has stressed that charisma is specifically foreign to routinized life, to rational economic activity, and to tradition, he has not been much concerned with attempting to specify the kinds of conditions which give rise to various types of charisma or account for its success with masses of people. Nor have sociological research and theory since his time done much to further our knowledge on this important topic. Weber does show the instability of charisma and its need to become transformed into established social forms if the charismatic movement is to survive and possess any future. He calls especial attention to the first succession crisis when the charismatic leader is no longer present and to the importance for the future of the movement of the kind of leadership which emerges in those circumstances. From this charismatic moment of origin there develops a routinization of charisma in which the charisma of institution and office replaces the older originating form. This transformation is at the same time a diminution and a containment of charisma within structured roles, rites, and procedures. This process of routinization may develop in either a rational or a traditional direction, or in some mixture of the two, as was the case with Christianity.[25]

What Weber has worked out in generalized categories of analysis, Troeltsch has done historically in his monumental *Social Teaching of the Christian Churches.* In this work Troeltsch traces the transformations in the inner structure of the church together with its changing relationship to the larger society in which it exists. He pays careful attention to the effects on Christian developments of both the content of the Christian Gospel and the social conditions under which the new church finds itself. He also points up the inner demands of the process of development itself as presenting problems to be solved by the developing church. The compromise of the church with classical society is the result of Christian ideas and values, of the orientations and needs of social classes to whom Christianity appealed, and of the needs of the developing organization. Here we see a sociological study which involves both an "external" and an "internal" view of the multiplicity of factors involved.[26]

Much of Weber's work concerned the sociological study of religion on a grand scale. Weber was concerned to show that religious ideas and institutions exerted a causal influence on human action and history and to oppose to a one-sided interpretation of Marxism a view in which both so-called "material" and "ideal" factors would be given their specific value as causal forces. This aspect of his work is best known from his essay on *The Protestant Ethic and the Spirit of Capitalism,* which Parsons translated in 1930.[27] But in recent years other portions of his study of the world religions have appeared in English. Weber's concern with ascetic Protestantism as a causal element affecting economic life, and with Christianity in general as one important cultural element influencing the rise of modern capitalism in Europe in contrast with the religions of Asia which presented the masses with no road to economic rationality, has influenced much sociological study on the relationship of religion to economic life.[28] In a part of his work translated into English and published under the title *The Sociology of Religion,*[29] Weber explores the relation between religious phenomena and a great variety of social factors. For example, he shows that religious messages have differential appeal to different social strata and that socially generated needs may coalesce with and affect religious needs. Thus lower classes show a tendency to embrace religions which preach a doctrine of salvation, while ruling classes display an elective affinity for religions which legitimate their position and function. Moreover, he shows the tend for lower-middle class groups, especially the artisan class, to embrace and develop rational ethcal religion, while peasants and warriors show a much greater predilection for magical phenomena. Furthermore, he points out the significance of the kind of internal differentiation that develops in a religious movement for its course of development. Thus the development of a rational theology must await as its necessary, though not necessarily its sufficient, condition the development of a priesthood enjoying a special status apart from the common run of membership. Weber also deals with religious surrogates and sees in nineteenth-century socialism such a functional equivalent of religion for the working classes of western Europe. Like Troeltsch, Weber shows a concern with the content of religious doctrines, with the social setting of religious groups and its effects on their development, and with internal structure in religious bodies. He is specially concerned with the effiects of religion on economic developments.

In his work on the Christian churches, Troeltsch has provided a model for the study of social movements and institutions which base themselves in some part on situationally transcendent ideals. For such movements and institutions, as for historic Christianity, practical adjustment to the world as it faces the religious body from without and as it penetrates that body in its own members comes into conflict with important aspects of its transcendent goals and ethic. Troeltsch proposed two sociological forms which embody the approach of compromise and the reaction against compromise in the development of such movements. The church represents the tendency to compromise with the world, to embrace universalism, and to come to peace with secular culture. In his study Troeltsch traces out this development in the spheres of family life, economic life, politics, and intellectual endeavor. He presents the sect as the embodiment of revolt against the whole spirit of compromise. A number of sociological studies have utilized this conceptualization in contemporary American sociology. These concepts have found further refinement in the works of J. Milton Yinger, H. Richard Niebuhr, and the present writer.[30] Troeltsch also deals with another alternative to the church-sect dichotomy: the more individualized and subjective reaction against highly institutionalized religion, mysticism. Unfortunately, sociologists have not paid much attention to this aspect of Troeltsch's conceptualization and have generally reduced his trichotomy of church-sect-mysticism to a church-sect dichotomy. This is more the pity because of the great importance of mystical reactions against the institutionalized church for long periods preceding and following the Reformation and also because of the importance of a sociological study of functionally equivalent phenomena in the secularized society of the West in our own day (for example, some aspects of existentialism, nationalism, the beatnik phenomenon, and some forms of secular quietism in the face of baffling social developments).

Thus the substantive and theoretical work of Troeltsch and Weber has enriched the sociology of religion with conceptualizations more adequate for the study of religion in complex modem societies and of religious movements and institutions in terms of their internal functional problems as well as their adjustment problems in the modern world. Glock has remarked that more case studies are needed in contemporary American sociology dealing with the conditions leading to the establishment and affecting the development of "several score of major and minor religions indigenous to America"[31]

Joachim Wach has reduced some of this rich complexity to

order, especially with respect to the internal structure and development of founded religions.[32] Starting with Rudolph Otto's treatment of the religious experience,[33] which in its basic outline presents a remarkable parallel to important aspects of Durkheim's treatment of the sacred, Wach presents a scheme of analysis which shows the religious movement proceeding from its original form of a charismatic leader and his circle of disciples, through an intermediate state of a loose and charismatic brotherhood, to become a fully institutionalized ecclesiastical organization. This course of development parallels in important ways Weber's treatment of the routinization of charisma and Troeltsch's analysis of the developments in early Christianity. A comparison of the three men offers a rich and many-sided view of what is involved in the institutionalization of religion and offers the sociologist a set of concepts for the formulation of problems and of hypothesis and the development of analysis. Moreover, Wach sees the institutionalization of religion proceeding on three levels, each separably identifiable with its own problems involved in the process.

He agrees with Troeltsch and the best insights of Durkheim concerning the sacred and of Weber with respect to charisma, in making the strategic level or aspect that of worship. Worship is central to the religious institution and continues in altered and symbolic form the original religious experience of the founding generation under new and changing conditions. The performance of cult, moreover, contains by implication much that is later developed as explicit doctrine and much that becomes institutionalized in the role structure of the religious organization. Thus the development of the Lord's Supper into the Mass contains the germs of both Trinitarian doctrine and the later defined idea of Christ's dual nature, and role of mediatorship, and the strategically significant inner differentiation of the church into two distinct orders, clergy and laity.

The second level or aspect is the intellectual expression of religion in myth and doctrine. Comparable to Weber's idea of two directions of the routinization of charisma, one tradititional, the other rational, is Wach's notion of two possibilities in the intellectual development from the religious experience, one in the direction of myth, the other toward rational theologies. Like

Weber, Wach sees also a long-term trend toward rationality.

The third level is that of organization, the development of the ecclesiastical body. These three aspects are seen as interpenetrating and affecting one another in the course of development. Wach, of course, sees this whole religious development taking place in specific social and cultural settings with which it is in reciprocal relationship. Such developments of religious bodies proceed from the immanent implications of the original religious experience of the founding generation and are strongly affected by the structural necessities of development itself and by the social and cultural conditions of their milieu. For example, gnosticism and its attendant threat of misinterpreting Christian ideas, together with the existence of Greek philosophy, as elements in the world of early Christianity intensified the normal tendency toward an intellectual expression of religious belief in a rational theology.

Wach introduces the important category of "protest," a universal category of analysis for the understanding of religious developments. New adjustments to the world, new specifications of points of doctrine, new changes in liturgy or in church organization, affect sections of the membership differently. There are groups unable to go along with the new developments, who have become alienated from the changing ecclesiastical organization, and who revolt. Such revolts either may become secessionist or may be reintegrated into the, larger church structure. Wach's thinking here follows closely that of Troeltsch on the sectarian response and its nonsecessionist variation, monasticism, though Wach proposes a more generic universal category, since protest may take other than sectarian forms, as may be seen in schism and the larger churches of the Reformation.

Wach's paradigm of religious development actually opens up the possibility of integrating into the sociological point of view the work of many students of religion, mythology, and symbolism. For example, the development of cult in the context of the developing religious body and developing myth and doctrine opens up to sociology the perspectives to be seen in the work of people like Susanne Langer,[34] Mircea Eliade, Van der Leeuw, and many others.[35]

The Study of Religion and Other Sociological Specializations

Other disciplines of sociology have also developed analytic concepts of help in the sociological study of religion. The institutionalization of religion in its ecclesiastical form results in a hierarchically organized church, whose functional problems resemble closely those characteristic of hierarchical bureaucracies generally. A body of theory, which owes much to Max Weber but has been considerably refined by American researchers, is available for an analysis of religious organizations.[36] The study of social disorganization has long been a concern of sociologists, as have the social forms developed by men in response to disorganization and anomie. For example, a study in which the present writer participated has shown that the formation of store-front churches among Puerto Rican migrants to New York represented an attempt to rebuild community in response to the personally and socially disorganizing impact of the metropolis on the newcomers.[37] The study of the assimilation and conflict involved in the integration of immigrants into American culture has opened up further areas of interest to sociological study. In this country, as well as in some other parts of the world, there is a tendency for religious identity to become synonymous with ethnic identity. A conflict, for example, between Catholics and Orthodox in Yugoslavia is at the same time a conflict between Croatians and Serbs, with their different cultural values and traditions and rivalry for power. This merger of religious with ethnic identity in social conflict has also been studied by sociologists, with results highly suggestive for future research.[38] For to fail to recognize in what Billington has called the Protestant crusade of the first half of the nineteenth century a nativist reaction against the Irish on the part of American Anglo-Saxons is to be insensitive to a large element involved. Moreover, a new religious identity can lead to the development in time and under propitious historical circumstances of a new ethnicity, as may be seen in the effects of the millet system under Turkish rule in the Middle East, or the quasi ethnicity of the Mormons whose development traversed a course from "near sect" to "near nation."[39]

American sociological research has been much interested in

voting behavior, and it has been gradually recognized that religious identification is among one of the most important variables affecting voting.[40] Even when others, such as social stratification, income, and education, are held constant, religious identity among Catholics and Protestants permits reliable prediction. The findings on voting behavior suggest the significance of the religious tradition for personal identification and perception of interests in this country.

Finally, the sociology of knowledge which is concerned with studying the relationship between cognition and social conditions stands in close relationship to the sociology of religion, a fact to be seen in Durkheim's treatment of it in his *Elementary Forms of the Religious Life.* The present writer has attempted to combine the two in a study of the problems involved in the intellectual life as it has developed in American Catholicism.[41]

Thus there exists in sociology a body of concepts useful in the analysis of the human situation in terms of its component of social structure and social process, and one specifically derived from and of utility in the study of religious behavior and religious institutions. This body of concepts and ideas comprises "theory" in the scientific sense of that word. It is "theory," not theories in the sense of empirical hypotheses about future or regular behavior, since it is a frame of reference and a system of analytical categories. In its context, problems may be defined and hypotheses stated as the basis of empirical research. Such a body of theory is continually corrected, made more adequate, and expanded in terms of empirical study itself. What actually exists for the study of religion represents a rich heritage of sociological work and thought.

This body of theory is not, however, without serious lacunae, and much work remains to be done in the theoretical as well as the empirical field. There is needed, first of all, more empirical research in which this body of theory is used. This is required in order both to enrich our knowledge of religion from the sociological perspective and to refine and develop the conceptual scheme itself. There is also a need for a clearer working through and systematization of the implications of the theory as it now stands. It may be safely declared that in neither the theoretical nor the empirical spheres has the sociology of religion realized its potentialities as these already exist.

Second, there is needed a greater cooperation and cross fertilization between the sociology of religion and psychology, especially depth psychology of the psychoanalytic and related schools. Although some work has been done in this area, there is still much to do.[42] Third, the sociology of religion must strengthen its relationship to history, since in modern complex societies a knowledge of past developments is often crucial to any adequate comprehension of the contemporary situations with which the sociologist deals. Finally, the sociology of religion must develop some degree of dialogue with theology and the philosophy of religion. Since the content of the particular religious view enters into the structuration of the religious institution and the norms which pattern behavior in it the sociologist must develop a degree of competence in his understanding of this content. The sociology of religion is not simply the study of religion in relation to society, as some sociologists seem to assume, but rather the study of religion in relation to social structure and social process, not only as these are to be observed between the religious organization and ideology and the general society but also as these enter into the development and functioning of the religious organization and its ideology.

This implies that sociology enters into the study of religion in three ways. First of all, as the sociology of religion it is concerned with the relation of religion to social structure and social process, including the function of religions in particular societies. Second, in the study of given societies or of separate institutions in any society, the sociologist is concerned with the functional relationships between religious institutions and the particular area of his concentration. Thus a study of social structure and motivation for achievement will have to take into account the effects of various religious identifications and backgrounds on its subject matter. Third, the study of particular religious groups or of particular religious problems must pay attention to the effects of social structure and social processes on the religious group and its ideas. Christopher Dawson once declared, "Most of the great schisms and heresies in the history of the Christian church have their roots in social and national antipathies, and if this had been clearly recognized by the theologians, the history of Christianity would have been a very different one"[43] To ignore the sociological level of study and analysis in the study of religion is to leave out of account important factors influencing the developments and adaptations, and the problems and crises, of religious groups and religious ideas.

What has been said points up the importance of sociology for adequate understanding of religious phenomena. It also defines its limitations. The sociology of religion is not the complete study of religion, but is rather one of a number of disciplines engaged in exploring the human meaning and significance of religion. To the student of religion it is an ancillary and complementary approach to his own central concerns, but one of considerable importance for him. To the sociologist studying religion, the work of the specialists in religious study offers also an ancillary and complementary approach to his own, and one with which he must have some acquaintance if he is to make the optimum use of his own theory and techniques.

NOTES

1. A detailed theoretical presentation of what is implied here may be seen in Talcott Parsons, *The Social System* (Glencoe: 1951).
2. See Werner J. Cahnman and Alvin Boskoff, eds., *Sociology and History* (London: 1964). Also Talcott Parsons, *The Structure of Social Action* (Glencoe: 1949).
3. Cf. Charles Y. Glock, "The Sociology of Religion," in Robert K. Merton, Leonard Broom, and Leonard S. Cottrell, Jr., eds., *Sociology Today: Problems and Prospects* (New York: 1959), pp. 154 ff.
4. See Bronislaw Malinowski, *Magic, Science, and Religion and Other Essays* (Glencoe: 1948), and William J. Goode, *Religion among the Primitives* (Glencoe: 1951), Chapter 1.
5. The chief reference is Emile Durkheim, *The Elementary*

Forms of the Religious Life, Joseph Ward Swain, tr. (Glencoe: 1954). Also particularly his French successors such as Marcel Mauss, *The Gift* (Glencoe: 1954). Interesting is the work of Francis M. Cornford, influenced by Durkheim, *From Religion to Philosophy* (New York: 1957).

6. Ernst Troeltsch, *The Social Teaching of the Christian Churches,* Olive Wyon, tr., Vols. 1 and II (London and New York: 1931).

7. See especially Max Weber, *The Theory of Social and Economic Organization,* A. M. Henderson and Talcott Parsons, trs. (New York: 1947); *The Protestant Ethic and the Spirit of Capitalism,* Talcott Parsons, tr. (New York and London: 1930); and *The Sociology of Religion,* Ephraim Fischoff, tr. (Boston: 1963).

8. Joachim Wach, *The Sociology of Religion* (Chicago: 1944).

9. See especially Talcott Parsons, "The Theoretical Development of the Sociology of Religion," in *Essays in Sociologicat Theory,* rev. ed. (Glencoe: 1954), pp. 197-211.

10. For a good overall view of the Marxist position, see Karl Marx and Friedrich Engels, On Religion (New York: 1964 Schocken paperback reprinted from the edition of 1957, published by The Foreign Languages Publishing House, Moscow, USSR); and Friedrich Engels, The Peasant War in Germany (New York: 1924).

11. R. H. Tawney, *Religion and the Rise of Capitalism* (New York: 1947), and Amintore Fanfani, *Catholicism, Protestantism and Capitalism* (New York: 1955).

12. For a sophisticated attempt to show this by mathematical method using factor analysis, see Alvin W. Gouldner and Richard A. Peterson, *Technology and the Moral Order* (Indianapolis and New York: 1962).

13. See the discussion of Robert K. Merton, "Manifest and Latent Functions: Toward the Codification of Functional Analysis in Sociology," in *Social Theory and Social Structure* (Glencoe: 1957). Chapter 1, pp. 19-84; and Goode. *op. cit.*, pp. 33 ff.

14. Quoted from Horace L. Friess, "Growth of Study of Religion at Columbia University, 1924-1954." *Review of Religion.* XIX Nos. 1–2 (November, 1954), 15.

15. For example, see David C. McClelland, *The Achieving Society* (Princeton: 1961).

16. The classic work on the topic of this paragraph is Ferdinand Toennies, *Community and Society—Gemeinschaft und Gesellschaft.* Charles P. Loomis, tr. and ed. (East Lansing, Mich.: 1957).

17. See the first essay in Malinowski, *op. cit.*

18. Durkheim, *op. cit.* See also the discussion in Talcott Parsons, *The Structure of Social Action* (Glencoe: 1949), pp. 435 ff.

19. Kingsley Davis, *Human Society* (New York: 1948). p. 529.

20. *Ibid.*, p. 531.

21. The entire background of this statement is explored thoroughly in terms of its significance for sociology in Parsons, *The Structure of Social Action.*

22. Glock, *op. cit.*, p. 155. See also Merton, *op. cit.*, pp. 30–32. 41–47; and Allan W Eister, "Religious Institutions in Complex Societies: Difficulties in the Theoretic Specification of Function." *American Sociological Review,* XXII, No. 2 (1957), 387–391.

23. For example, see Daniel Lerner, with Lucille W. Pevsner, collaborator. "Modernizing the Middle East," in *The Passing of Traditional Society* (Glencoe: 1958). Also Jules Monnerot, *Sociology and Psychology of Communism,* Jane Degras and Richard Rees. trs. (Boston: 1960), especially "Psychology of Secular Religions," Chapter 10, and "Projections of the Sacred," Chapter 14.

24. See Chapter 13 in the present volume.

25. Weber, *The Theory of Social and Economic Organization,* pp. 358 ff.

26. See Troeltsch. *op. cit.,* Vol. I.

27. Weber, *The Protestant Ethic and the Spirit of Capitalism,* Talcott Parsons, tr. (New York and London: 1930).

28. In addition to the works of Weber listed above, this is discussed in the following translations of his works: *The Religion of China: Confuciantsm and Taoism,* Hans H. Gerth, tr. (Glencoe: 1952); *Ancient Judaism,* Hans H. Gerth and Don C. Martindale. trs. (Glencoe: 1951); *General Economic History,* Frank Knight, tr. (New York: 1927).

29. See footnote 7 above.

30. See J. Milton Yinger, *Religion and the Struggle for Power* (Durham: 1946); H. Richard Niebuhr, *The Social Sources of Denominationalism* (New York: 1929); Bryan R. Wilson, *Sects and Society* (Berkeley, Calif.: 1961), and "An Analysis of Sect Development," *American Sociological Review,* XXIV (February, 1959), 3–15. Aiso Chapter 6 in the present volume. For a further exploration of the problems opened up in Troeltsch's work in terms of theological alternatives, see H. Richard Niebuhr, *Christ and Culture* (New York: 1951).

31. Glock, *op. cit.,* pp. 159–160. The studies suggested as examples by Glock are: Marshall Sklare, *Conservative Judaism* (Glencoe: 1955); Thomas F. O'Dea, *The Mormons* (Chicago: 1957); H. H. Stroup, *Jehovah's Witnesses* (New York: 1945); and Hadley Cantril, "The Kingdom of Father Divine." in Cantril, ed., *The Psychology of Social Movements* (New York:1941).

32. Wach, *op. cit.*

33. Rudolf Otto, *The Idea of the Holy,* J. W. Harvey, tr., 2d ed. (London: 1950).

34. Susanne K. Langer, *Philosophy in a New Key* (Cambridge: 1951).

35. See, for example, Mircea Eliade, *Patterns of Comparative Religions,* Rosemary Sheed, tr. (New York: 1958).

36. For example, see Peter M. Blau and W. Richard Scott, *Formal Organizations* (San Francisco: 1962), or Robert K. Merton, *et al., Reader in Bureaucracy* (Glencoe: 1952).

37. See Chapter 10 in the present volume.

38. See, for example, Kenneth W. Underwood, *Protestant and Catholic* (Boston: 1957), and John J. Kane, *Catholic-Protestant Conflicts in America* (Chicago: 1955).

39. See Werner J. Cahnman, "Religion and Nationality," in Cahnman and Boskoff, *op. cit.*, pp. 271–279, and Chapter 6 in the present volume.

40. For a good summary, see Seymour Martin Lipset, "How Big Is the Bloc Vote? " *New York Times Magazine*, October 25, 1964, pp. 32 ff.

41. Thomas F. O'Dea, *American Catholic Dilemma* (New York: 1958).

42. See, for example, W. Earl Biddle, *Integration of Religion and Psychiatry* (New York: 1962), and O. Hobart Mowrer, *The Crisis in Psychiatry and Religion* (Toronto, New York, and London: 1961).

43. Christopher Dawson, "Sociology as a Science," republished in *Cross Currents*, IV, No. 28 (Winter, 1965), 136.

THE SOCIOLOGICAL STUDY OF RELIGION

Important Books of Similar Interest Published Recently

Encyclopaedia of Sociology of Religion, in 3 Volumes
Edited by V. G. Nayar and M. G. Nayar

Encyclopaedia of Sociology of Politics, in 3 Volumes
Edited by K. Motwani and R. D. Saksena

International Encyclopaedia of Non Violence, in 5 Volumes
Edited by S. R. Sharma

Encyclopaedia of Ethics and Logic, in 10 Volumes
Edited by John H. Piet and Ayodhya Prasad

International Encyclopaedia of Anthropology, in 12 Volumes
Edited by Subhadra M. Channa

Encyclopaedia of Tribal Religion, in 12 Volumes
Edited by Subhadra M. Channa